D1590875

"In the Hands of a Good Providence"

"IN THE HANDS OF A GOOD PROVIDENCE"

Religion in the Life of George Washington

Mary V. Thompson

University of Virginia Press
Charlottesville and London

University of Virginia Press
© 2008 by the Rector and Visitors of the University of Virginia
All rights reserved
Printed in the United States of America on acid-free paper

First published 2008

1 3 5 7 9 8 6 4 2

LIBRARY OF CONGRESS CATALOGING-IN-PUBLICATION DATA

Thompson, Mary V., 1955–
"In the hands of a good providence" : religion in the life of George Washington /
Mary V. Thompson.
p. cm.
Includes bibliographical references and index.
ISBN 978-0-8139-2763-3 (alk. paper)
1. Washington, George, 1732–1799—Religion. 2. Washington, George, 1732–1799—
Political and social views. 3. Washington, George, 1732–1799—Family. 4. Washington
family. 5. Anglicans—Virginia—Biography. 6. Virginia—Religious life and customs.
7. Chesapeake Bay Region (Md. and Va.)—Religious life and customs. 8. Christianity
and politics—United States—Church of England—History—18th century. I. Title.
E312.17.T466 2008
973.4'3092—dc22
2008011310

For my parents, Chaplain Parker Campbell Thompson,
U.S. Army (retired), and the late Irene Kirkpatrick Thompson,
who overcame many obstacles to join the church and
serve the Lord who means so much to them

and

For Mrs. Alexander L. Wiener, Mount Vernon's late
Vice Regent for Michigan (1964–1989), who always
wanted the story in this book to be told

CONTENTS

PREFACE

Mount Vernon has attracted visitors in large numbers, beginning in George Washington's lifetime with those who were curious to see this famous man who had been something of an international celebrity since the age of twenty-two. In the nineteenth century, the estate itself developed almost religious connotations as a pilgrimage site or shrine. In the twentieth and twenty-first centuries, Mount Vernon has become a tourist center, each year welcoming roughly one million visitors, who see evidence of George Washington's taste in decorative arts and clothing, study Martha Washington's needlework and expertise at domestic management, and marvel at the agricultural innovations directed by Washington and put into practice by his slaves. Until the opening of a new museum and education center at the end of October 2006, however, what they did not get a sense of was the spiritual life of the people who lived on the plantation. While this topic has, at last, been touched on, still, the constraints imposed by the medium of an exhibit case leave a lot of room for questions. Much of the lack of interpretation on this subject has reflected not only a modern reticence to discuss a potentially emotional issue and the secularism of our society, but, perhaps even more, the reserve of the estate's most famous resident regarding his own religious beliefs and those of the other individuals with whom he lived.

This is unfortunate, because the Washington family at Mount Vernon lived in a period of incredible turmoil in the religious life of England and its colonies. Some of this unrest even led to the family's emigration to America in the mid-seventeenth century. Following their arrival in the New World, the Washingtons, like others in Virginia, had to find ways to adapt the Anglican practices they had known in the mother country to the very different conditions found in America. During George Washington's lifetime, the modern evangelical movement was born; other denominations, especially Baptists, Methodists, and Quakers, challenged the state church for the right to worship freely; the Anglican Church itself went through major changes before and after the Revolution; and Unitarians and Universalists were talking and writing about new ideas regarding God and Christianity. Because of his prominence in both national and international affairs, George Washington drew into his orbit many of the leading figures in the religious history of the eighteenth century. Washington's death came just two weeks before the start of the nineteenth century. Within five years of his demise, a new spirit broke out in the church in which he had spent his entire life. That change influenced younger members of his family, who found themselves caught up in the great movements of nineteenth-century Christianity, such as the Sunday School and missionary societies. In many ways, the history of the American church through two hundred years can be read in the history of this one prominent family.

This work began with a question from a person who wrote to Mount Vernon via the Internet in the spring of 1997, asking simply about George Washington's religious beliefs. When asked that question in the past (which was not often, because such questions would typically have gone to the staff in the library), I had answered, as I had been taught, that George Washington was a Deist. For some reason, this particular inquiry came to me and arrived at an unusually slow period, when I had the luxury of time to investigate my answer. I very quickly came to the conclusion that Washington was not a Deist, but it has taken many years to flesh out the story of where he fit in the religious milieu of the time in which he lived.

The chapters that follow will explore the place of religion in the life of George Washington. While the primary focus will be him (he is, after all, the member of the family in whom most people are interested), Washington came to believe the way he did through the influence of generations of those who lived before, and he, in turn, would influence the religious practices of younger members of the family and generations to come. It will be necessary, therefore, to examine the lives of other members of this extended family, as well as trends within the Anglican/Episcopal Church, which served as the framework for their actions.

Some readers may be wondering who I am and what I bring, both positively and as baggage, to this study of religion in the life of George Washington. Perhaps I should start by admitting that I am not, and never wanted to be, an academic historian. My interest has always been in museums and what is now termed public history. In high school, I did volunteer work at one of the U.S. Army museums. As an undergraduate, I majored in history, with a minor in folklore, and worked on a project, funded by the National Endowment for the Humanities, to identify practitioners of traditional folk crafts in a five-county area around Birmingham, Alabama. In graduate school, I specialized in the history of early modern Europe and colonial America. The focus of my thesis was on the relationships between colonists and Native Americans in the Carolinas and Georgia. Between graduate school and finding a paying job in the museum field, I volunteered for several months with a second army museum.

Since 1980 I have been on the staff at Mount Vernon, as an employee of the Mount Vernon Ladies' Association, the oldest national preservation group in the United States. After five months as an interpreter (docent/tour guide), which gave me invaluable experience with the visiting public and what they know and don't know about history, I was moved to the Curatorial Department, where I remained for the next eighteen years. There I did research for the curator, was responsible for the cataloguing and management of a collection of about fifteen thousand objects, trained interpreters, put together exhibits, and was assigned several long-term research topics dealing with domestic life at Mount Vernon and the Washington family. In 1998 I was transferred again, becoming a department of one, as the research specialist. Here the focus has been more on working with public inquiries, assisting visiting scholars, reading and commenting on manuscripts submitted by an assortment of authors, and telling the story of the Washingtons and Mount Vernon through publications and lectures, while continuing with my own long-term research projects. My years at Mount Vernon have given me a pretty thorough grounding in the "stuff" the Washingtons owned, an understanding of how those things were used, and a familiarity with the surviving family manuscripts, Washington historiography, and scholarship on both social history and George Washington.

By way of full disclosure, I should probably say that I am a member of a Southern Baptist church but have not always been Baptist, having joined that denomination in my late twenties. Both of my parents were raised in non-Christian homes and became Baptists as young adults before they met. My father served as a U.S. Army chaplain for thirty-two years (he is still an active Baptist pastor), during which he was the first curator of the

Army Chaplains Museum and edited a five-volume history of the Chaplain Corps, for which he wrote the first volume. I grew up as an army brat, being raised in a nondenominational Protestant setting. Army services tend to mix elements of liturgical and nonliturgical denominations: during prayers, worshippers are free to kneel or sit in the pews, as they prefer; communion is offered both in the pews and at the altar rail in the same service; and responsive readings and recitations of creeds are typical, although most of the hymns come out of the evangelical tradition. In addition, I have happily worshipped at various times with Moravian, Presbyterian, Lutheran, Catholic, Church of Christ, and Pentecostal congregations and feel quite comfortable with everything from prayer books to raised hands during prayers as well as clapping along with the music in services.

Turning to the subject of the chapters that follow, I have tried as much as possible to use contemporary eighteenth-century sources, rather than the secondary works of other historians, although the latter have been very helpful for providing context, and the reader will find a number of them cited in the endnotes and bibliography. An exception has been made for statements made in the nineteenth century by younger members of George and Martha Washington's families who had spent time in the Washington household and knew them well. These young people, Martha Washington's grandchildren (two of whom had been raised by the couple) and two of George Washington's nephews (who had worked as aides or secretaries to their uncle), were asked for their opinions about the faith of their most-famous relative in the late 1820s and early 1830s, at a time when the deaths of John Adams and Thomas Jefferson moved their countrymen to start asking questions about the founding generation. Statements had been made that questioned George Washington's belief in Christianity, and biographers were taking the opportunity to interview remaining family members, who now ranged in age from their late forties to their early sixties, about what they remembered. Modern historians have largely ignored these sources, primarily because of their concern that these no-longer-young people would not remember things correctly, either because of the passage of years or out of a belief that they had to defend Washington's orthodoxy as a means of protecting his honor. Others have felt that, since many of these younger relatives went on to become pillars of the nineteenth-century Episcopal Church in Virginia, they would not be able to separate their own, decidedly more evangelical, beliefs and practices from those of the earlier generation. While these are all valid points, I believe that these historians have been remiss in almost totally ignoring the testimony of Washington's family members. All of these individuals knew the Washingtons as adults (the youngest grandchild was eighteen when George Washington died and twenty-one at the time of Martha Washington's death; the nephews were both in their twenties when they worked for George Washington). One has to ask if they, as the devout Christians most of them seemed to be, would go so far as to deliberately mislead friends and the public about this issue, when it would have been a more powerful testimony to say to someone, "With all the great and wonderful things that George Washington did over the years, he lacked the one thing that counts most when you come to the end of life. And if he could be so good and is still lost, what hope do you have?" These younger relatives were generally reliable on other issues about life at Mount Vernon (where they are not, the discrepancies can be fairly easily explained), and they should at least be given a hearing on a matter of this importance.

In the following pages, I will first take a look at the controversy about Washington's religious beliefs and then go on to examine topically various aspects of his life that might shed light on those beliefs. (Many of these topics have been used by those skeptical of Washington's orthodoxy to discredit his faith.) From there I will look at Washington's writings to see what they can tell us about what he believed and then move on to his actions relating to religion on the national stage. I hope, in this way, to allow readers to quickly find information on areas of particular interest, without bogging them down in a more biographical or chronological approach. Those who would like a firm stand on the issue of whether or not George Washington was "really a Christian" are likely to be disappointed. I genuinely believe that Washington was a devout eighteenth-century Anglican, a person who today might be called a liberal, low-church (or even Broad Church) Episcopalian, but would then have been known as a Latitudinarian. It is also my belief, which I'll discuss more fully in the conclusion, that it is impossible for any of us to see into another person's heart and know what he or she really believes. There might be indications in a person's statements, either oral or written, but people can rather cynically use religion for personal gain. Even if someone's statements or actions suggest that he or she is not particularly religious, or even is antireligion, things can change when death is near and the possibility of meeting God face to face is confronted. As British antiquarian and topographer William Camden wrote many years ago, in a poem entitled *Remains: Epitaph for a Man Killed by Falling from His Horse*:

> My friend, judge not me,
> Thou seest I judge not thee.
> Betwixt the stirrup and the ground
> Mercy I asked, mercy I found.

In addition, various readers will disagree about "true" Christianity. Many contemporary evangelicals would only consider someone Christian who has walked down an aisle at the close of a service, knelt in tears to confess his or her sinful nature, and made a public profession of faith in Jesus as savior. Others in the evangelical tradition would only count as Christian a person who has done these things and then gone on to be baptized (immersed) immediately after coming forward. Conversely, people who come out of a more liturgical tradition might say that someone is Christian if he or she was christened as an infant, catechized and confirmed at the appropriate stage of life, and regularly attends services. Diehards within all of these groups often have trouble accepting the others as "real Christians."

Over the years, I have had both atheists and evangelical Christians tell me that Washington was not Christian, probably because both expected a Christian to have had an emotional conversion experience and to talk about it publicly. This is, I feel, a real disservice to fellow Christians who come out of a liturgical background that does not emphasize the need for an emotional conversion experience. Why can't someone be seen as Christian who is daily doing their duty to God and their fellow man (as Washington and other eighteenth-century Anglicans were taught was the chief responsibility of a good Christian) and who is quietly making the choice to live uprightly, to attend and support the church, to see that there is a religious structure set up to meet the needs of the community (as Washington did as a vestryman and on the religion committee in the House of Burgesses), to see that the next generation is raised in the church, even if they have not "walked the aisle"? How do you know that this individual hasn't privately given his or her soul to God? Ultimately, there is no more or no less evidence that this person is Christian in their heart (the only place it matters) than the supposed evangelical who wears his or her religious beliefs on their sleeve, or T-shirt, but who is only spouting rhetoric. I think it is presumptuous for anyone on earth to make that judgment, which is why, absent really strong evidence to the contrary, I would tend to consider both of these hypothetical individuals Christian. The only judgment that counts is God's.

Having said that, however, in getting to know someone and perhaps faced with deciding on the sincerity of their stated religious beliefs, there are certain things to look for: whether or not they attend church; if they pray; whether they look after those less fortunate than themselves; and if they treat other people in a gentle, loving manner. Jesus himself suggested some things, which will be discussed much later in the book. Recently, Professor David L. Holmes, the Walter G. Mason Professor of Religious Studies at William and Mary, in looking at the founding generation of Americans, has suggested several criteria for distinguishing a Deist from an orthodox Christian: sporadic versus regular church attendance; participation in ordinances or sacraments of the church, especially those in which they had a choice, such as confirmation and communion; level of activity and participation in rituals, such as regular church attendance, confirmation, and communion; and use of religious language that is specifically Christian rather than deistic.[1] I also will be looking at these issues. However, I contend that, while others have certainly examined these aspects of Washington's life, they have done so in a rather simplistic manner and have not looked for explanations of a given action or inaction that point to anything but unbelief.

In this work, I am seeking to move the discussion past "was he or wasn't he," in order to see the place religion had in Washington's life. This approach allows the reader the opportunity to weigh the evidence and make up his or her own mind about where they think Washington fits in the eighteenth-century religious spectrum. The contribution I hope to make to the field is to present the evidence to the reader, being very clear to document sources (something that was not often done in the past); to look at issues other historians have not, such as Washington's work on the religion committee of the House of Burgesses, the books and artwork touching on religion in Washington's home, and the charities he supported; and to try to put Washington into the context of his family and his church.

Throughout this work, biblical quotations will be taken from the King

James version of the Bible, which is the version used by George Washington and his contemporaries in England and America. The idiosyncratic spelling of the eighteenth-century writers has been maintained, with the exception that missing letters in contracted words have been filled in with bracketed material and some adjustments have been made to make the punctuation more clear.

Acknowledgments

There are quite a few people to whom I owe a debt of thanks for their help and support on this project. Foremost among them are the members of the Mount Vernon Ladies' Association, those "pioneers in preservation" who are still making waves 150 years after their founding. Singled out for special remembrance are the current regent, Gay Hart Gaines, who has always been an enthusiastic booster, and the estate's executive director, Jim Rees. My current colleagues in the Collections Department have endured my eccentricities with good grace. I'd especially like to thank Linda Ayres, our associate director for collections, for her friendship; our curator, Carol Borchert Cadou, for her shared interest in the topic of religion; Dawn Bonner, for her help with the photographs; Laura Simo, for volunteering to look over the manuscript for glaring copyediting problems (because she thinks bibliographies and endnotes are fun); research librarian Jennifer Kittlaus, a never-ending font of helpful suggestions, for making me laugh; and John Rudder, for keeping me supplied with current events in the world of barbecue, as well as for dragging my chair each week from the office to our department staff meetings. The rest of you, although unnamed, are very much appreciated just for being there. My former boss, Mount Vernon's long-time curator, Christine Meadows, will always have my heartfelt affection and loyalty for giving me a chance when no one else would. From other departments, I'd like to thank Ann Bay, the deputy director for education, for reading the manuscript, and Sue Keeler and Sandy Newton, who never stopped pushing me to finish. Licensing director Beverly Addington kept me sane. (The rest of you should be extremely grateful to her.)

Outside of Mount Vernon, there are additional colleagues and friends who deserve recognition: historians Ken Bowling, Pat Brady, Bruce Chadwick, Phil Chase, Frank Grizzard, Peter Henriques, Don Higginbotham, Robert Jones, Jean Lee, Phil Morgan, and Jack Warren keep me on my toes, and, although we don't always agree on interpretation, have strongly encouraged me to publish. To Dr. Joseph Whitehorne of Lord Fairfax Community College and Dr. Thomas McDaniel of Eastern Baptist Theological Seminary, many thanks for reading over and commenting on a very early draft of this manuscript. Michael and Jana Novak have been active supporters of this project since they first read the manuscript several years ago; Michael's kindness has been overwhelming. Peter Lillback and I were thrilled to discover that we had come to a number of the same conclusions about the place of religion in Washington's life, even though we were working independently and using some very different material as evidence. Henry Wiencek was always there, passing along a pertinent piece of information he'd run across in his own research, which was applicable to my project; thank you so much for pushing me. Roxanne Merritt, director of the U.S. Army Special Warfare Museum, and I worked together at the Army Ordnance Museum; she not only encouraged a newcomer to the museum field, but also taught me to write. Dona McDermott, the archivist at Valley Forge, and I have found so many parallels in both our private and work lives that we suspect we might be twins who were separated at birth; she also has my undying gratitude for sticking up for my position on Washington's religious beliefs during a contentious session at a symposium several years ago. Ellen McCallister Clark, the charming head of the library of the Society of the Cincinnati, is a former Mount Vernon colleague who is still interested in what happens—and what our research is uncovering—at this very special place. Most of all, I owe a great debt to Scott Casper of the University of Nevada at Reno for reading over this entire manuscript and making detailed suggestions. His enthusiasm for history and museums is infectious and much appreciated.

To the Library of Congress mafia—Sheridan Harvey, Cheryl Adams, Josephus Nelson, Norman Middleton, and Stanley Bandong—thank you for expressing interest and putting up with the latest on George Washington over dinner, time and again. My former coworker, Anne Huber Gorham, who is working on the history of Pohick Church, and newer friend Eleanor Wilson, who shares a similar interest in Christ Church in Alexandria, have each been strong sources of support since the first day we met, as have the members of my Sunday School class (of whom Chris Amrhein, Tony Clarke, Kay Herring, Luci and Jerry Rodgers, and Jim and Debra Downing have to be singled out for their special interest in this project, and Lena Schmucker for her caring).

Acknowledgments

Closer to home, my siblings and their spouses, Robert Avery and Monica Sine Thompson, and Jeff and Laura Thompson Pennington, have provided love, caring, and a ready source of funny e-mails, movie suggestions, and stories about their respective households. My wonderful father, Parker Thompson, introduced me to museums and history as a young child—just look what you started!

Lastly, I owe an enormous thank you to my "best guy," my husband Tony Bates, who has believed in me from the very beginning. A fellow global nomad, he always understands, often without my saying anything. And to Geordie the dog, and the feline trio, Xander, Jerusha, and Nathina—the best four-legged helpers a person could have, whether reading or napping, or contemplating life in the eighteenth century—extra treats all around!

"In the Hands of a Good Providence"

1

CONTROVERSY

A Man of Many Questions

TWO HUNDRED YEARS after the deaths of the men and women who
founded the United States, the question of their religious faith still
elicits strong opinions.[1] The issue has become quite heated and
sometimes even strident. Particularly in the last few decades, what the
Founding Fathers believed has been a bone of contention between the
political left and right. What would otherwise have been just a matter
for those interested in history has broader implications when applied to
things like the interpretation of the Constitution by the Supreme Court.
At least in the case of George Washington, however, this speculation is
nothing new, for the subject of his personal religious beliefs has been a
matter of some controversy for many years. Washington has been called a
near-atheist by some and an extremely religious man by others. His one-
time colleague and later political adversary, Thomas Jefferson, once described him in rather harsh terms to a young Englishman, closing with
the remark that Washington "has divines [ministers] constantly about him
because he thinks it right to keep up appearances but is an unbeliever."

Jefferson's views have been seconded in recent years by a site on the
Internet, which has sought to get out the message that Washington was
not only neither a communicant of the Episcopal nor any other church,
but was not even a "believer in the Christian religion."[2] Conversely, a
eulogy delivered shortly after Washington's death extolled that, "The
virtues of our departed friend were crowned by piety. He is known to

have been habitually devout. To Christian institutions he gave the countenance of his example; and no one could express, more fully, his sense of the Providence of God, and the dependence of man." These same views have recently been expounded by a contemporary member of the clergy, who has used his television ministry to spread the word of Washington's "STERLING CHARACTER . . . CHRISTIAN HERITAGE . . . FERVENT PRAYERS . . . DEVOTIONAL LIFE . . . CHRISTIAN WALK . . . ," and his life as "A TRULY DEVOUT CHRISTIAN."[3]

To muddy the waters further, still other sources, as disparate, and mainstream, as the popular *Encyclopaedia Britannica,* along with prominent Washington biographer James Thomas Flexner, indicate that George Washington was a "Deist" rather than a Christian. Deism developed in the late seventeenth century, growing out of several centuries of discovery in the sciences (for example, astronomers' contention that the earth revolved around the sun, which challenged the teachings of the church that the earth was the center of the universe), as well as geography, as explorers from Europe traveled to other parts of the world and brought back news of other cultures, with vastly different religious traditions. In an attempt to reconcile these new ideas, Deists propounded the notion that knowledge of God is either born into each person or can be found through reason, rather than through revelation or the teachings of any specific religious group. This system flowed from a strong belief in the human ability to reason, a disenchantment or repugnance with religious teachings based solely on revelation, which it was thought led to dogmatism and intolerance, and an image of God as the rational creator of a logical and ordered universe. One well-known example of the latter is the idea that the universe was a watch, which God (the watchmaker) had constructed, set properly, and then walked away from, allowing his creation to tick away without divine interference.[4]

It has been suggested that Deist thought can be reduced to five main propositions: first, that "all men possess the faculty of reason adequate to all the important needs of human life"; second, that "reason, the image of God in man, can know God and God's will"; third, that "man's duty is to do God's will"; fourth, that "man has always had this possibility of knowledge of the good, or natural religion"; and last, that "no religion can be higher than natural religion."[5] That last point, of course, put the Deists at odds with the Christian establishment, which said that Christianity is definitely superior to both natural religion and any of the other religions found in this world.

The Anglo-American church fought back against the Deists in the eighteenth century. Puritan cleric and theologian Jonathan Edwards wrote scathingly that they had "wholly cast off the Christian religion, and are professed infidels. They are not like the Heretics, Arians, Socinians, and others, who own the Scriptures to be the word of God, and hold the Christian religion to be the true religion, but only deny these and these fundamental doctrines of the Christian religion: they deny the whole Christian religion." He went on to say that:

> They own the being of God; but deny that Christ was the son of God, and say he was a mere cheat; and so they say all the prophets and apostles were: and they deny the whole Scripture. They deny that any of it is the word of God. They deny any revealed religion, or any word of God at all; and say that God has given mankind no other light to walk by but their own reason.[6]

Reviled as they might have been by contemporary divines, the Deist philosophers have since been viewed as the progenitors of the secular Enlightenment of the later eighteenth century and described as "powerful agents of modernity."[7]

The truth about Washington's religious beliefs appears to lie between the extremes, pietism and deism, often claimed for him. One of the earliest biographies of Washington was written by Chief Justice John Marshall, whose five-volume work was published between 1804 and 1807, with the cooperation of his subject's family. Marshall knew Washington personally, and wrote simply in his summation of the first president's character: "Without making ostentatious professions of religion, he was a sincere believer in the Christian faith, and a truly devout man."[8] In the catalogue to a 1998 exhibition at the Library of Congress on the role of religion in the founding of the United States, the author wrote that it was difficult to fit Washington into the Deist category at all:

> Judging from his public conduct, he was a loyal Episcopalian. If he was a deist, he did not consider his views incompatible with full participation in his church, because for years he served faithfully as a member of his local vestry. The larger point here is that deism in America, such as it was, did not veer

off into anticlericalism, as it did in Europe; it accommodated itself, without exception, to existing religious institutions.[9]

More recently scholars are recognizing various gradations along the Deist/Christian divide. Charles B. Sanford indicates that Thomas Jefferson, often depicted as a Deist, should more properly be viewed as a theist, someone who believes that God not only exists, but is active in the world and, thus, has attributes that are knowable.[10] Peter Henriques suggests that Washington might best be seen as a "theistic rationalist," someone who followed a "hybrid belief system mixing elements of natural religion, Christianity, and rationalism, with elements of rationalism being the predominant element."[11] David L. Holmes, who has referred to Washington as a "Deistic Episcopalian," argues that the founding generation of Americans should be divided into three categories, rather than two: non-Christian Deists, Christian Deists, and orthodox Christians. Holmes places Thomas Paine and Ethan Allen in the first category, George Washington and Abigail Adams in the second, and Samuel Adams, Elias Boudinot, Patrick Henry, and John Jay in the third.[12] Nicholas Gier suggests that Washington and a number of other founders could be styled "constructive" Deists, rather than "critical" Deists (he defines the latter as "those who were openly anti-Christian and anti-Bible"), but indicates that he prefers the term "religious liberal" as "a far better way of characterizing the religious thought of these founding fathers."[13]

At least three scholars have proposed that the first president was a Latitudinarian, subscribing to a movement within the Anglican Church in the seventeenth and eighteenth centuries, strongly influenced by rationalism (from which deism flowed, as well), which sought to bring people back to the Anglican Church through an appeal to reason and intellect, rather than emotion.[14] In the last half of the seventeenth century, Latitudinarianism grew out of a weariness and disgust with the religious conflicts that had rocked Europe for almost 150 years and culminated in the barbarities of the Thirty Years' War and the English Civil War. Proponents of this movement emphasized the "reasonableness" of Christianity, striving for balance between the contending ideas of the various Protestant denominations and claims for infallibility on the part of Catholic tradition. The Latitudinarians also limited Christian doctrine to a few beliefs, which they considered to be fundamental and had to be accepted as vital to the Christian faith. They were, however, quite accepting, or "allowed for latitude," on other teachings and practices, which they felt were not critical, stressing that the doctrinal differences between Protestant Christians were less important than the beliefs they shared.[15]

The core beliefs of the Latitudinarians seem to have varied from one theologian to the next. One early proponent, for example, reduced the Thirty-Nine Articles of the Anglican Church to five: "That God exists, that he should be worshiped, that man should order his faculties as the principal part of divine worship, that everyone is duty bound to repent his sins, and that rewards and punishments will follow our brief passage here." According to another, if one's neighbors "be Christians in their lives . . . if they acknowledge the Son of God as their master and Lord and live as becomes persons making these professions, . . . why then should I hate such persons . . . because their understandings have not been brought up like mine, have not had the same masters, have not met with the same books, nor the same company." Still others included in their basic theology "the existence of God, the revelation of his word, the atonement and resurrection of his son, the indwelling of the Holy Ghost, and the church universal." This was a tolerant system, in which, as one historian has described it, "the one thing which could not be tolerated was active intolerance in any form."[16] A close examination of Washington's religious education, along with his customary practices and public statements, lends credence to the idea that he may well have been a Latitudinarian. This was a man, after all, who once wrote that "in religion my tenets are few and simple."[17]

The questions about Washington's religious beliefs began during his lifetime. The Reverend Dr. James Muir was the Presbyterian minister in Alexandria, Virginia, in the last years of Washington's life and also served as the chaplain for the local Masonic lodge. He knew Washington better than the average man on the street did, having seen him around the city and known him personally both through the lodge and mutual acquaintances. In a funeral sermon delivered about two weeks after Washington's death, Reverend Muir praised the deceased leader for his public role in furthering the interests of the church:

> Zion mourns his loss for he was her protector. Enumerating in his offi-
> cial papers, events prosperous, or adverse in the most pointed, in the most
> express, in the most devout manner, he acknowledges the interposition of
> a particular Providence. He had always been exemplary at the head of the

army, and in the first office of Government giving regular countenance to public worship. Of the religious rights of his country he was as tender as of her civil. . . . There is levity in some minds whereby they are easily amused by any thing novel in doctrine or in practice. . . . In no age has the influence of such levity been more remarkable than in our own. It has had an effect upon the more experienced, and steady. God, and a superintending Providence has been too much despised. But the illustrious American whose loss we all lament, possessed a strength of mind which such folly could not impress. Whatever proceeded from him in his official character, breathes a reverence for God; a respect for his Government; and a deep sense of the importance of Religion to secure men's best interest both in this, and in the other world.[18]

Despite the Reverend Muir's strong and fairly certain words regarding the public Washington, a letter written by him within a month of this sermon suggests that he may have had some questions about the private George Washington's soul. In answering an unidentified minister about the last hours of Washington's life and, apparently, if he had died in a state of grace, Muir responded by sending a copy of his funeral sermon and stating that, "The Inclosed gives all the answer in my power to give to the important inquiries which you propose. Our illustrious neighbour was a member of the Episcopal Church, and occasionally attended Public worship." Noting that the suddenness and violence of his final illness had prevented the retired president from saying more than twenty sentences throughout the ordeal, he said that Washington's last words included the following statements to his physician: "I die hard . . . will this Struggle last long?—I hope I have nothing to fear." Muir went on to state, "I believe he said no more on this all important Subject." The minister acknowledged that Washington's mind was firm to the end and that he had not been rambling in his final hours. He closed somewhat ambiguously by saying that Americans "lamented his loss, and leave him with him who Judgeth righteously. . . . How happy it would be were all our great men *good* men, nursing fathers and nursing mothers to the church."[19] Muir's account of Washington's final words differs considerably from that of the late president's secretary and long-time friend, Tobias Lear, who was present when Washington died. According to Lear, Washington actually said, "Doctor, I die hard; but I am not afraid to go; I believed from my first attack that I should not survive it; my breath can not last long."[20] The latter statement, of course, expresses no fears about dying and a meeting with the Almighty.

In the forty years after Washington's death, questions continued to be asked about the orthodoxy of the late president's religious beliefs. Less than two months after Washington's demise, Thomas Jefferson recorded a bit of gossip on this subject in a private journal:

Doctor [Benjamin] Rush tells me that he had it from Asa [Ashbel] Green, that when the clergy addressed General Washington on his departure from the Government, it was observed in their consultation, that he had never, on any occasion, said a word to the public which showed a belief in the Christian religion, and they thought they should so pen their address, as to force him at length to declare publicly whether he was a Christian or not. They did so. However, he observed, the old fox was too cunning for them. He answered every article of their address particularly except that, which he passed over without notice. Rush observes, he never did say a word on the subject in any of his public papers, except in his valedictory letter to the Governors of the States, when he resigned his commission in the army, wherein he speaks of "the benign influence of the Christian religion."

I know that Gouverneur Morris, who pretended to be in his secrets and believed himself to be so, has often told me that General Washington believed no more of that system than he himself did.[21]

Jefferson's statements, published after his own death, have been widely used by those who would like to see Washington as a freethinking icono-clast in matters pertaining to religion.[22] They were rebuffed, however, by one of the men who served as Washington's pastor during his presidency. In answer to an inquiry, Episcopal Bishop William White of Pennsylvania recalled Washington's meeting with a number of local ministers shortly before his retirement and the address, "prepared by Dr. Green, and deliv-ered by me," so he knew exactly the contents of the address and the intent behind it. He went on to note that,

It has been the subject of opposite statements, owing to a passage in the posthumous works of Mr. Jefferson. He says, giving Dr. Rush for his author, who is said to have had it from Dr. Green, that the said address was intended to elicit the opinion of the President on the subject of the Christian religion. Dr. Green has denied this, in his periodical called "The Christian Advocate," and his statement is correct. Dr. Rush may have misunderstood Dr. Green, or the former may have been misunderstood by Mr. Jefferson; or the whole may have originated with some individual who mistook his own conceptions for the sense of the body.[23]

How is it possible that so much doubt could exist about this one facet in the life of a man about whom volumes have been written? George Washington was a reticent man by nature. A visitor who came to Mount Vernon shortly after the close of the American Revolution described his host as "a silent man, but when he gave his opinion on any subject it was done with plain good sense."[24] Abigail Smith Adams, the wife of Washington's vice president, John Adams, commented upon getting to know him that, "Our August President is a singular example of modesty and diffidence," while another Mount Vernon visitor noted that Washington had been "reproached for his reserve and his taciturnity," and that he found him "somewhat reserved in speech."[25] Many years later, the man who was his pastor during the presidency, also recalled that Washington was terribly reserved and rarely said anything about himself:

> Although I was often in company of this great man, and had the honour of dining often at his table, I never heard any thing from him that could manifest his opinions on the subject of religion. I knew no man who seemed so carefully to guard against the discoursing of himself or of his acts, or of any thing pertaining to him: and it has occasionally occurred to me, when in his company, that if a stranger to his person were present, he would never have known, from any thing said by the President, that he was conscious of having distinguished himself in the eyes of the world. His ordinary behaviour, although unexceptionably courteous, was not such as to encourage obtrusion on what might be in his mind.[26]

In another letter to the same clergyman, this Episcopal bishop more pointedly linked the lack of evidence about Washington's religious beliefs to his habitual reluctance to discuss personal matters: "I do not believe that any degree of recollection will bring to mind any fact which would prove General Washington to have been a believer in the Christian revelation; further than as may be hoped from his constant attendance on Christian worship, in connection with the natural reserve of his character."[27]

On the subject of his religious beliefs and what he might have confided in her on that subject, Eleanor Parke Custis Lewis, the step-granddaughter Washington had raised, stated:

> I should have thought it the greatest heresy to doubt his firm belief in Christianity. His life, his writings, prove that he was a Christian. He was not one of those, who act or pray, "That they may be seen of men." He communed with his God in secret. . . . He was a silent thoughtful man. He spoke little generally; never of himself. I never heard him relate a single act of his life during the war. . . . I was, probably, one of the last persons on earth to whom he would have addressed serious conversation.[28]

Nelly went on to say, however, that one of the reasons why Washington might not have felt compelled to make more explicit statements on the subject of religion to the young woman placed in his care was that he knew his wife, Martha Dandridge Custis Washington, Nelly's paternal grandmother, was a devout Christian woman, who would set a proper example and bring up the girl in her own image. As Nelly remembered her grandmother and the relationship between the Washingtons, she also made several inferences about her step-grandfather's religious beliefs. She noted that Martha Washington "never omitted her private devotions, or her public duties; and she and her husband were so perfectly united and happy, that he must have been a Christian. She had no doubts, no fears for him."[29]

Nelly's statements about the Washingtons' shared faith and Mrs. Washington's influence on her grandchildren were echoed by one of her older sisters. In a long letter to her own grandson, written on the occasion of his thirteenth birthday, Eliza Parke Custis (Law), then divorced and in the last year of her life, noted that it was from her grandmother that she "learn'd the lessons of duty & religion, which have sustain'd me under trials so afflicting, that I pray no others may suffer in the same degree." She went on to say that Martha Washington was the kind of woman "who shared every thought, who kept pace with him [her husband] in the road of righteousness."[30]

Beyond his own reserve, after so many years in the public eye, it may well have been another trait the Washingtons shared, the desire for privacy, that led to the current uncertainty about a number of issues in their lives, religion being only one. Two important sets of family correspondence are known to have been lost in the last years of the eighteenth and the first years of the nineteenth centuries. First, the majority of the letters written by George Washington to his cousin, Lund Washington, who managed the Mount Vernon estate during the Revolution, were destroyed by Lund's widow in accordance with her late husband's wishes. Second, according to another family tradition, sometime between her husband's death in December 1799 and her own demise in the spring of 1802, Martha Washington burned the many letters exchanged by the couple over a period of about forty years. Only a very few escaped the flames.[31] It is almost impossible not to think, given the friendship between Washington and his cousin, and, more especially, the closeness of the relationship with his wife, which is described by the grandchildren and family friends and can be inferred from other family papers, that Washington would have confided, or allowed to slip out, those things he considered private, including the depth, or lack thereof, of his religious faith, to one or both of these two individuals, particularly his wife. True to their natures, but sadly for the generations of historians and fellow citizens who followed, both Lund and Martha Washington kept the trust that had been placed in them. Still, from surviving family records and statements by the Washingtons and those who knew them well, we can learn something about the practice of George Washington's religious beliefs, as well, perhaps, as the philosophy or theology behind them.

2

FOUNDATIONS

Early Influences

OTH GEORGE AND MARTHA Washington could claim Anglican ministers among their ancestors. George Washington's great-great-grandfather, the Reverend Lawrence Washington, was something of a scholar, who studied at Oxford University's Brasenose College between 1619 and 1623, earning a bachelor's degree and then becoming a fellow at the same school, where he received a master's degree in 1626. The following year, he was made lector of Brasenose College, a position described by one historian as "the chief disciplinarian of undergraduates," and in 1631 he became a proctor for the University of Oxford. The proctorship came as a result of a political move by the Bishop of London (and later Archbishop of Canterbury), William Laud, the university's chancellor, who was working at the behest of King Charles I to stamp out Puritanism at the school. After several members of the administration, including two of the four proctors, were dismissed for their Calvinist leanings, Lawrence Washington was chosen to fill one of those empty slots. This appointment suggests that his theology was close to Laud's and that he may have subscribed to Arminianism, a theological movement begun in the seventeenth century, in reaction to the strict Calvinist belief in predestination.[1]

Within a short time, however, Lawrence Washington's life changed course. Marriage necessitated leaving his position with the university, a job open only to bachelors, and going into the ministry. Reverend

Washington began serving as the rector at All Saints Church in the Essex village of Purleigh about 1632. This position provided a "substantial living" and was probably awarded to him through his ties with the university and Bishop Laud, or, in the words of one historian, as a favor to "a don who had served his college and university exceptionally well, had pleased the Caroline hierarchy, and was ready to take up the benefice to which a university career was expected to lead."[2]

When civil war broke out about a decade later between forces loyal to King Charles I and those backing Parliament under Oliver Cromwell, Reverend Washington remained a firm Royalist, a political position that led to the loss of his parish in 1643 and charges that he was "Malignant," a term often used for those who were loyal to the deposed king. In the ensuing seventeen years until the restoration of the monarchy in 1660, Parliament persecuted almost 2,800 Royalist clergymen.[3] A pamphlet prepared at the behest of the Parliament in 1643 outlined six reasons why the largely Puritan government had moved against one hundred ministers and replaced them with "godly, learned, orthodox Divines, diligent Preachers of the Word of God." The first reason was probably most important in the eyes of the government:

> The present Church Government by Arch-bishops, Bishops, their Chancellours, Commissaries, Deanes, Arch-deacons, and other Ecclesiasticall Officers, depending upon the Hierarchie, is evill and justly Offensive and burdensome to the Kingdome, a great Impediment to Reformation and growth of Religion, and very prejudicial to the State and Government of this Kingdome, and therefore to be taken away.[4]

The author went on to accuse many of the persecuted ministers of neglecting their duties, of "Weighty trust," of preaching the gospel, and of being drunkards, adulterers, and homosexuals who had been unduly influenced by Catholicism.[5]

Among the actions recorded in the little publication was the following, outlining the charges against George Washington's great-great-grandfather:

> The Benefice of *Lawrence Washington,* Rector of *Purleigh* in the County of *Essex,* is sequestred, for that he is a common frequenter of Ale-houses, not only himselfe sitting daily tippling there, but also incouraging others in that

beastly vice, and hath been oft drunke, and hath said, *That the Parliament have more Papists belonging to them in their Armies, then the King had about him or in his Army, and that the Parliaments Army did more hurt then the Cavaleeres, and that they did none at all;* And hath published them to be Traitours, that lend to or assist the Parliament.[6]

A county justice of the peace, who personally knew the Reverend Lawrence Washington, later recorded, however, that

> he took him to be a very Worthy, Pious man; that as often as he was in his Company, he always appeared a very Modest, Sober Person; and that he was Recommended as such, by several Gentlemen, who were acquainted with him before he himself was; Adding withal, that he was a Loyal Person, and had one of the best Benefices in these Parts; and this was the ONLY Cause of his Expulsion, as I verily believe.[7]

Reverend Washington was financially ruined by the loss of his parish, but was given the opportunity to serve the church at a smaller, less wealthy parish in Little Braxted, also in Essex, until his death in 1652.[8]

Their father's persecution at the hands of the Parliamentary government, and its implications for their own futures, probably led Reverend Washington's sons, John and Lawrence, to immigrate to Virginia several years after he died. While they might have become bitter and angry toward God for the way their father had been treated, the young men's faith seems to have weathered the storms in their father's life. Within just a few years of coming to America, John became a vestryman for Appomattox (later called Washington) Parish on July 3, 1661. Taking up this office required him to sign a statement attesting that he had taken an "oath of Alegiance & Supremacie & doe subscribe ye following words: as, I doe Acknowledge my self a true sonn of ye Church of Engld so I doe beleeve ye Articles of faith there professed & oblige myself to bee Conformable to ye Doctrine & Diceline there taught & established."[9]

Virginians at this period often opened their wills with statements about their religious beliefs.[10] As he made preparations for his own death, John, who would become George Washington's great-grandfather, noted that he was "of good & perfect memory," for which he gave thanks to God. He went on to say that he was "hartily & sorry from the bottome of my hart for my sins past," and "most humbly" asked for forgiveness

from the Almighty god (my saviour) & redeimer in whome & by the merrits of Jesus Christ, I trust & beleive assuredly to be saved & to have full
remission & forgiveness of all my sins & yt my soule wth my body at the
generall day of ressuriction shall arise againe wth Joy & through the merrits
of Christ['s] death & passion, possess & inherit the Kingdom of heaven,
prepared for his ellect & Chossen.[11]

After asking that a funeral sermon be preached for him at his church,
John Washington requested that some of the money he still had in England be used to purchase a set of the Ten Commandments and the royal
arms to decorate the "Lower Church of washing[ton] parish," near his
home in Westmoreland County, Virginia.[12]

In a similar fashion, the first point in the will of John's brother, Lawrence, was a statement giving his soul "into the hands of Almighty God,
hoping and trusting through the mercy of Jesus Christ, my one Savior
and redeemer, to receive full pardon & forgiveness of all my sinns, and
my body to the earth, to be buried in comely & decent manner." Later in
this document, he spoke of his "loving wife, Jane Washington, & the two
children God hath given me by her."[13] In the next generation, Lawrence
Washington, who became George Washington's grandfather, left a long
statement of faith in his will, very similar to that of his father, John, and
went on to give directions on the settlement of his "Temporal Estate and
such goods Chattles & Debts as it hath pleased God far above my desarts
to bestow upon me."[14]

Considerably less information is available about the religious beliefs of
Martha Washington's earliest ancestors in Virginia. Her maternal great-
great-grandfather, Rowland Jones, was a minister in Oxfordshire, England, while her great-grandfather, also named Rowland Jones, was an
Oxford graduate and served as the first pastor at Williamsburg's Bruton
Parish Church from 1674 until his death. The younger Jones was initially
paid a salary of £100 per year, but at some point agreed to take sixteen
thousand-weight of tobacco instead, because his congregants claimed that
they could not raise the required amount in cash. In addition to Bruton
Parish Church, for at least a time around 1680, he also ministered to the
congregations at Jamestown and Martin's Hundred.[15]

According to one historian of Anglican Church practices in Virginia,
during the first half of the seventeenth century when the ancestors of
George and Martha Washington were putting down roots in the colony,

their fellow colonists gradually came to realize that, in order to survive and be economically successful, it would be necessary to play down differences between various Christian denominations. Described as "neither toleration nor religious freedom, but . . . a step in that direction," this mind-set "solved the problem of unity and identity by creating a system that left faith a private matter," and stressed "the colonists' common Christian inheritance, rather than the religious factionalism typical of Europe."[16] By the last part of the seventeenth century, and the early years of the eighteenth century, when George and Martha Washington's parents were born and raised, the Latitudinarian message being preached by at least some Anglican clergymen in England was reaching Virginia through published sermons and religious texts, which would have reinforced the earlier moves toward toleration in the colony.

In the years when the Washingtons were growing up, the Anglican Church in Virginia was hampered by a number of factors, including the lack of a bishop to provide leadership and see that children were properly catechized and brought into the church at the appropriate age, a shortage of ministers, and the scattered, rural pattern of land settlement, which meant that parishes tended to be large and pastors were forced to rotate between their flocks. The colonial church saw its purpose as a practical one of providing spiritual sustenance and teaching to individual members, as opposed to a more intellectual involvement in theological and philosophical theorizing or a more emotional regard for "mysteries," such as miracles. There was an emphasis on "low-key piety," which, while it was a deep and pervasive element in the life of an individual believer, "was given to order rather than to passion or ecstasy." A typical Virginia Anglican at this period saw religion as one of life's duties and believed that the proper response to God's love was obedience. As played out in daily life, this duty was manifested by "a well-ordered life of prayer and obedience to God's laws." Eminently practical, a believer's faith would reveal itself through actions, such as prayer and the reading of devotional literature, including the Bible, the Book of Common Prayer, and numerous others. In the words of one historian, "Doing one's duty was a statement of faith and the product of a sincere devotional life."[17] The logistical problems facing the church in Virginia meant that church attendance, while important, was emphasized less than private devotions, which could be done at home.[18]

The revival movement known as the First Great Awakening began in England in the mid-1720s, several years before George and Martha Washington were born, and spread to Britain's American colonies over the next few decades. Evangelicals within the Anglican Church, under the influence of George Whitefield and John Wesley, stressed the need for individual repentance from sin and commitment to God, rather than reliance on ritual and good works within the church setting.[19] Wesley, for example, emphasized the importance of individual salvation and opened his arms to all, not just the educated and moneyed classes, but also the poor, with the message that God loved them and Christ had come to save them. Where the church had previously stressed doing one's duty, both to the church and to society at large, within the sphere in which one had been placed, as well as the need to help and educate those who were less fortunate, Wesley's emphasis was on love, the equality of all believers, and the need for personal salvation.[20] The evangelical movement in eighteenth-century Virginia seems to have been strongest among the Presbyterians and Baptists but reached only a few Anglican pastors and their congregations before the Revolution.[21]

According to the family Bible owned by his mother, George Washington was born in Westmoreland County, Virginia, in February of 1732 and was christened two months later on April 5th into the Anglican Church, the state church of that colony. Officiating at the ceremony that day was probably the Reverend Roderick McCullough, who was the rector of Washington Parish in that county from 1731 until his death.[22] George Washington's family, in the wealthiest tenth of Virginia's population, was part of what has been called the "second tier" of the Virginia aristocracy, having little in the way of prominence or influence outside their home county.[23] His father, Augustine Washington, a planter and businessman, had three surviving children from his first marriage. Augustine's second wife was a young woman named Mary Ball, who had been orphaned at a fairly young age. Like her husband, she had been born in Virginia, to a family that had come to the New World from England. George was the first of six children they would have together before Augustine himself died, when their oldest son was just eleven years old.[24] Unlike the wills of his immediate ancestors, Augustine's, probably made on his deathbed, contained no statement of faith, although he is known to have taken an active role in his local parish, where he served as a vestryman between 1735 and 1737.[25]

Because of the lack of ministers in the colony and the distances involved, it was typical in Virginia during the seventeenth and eighteenth

Page from the Washington family Bible with the entry for George Washington's birth and christening. Like many of his fellow colonists, George Washington was welcomed into the Anglican Church, as an infant, at the time of his christening. He would remain a member of that denomination for his entire life. (Courtesy of the Mount Vernon Ladies' Association)

centuries for religious instruction to take place within the home, rather than at the church. One Anglican minister, born in Virginia the year after George Washington's birth, to parents who did not attend church services, noted that his parents had still schooled their children on the subject of religion, and had "made us perfect in repeating the Church Catechism."[26] Historians looking into the practices of colonial Virginians at this period have found "recollections of the devotional regimen of Anglican mothers, the stern rectitude of Anglican fathers, and the common parental practices of teaching young Anglican children to read with the Bible as their primer, drilling them in the catechism, and stocking their households with books of sermons and other religious treatises."[27]

Given the dearth of substantial information about George Washington's childhood, including his religious training, myth has tended to substitute for hard evidence. An early biographer, Parson Mason Locke Weems, an Episcopal minister and itinerant bookseller, recorded a number of rather fanciful and sentimental, if not saccharine, stories about the religious education provided for the young Washington by his parents, more specifically, his father. At least one of Weems's anecdotes has become imbedded in the American public's understanding of Washington's life and character. A fellow clergyman later recorded that Weems was a kind, gentle, charitable man who had a gift for making people laugh: "Whether in private or public, in prayers or preaching, it was impossible that either the young or old, the grave or the gay, could keep their risible faculties from violent agitation." Even this minister, however, felt obliged to remind his readers that Weems was never one to let truth stand in the way of a good story. Writing in 1857, when there were still people alive who had known Weems, he noted, "Some of Mr. Weems's pamphlets on drunkenness and gambling would be most admirable in their effects, but for the fact that you know not what to believe of the narrative." He went on to say that Weems's biographies of Washington and Francis Marion were "very popular, but the same must be said of them. You know not how much of fiction there is in them."[28]

The best-known of Weems's tales relates the story of how Washington, as a six-year-old, fatally damaged his father's cherry tree with a new hatchet and later confessed the act when questioned about it. In another, Weems has Washington's father deliver a lesson on the benefits of sharing, an activity that would bring down blessings from God.[29] Even more interesting is one in which Washington's father wrote the boy's name in seeds in the garden and then covered them over. A few days later, the seeds had come up, startling the child, who ran to tell his father about his amazing find. The two discussed the possibility that the seeds had grown that way by chance, giving the father the opportunity to confess his role in the trick, and to teach his son "a great thing which I wish you to understand. I want, my son, to introduce you to your *true* Father." As related by Weems, the senior Washington expounded, "As my son could not believe that *chance* had made and put together so exactly the *letters* of his name, (though only sixteen) then how can he believe that *chance* could have made and put together all those millions and millions of things that are now so exactly fitted to his good?" In the story, the young George eventually concluded, with his father's guidance, that God had made the world and that everything his family had was a gift from the Almighty. Weems closed this section of his book with the words:

> At this, George fell into a profound silence, while his pensive looks showed that his youthful soul was labouring with some idea never felt before. Perhaps it was at that moment, that the good Spirit of God ingrafted on his heart that germ of piety, which filled his after life with so many of the precious fruits of *morality*.[30]

Leaving the problems with the Weems account aside, however, it is still possible to determine something about the religious education with which the boy was raised. Augustine's death left Mary Ball Washington and their five surviving children in straitened circumstances. Where George Washington's father and two older half-brothers had been schooled in England, that option was now closed to the family. George and his younger siblings would have to be educated in Virginia, by his mother and whatever local schoolteachers were available. As an adult, Washington would feel that his basic education had been "defective." Unlike others of his class, he could not read Latin, Hebrew, Greek, or French, and throughout his life he sought to improve himself through reading on his own and amassing a large library.[31]

While not enough material survives to corroborate the family's own oral history, George Washington's mother was remembered in the family as an extremely devout woman. According to Martha Washington's grandson, Mary Ball Washington had been "always pious" and, as an elderly woman, "her devotions were performed in private. She was in the habit of repairing every day to a secluded spot, formed by rocks and trees near to her dwelling, where, abstracted from the world and worldly things, she communed with her Creator in humiliation and prayer."[32]

The recollections of Mary Ball Washington's own grandsons provide some indication of the influence she may have had on the spiritual development of her children many years earlier. Lawrence Lewis was a son of Fielding Lewis and George Washington's younger sister, Betty, who lived nearby and served as primary caregiver for her aging mother. As a result, Lawrence, who married Martha Washington's granddaughter, Nelly, had many years of close contact with his grandmother. He recalled much later that she had a favorite rock, which gave a lovely view of the surrounding countryside, and that it "was upon this spot, rendered forever dear to my recollection, she impressed on our infant minds the wonderful works of the Great Creator of all things, his goodness, his mercy to all who love and obey him."[33] Another grandson, Lawrence's younger brother Robert, remembered spending Sunday evenings looking through the pictures illustrating the Washington family Bible with his grandmother, as she read aloud to him from it.[34] There is no reason to think that she had not given similar lessons to her own children, including her oldest son George, during his boyhood.

In May of 1788, Mrs. Washington drew up her will, which began with a one-paragraph statement of faith. It started, as was typical, with the words, "In the Name of God! amen." Noting that she was in good health, but "calling to mind the uncertainty of this life," the elderly woman recommended her soul "into the Hands of my Creator, hoping for a remission of all my Sins through the merits & mediation of Jesus Christ, the Saviour of mankind."[35] Upon her death a little over a year after drawing up the will, Mary Ball Washington was eulogized with the words: "It is usual when virtuous and conspicuous persons quit this terrestrial abode, to publish an elaborate panegyric on their characters—suffice it to say, she conducted herself through this transitory life with virtue, prudence and Christianity, worthy the mother of the greatest Hero that ever adorned the annals of history." This statement, taken from her death notice, suggests that Mary Ball Washington was considered a religious woman, not just by her family, but also by others who actually knew her.[36]

While no books were recorded in the estate inventory taken the summer after Augustine Washington's death, relying on the inventory alone would give an incomplete or false picture of life in the Washington household.[37] In addition to the family Bible mentioned earlier, other books in Augustine and Mary Ball Washington's home could have been used for the religious education of their children. Only a handful of the objects once owned by George Washington's mother have retained their association with her over the years; one of those things is a book entitled *The Christian Life,* which was written by John Scott, one-time rector of St. Giles's in the Fields, and published in London in 1700. Signed "Mary Ball, 1728," it suggests that, as a young woman of twenty, Washington's mother had an interest in the Anglican religious thought of the period, a concern she may well have shared with her children, the first of whom, George Washington, would be born only four years after she received this book.[38] Mary Ball Washington also owned, and signed, a 1685 edition of *Contemplations, Moral and Divine,* by Sir Matthew Hale, which later came into the library of her son at Mount Vernon. There is a family tradition that Mrs. Washington read aloud from this volume to her children.[39] The book's author is best known today as a jurist and expert on English common law. Hale was tolerant on religious matters, numbering both nonconformists and liberal Anglicans among his friends. Having been raised as a Puritan, he managed to remain neutral during the conflict between the king and his largely Puritan Parliament in the 1640s, and even defended Royalists in court.[40]

These were not the only books in the family library that might have influenced the boy's religious development. Among the few other surviving artifacts from this formative period in his life are two books now in the collection at the Boston Athenaeum. The first, by Thomas Comber, is entitled *Short Discourses upon the Whole Common-Prayer. Designed to Inform the Judgment, and Excite the Devotion of Such as Daily Use the Same,* which was published in London in 1712. It was signed by both of his parents and later by George Washington himself, as a thirteen-year-old. The second is a book of sermons dating from 1717, *The Sufficiency of a Standing Revelation in General, and of the Scripture Revelation in Particular . . . In Eight Sermons, Preached in the Cathedral-Church of St. Paul, London,* by Offspring Blackhall, in which Washington, then probably eight or nine, signed his name twice.[41] Blackhall was educated at St. Catharine's College in Cambridge, served as rector at several parishes, and later became chaplain to King William III. He was made Bishop of Exeter in 1708. The book in the Washington home was based on lectures given by Blackhall in the year 1700 as part of a series, known as the Boyle Lectures, which were instituted by the scientist Robert Boyle "as a bulwark of Christianity— more particularly, of Low Church Anglican Christianity—against a rising tide of infidelity." Here, again, was a liberal, Latitudinarian world view, in which, in the words of one scholar, the lecturers sought to

> expound a theology based on the "two books" of Nature and Scripture, with minimal dependence on the traditions of the Church. . . . [They] sought to articulate an Anglican theology sufficiently broad and inclusive to "comprehend" many of the dissenters, and were prepared to make concessions on points of doctrine and practice to achieve that end. They were keen to em-

phasize, with [John] Locke, the *reasonableness* of Christianity, and to explain away its mysteries and seeming paradoxes. They were prepared to argue against atheists and deists on their own terms, i.e. to defend the credibility of the Christian revelation in terms of ordinary human reason, experience and testimony.[42]

From this description, one can perhaps see the genesis of Mary Ball Washington's lessons to her grandsons and presumably to her son many years before, in which she used examples from nature to teach about the nature of God.

It was not only works by Anglican churchmen that might have helped to shape Washington's religious development. As a schoolboy, sometime before his sixteenth birthday, Washington copied out a list of 110 "Rules of Civility & Decent Behaviour in Company and Conversation," as both a penmanship exercise and moral instruction. Based on a seventeenth-century English etiquette book, which in turn had been translated from a late sixteenth-century French Jesuit text on behavior, four of those rules, which influenced Washington throughout his life, dealt with God, religion, and the clergy. The first, number 26, included "Churchmen" among those "Persons of Distinction" in whose presence one was to remove one's hat, while number 109 cautioned the young Washington to "Let your Recreations be Manfull not Sinfull," and number 110 reminded him to "Labour to keep alive in your Breast that Little Spark of Celestial fire Called Conscience." Evidence from his later writings indicates that Washington took the fourth rule, number 108, very much to heart: "When you Speak of God or His Attributes, let it be Seriously & with Reverence."[43]

It would have been when Washington was in his late teens that whatever lessons he may have been taught by his mother and/or his church about the need for private toleration of differences between Christian denominations were reinforced by the activities of his older half-brother, Lawrence Washington. With a number of other gentlemen, Lawrence was then involved in a business enterprise known as the Ohio Company, which was trying to arrange for the sale of 50,000 acres of frontier lands to settlers from Germany. Lawrence had talked with German immigrants in Pennsylvania and found that, while they were very interested in moving to the Ohio country, their chief objection was "the paying of an English clergyman, when few understood, and none made use of him," a reference to the fact that they would have to pay taxes to support the Church of England. Lawrence was appointed to convince the British government to exempt the German settlers from those levies. In letters to government officials, he began by explaining the problem and then went on to give his personal opinion that "restraints on conscience are cruel, in regard to those on whom they are imposed, and injurious to the country imposing them." As he continued his argument, Lawrence stated that he hoped the English government would procure "some kind of charter to prevent the residents on the Ohio and its branches from being subject to parish taxes." The people to whom he had spoken indicated that large numbers of new settlers would come from Germany, "could they but obtain their favorite exemption." He did not believe that the Virginia legislature would approve such an exemption, but hoped that the mother country would. He compared the settlement pattern in Virginia with those in places with more liberal laws respecting religion, suggesting that the colony would benefit by allowing this small step toward religious freedom:

> This Colony was greatly settled in the latter part of Charles the First's time and during the usurpation by the zealous churchmen; and that spirit which was then brought in, has ever since continued, so that except a few Quakers we have no Dissenters. But what has been the consequence? We have increased by slow degrees except Negroes and convicts whilst our neighboring Colonies whose natural advantages are greatly inferior to ours have become populous.[44]

The governor of Virginia, then in England, responded favorably, but with a degree of caution: "I fear this will be a difficult task to get over; and at present the Parliament is so busy with public affairs, and the Ministry in course engaged, that we must wait some time before we can reply; but be assured of my utmost endeavours therein."[45] Although nothing further was done at this time about Lawrence's request, the seeds planted, probably through conversations with this half-brother, would begin to bear fruit in George Washington's life as an adult.

There is evidence in George Washington's writings that he had absorbed the stories, language, and practices of the Judeo-Christian scriptures to which he, like children in other Anglican families throughout the colony, was undoubtedly exposed during the course of his education. An undated entry in a memorandum book he kept during his teenage years indicates that he was studying the Bible at a period when he was spending little time with his mother and was beginning to make a career for himself as a surveyor. Among the many notes to himself in that little book was one suggesting, "If you cant find it in the Book of Ezekiel look for it in Israel."[46] Later in life, Washington's letters show a familiarity with people or characters mentioned in the Bible. In a teasing note to his brother-in-law, he once wrote that his tobacco crop was being "assailed by every villainous worm that has had an existence since the days of Noah," commenting that it was "unkind . . . of Noah now I have mentioned his name to suffer such a brood of vermin to get a birth in the Ark."[47] Concern about profiteers and others he considered "the greatest Enemys we have to the happiness of America" led Washington to write during the Revolution that, "I would to God that one of the most atrocious of each State was hung in Gibbets upon a gallows five times as high as the one prepared by Haman." Haman, of course, was the villain in the Old Testament book of Esther, the adviser to the Persian king, who plotted to have all the Jews in the kingdom killed but ended up being hanged on a gallows fifty cubits high, which he had intended for someone else.[48]

Washington's thinking shows that he had internalized certain principles expounded in the Bible. During the Revolution, he cautioned a friend that, "To trust altogether in the justice of our cause, without our own utmost exertions, would be tempting Providence," an allusion to a phrase that appears more than once in the scriptures, including in the story of Jesus's temptation in the wilderness, when he rebuked Satan with the words, "Thou shalt not tempt the Lord thy God."[49] In a discussion about some of the problems facing America during the war, especially price gouging and other actions that took advantage of the government and the army, Washington confided to a friend his belief that, "Our conflict is not likely to cease so soon as every good Man would wish. The measure of iniquity is not yet filled; and unless we can return a little more to first principles, and act a little more upon patriotic ground, I do not know when it will, or, what may be the Issue of the contest." The idea that the outcome of an event such as the war would be determined by the merits of those involved in the conflict, and that the United States could still turn things around, because the "measure of iniquity is not yet filled," alludes to a statement in the book of Genesis which reads, "But in the fourth generation they [Abram's descendants] shall come hither again: for the iniquity of the Amorites is not yet full."[50] In the circular letter he wrote to the governors of the states at the end of the American Revolution, Washington closed with the prayer that God would "most graciously be pleased to dispose us all, to do Justice, [and] to love mercy." In this case, he borrowed almost directly from an Old Testament prophet: "What doth the LORD require of thee, but to do justly, and to love mercy, and to walk humbly with thy God."[51]

Phrases from the Bible came to Washington's mind in letters to friends, and especially when he was giving advice to young relatives. In thanking a French correspondent for a recent letter, Washington remarked, "Every fresh assurance you give me of the continuation of your friendship is pleasing: it serves (to borrow an Indian phraze) to brighten the chain, and to convince me that you will not suffer moth or rust to injure or impair it."[52] While Native Americans may have used the phrase "brighten the chain," Washington clearly took the last part of the sentence from Jesus's injunction to his followers, in the Sermon on the Mount: "Lay not up for yourselves treasures upon earth, where moth and rust doth corrupt, and where thieves break through and steal: But lay up for yourselves treasures in heaven, where neither moth nor rust doth corrupt, and where thieves do not break through nor steal: For where your treasure is, there will your heart be also."[53] To several neighbors, who were hunting on Washington's land without permission, the retired president gave a reminder that many of his deer, descended from several brought from England for his deer park, looked very different from the native American variety. He then went on to paraphrase the Golden Rule, expressing the hope "that upon the principle of doing as one would be done by, they [the deer] would not have been injured by my Neighbours."[54]

Several times, in reference to charity, Washington wrote of contributing "my mite," or he encouraged a young relative to "never let an indigent person ask, without receiving something, if you have the means; always recollecting in what light the widow's mite was viewed," a clear reference to a famous story from the life of Jesus about an elderly widow in the temple at Jerusalem.[55] At one point, Washington tried to encourage his step-grandson to pay more attention to his school books and less to a young woman, counseling that he should "recollect again the saying of the wise man, 'There is a time for all things,' and sure I am this is not a time for a *boy of your age* to enter into engagements which might end in sorrow and repentance," an allusion to the beginning of the third chapter of the Old Testament book of Ecclesiastes, which states, "To every thing there is a season, and a time to every purpose under the heaven."[56] In a similar vein, when writing to a twenty-two-year-old nephew who was briefly managing Mount Vernon for him, Washington advised:

> I will mention a proverb to you which you will find worthy of attention all the days of your life; under any circumstances, or in any situation you may happen to be placed; and that is, to put nothing off 'till the Morrow, that you can do to day. The habit of postponing things is among the worst in the world; doing things in season is always beneficial; but out of season, it frequently happens that so far from being beneficial, that oftentimes, it proves a real injury. It was one of the sayings of the wise man you know, that there is a season for all things, and nothing is more true; apply it to any occurrence or transaction in life.[57]

Washington also made the phraseology of the scriptures his own. In a letter on wartime problems to his favorite brother, he referred back to the writings of St. Paul when he noted that unless something was done to curtail these damaging practices, "it does not require the gift of prophecy to foretell the consequences."[58] Several years earlier, he told this same brother about the reaction of those Bostonians who had remained loyal to the Crown to the news that the British were evacuating the city: "When the Order Issued therefore for Imbarking the Troops in Boston, no Electric Shock, no sudden Clap of thunder, [i]n a word the last Trump, could not have struck them with greater Consternation." Here, too, he used a phrase of St. Paul's: "Behold, I shew you a mystery; We shall not all sleep, but we shall all be changed, In a moment, in the twinkling of an eye, at the last trump: for the trumpet shall sound, and the dead shall be raised incorruptible, and we shall be changed."[59] Washington's use of language in a letter to General Benjamin Lincoln, in which he said that, "I trust in that Providence, which has saved us in six troubles yea in seven, to rescue us again from any imminent, though unseen, dangers," harkens back to the Old Testament book of Proverbs, where the writer noted that, "These six things doth the Lord hate; yea, seven are an abomination unto him."[60] After his retirement from the presidency, Washington wrote of his approaching demise—"The scene will close; grateful to that Providence which has directed my steps, and shielded me in the various changes and chances, through which I have passed, from my youth to the present moment"—in words reminiscent of a statement in the book of Proverbs: "A man's heart deviseth his way: but the Lord directeth his steps."[61]

One of the best examples of Washington's use of Biblical language comes from a very warm letter to the Marquis de Lafayette, written a few years after the conclusion of the American Revolution, which overflows with affection and good spirits:

> As the clouds which overspread your hemisphere are dispersing, and peace with all its concomitants is dawning upon your Land, I will banish the sound of War from my letter: I wish to see the sons and daughters of the world in Peace and busily employed in the more agreeable amusement of fulfilling the first and great commandment, *Increase and Multiply:* as an encouragement to which we have opened the fertile plains of the Ohio to the poor, the needy and the oppressed of the Earth; any one therefore who is heavy laden, or who wants to cultivate, may repair thither and abound, as in the Land of promise, with milk and honey: the ways are preparing and the roads will be made easy, thro' the channels of Potomac and James river.[62]

Here Washington pulled together a variety of images from both the Old and New Testaments. The "first and great commandment" harkens back to the very beginning of the Bible, when God told the first humans, "Be fruitful, and multiply, replenish the earth, and subdue it."[63] The reference to opening the West to those who were "heavy laden" recalls the words of Jesus, "Come unto me, all ye that labour and are heavy laden, and I will give you rest," while the "land of promise," which abounded with "milk and honey" was taken from descriptions of Canaan, the land to which the Israelites headed after their release from slavery in Egypt.[64] Washington's statement that the way to the West had been made easy refers back to John the Baptist's message: "Prepare ye the way of the Lord, make his paths straight. Every valley shall be filled, and every mountain and hill shall be brought low; and the crooked shall be made straight, and the rough ways shall be made smooth; And all flesh shall see the salvation of God."[65]

Three years later, Washington paraphrased scripture as he wrote to another correspondent in France about his hopes for peace in the future. In expressing those thoughts, he turned to the second chapter of the book of Isaiah, in which the prophet described the coming kingdom of God:

> For the sake of humanity it is devoutly to be wished, that the manly employment of agriculture and the humanizing benefits of commerce, would supersede the waste of war and the rage of conquest; that the swords might

be turned into plough-shares, the spears into pruning hooks, and, as the Scripture expresses it, "the nations learn war no more."[66]

Washington would turn to this vision of implements of war being transformed into tools needed in peacetime in at least three other letters.[67]

Probably the best-known example of a Biblical phrase used by Washington over and over again was that of the vine and fig tree. For instance, in a letter to the Jewish congregation in Newport, Rhode Island, he wrote, "May the children of the Stock of Abraham, who dwell in this land, continue to merit and enjoy the good will of the other inhabitants, while everyone shall sit in safety under his own vine and fig-tree, and there shall be none to make him afraid." That particular phrase was used in at least two places in the Old Testament. The first instance comes from the history of the kingdoms of Judah and Israel, in which it was recorded at one point, "And Judah and Israel dwelt safely, every man under his vine and under his fig tree"; the second is from one of the prophets, who foretold, "But they shall sit every man under his vine and under his fig tree; and none shall make them afraid: for the mouth of the Lord of hosts hath spoken it."[68]

The image of a person resting peacefully under his own grape vines and fig trees was appealing to eighteenth-century Americans of all denominations. When they wrote to Washington of their concerns about religious freedom at the beginning of his presidency, the Baptists in the state of Virginia noted that they were making fervent prayers, on behalf of both the country and himself,

> that the federal government, and the governments of the States, without rivalship may so co-operate together as to make the numerous peoples, over whom you preside, the happiest nation on earth, and you, Sir, the happiest man, in seeing the People, whom you saved from vassalage by your martial valor, and made wise by your maxims sitting securely under their vines and fig-trees, enjoying the perfection of human felicity.[69]

An example from his first inauguration suggests that Washington himself had developed a respect for the scriptures, which had probably served as his earliest school text. As he took the oath of office as president of the United States on April 30, 1789, Washington laid his hand on a Bible, borrowed from a nearby Masonic lodge, which had been opened to the forty-ninth and fiftieth chapters of Genesis.[70] Then, in a very public display before a crowd of thousands standing outside Federal Hall in New York City as he finished taking the oath that day, according to witnesses, Washington leaned over and "reverently" kissed the open pages of the Bible.[71] Many years after these events, Eliza Morton Quincy, the wife of Josiah Quincy (later the president of Harvard University), left the following account of what she witnessed at the inauguration as a fifteen-year-old girl:

> The balcony of the Hall was in full view of this assembled multitude. In the centre was placed a table, with a rich covering of red velvet, and upon this was a crimson velvet cushion, on which lay a large and elegant Bible. This was all the paraphernalia of this august scene. All eyes were fixed upon the balcony where at the appointed hour, Washington entered, accompanied by the Chancellor. . . . The populace appeared to understand that the scene had overcome him [Washington], and were at once hushed into profound silence. After a few moments the General arose and came forward. Chancellor Livingston read the form of oath prescribed by the Constitution; Washington repeated it, resting his hand upon the table. The chancellor took the Bible to raise it to the lips of Washington; he stooped and kissed the book.[72]

3

CHURCH AFFILIATION

A Lifelong Anglican

THROUGHOUT HIS LIFE, George Washington remained a member of the Anglican Church and, after the Revolution, of its American successor, the Episcopal Church. The officiating ministers at both his wedding and his funeral, two significant events separated by forty years, were Anglican/Episcopal clergymen.[1] He was married on January 6, 1759, by the Reverend David Mossom, in New Kent County, Virginia, at a plantation called White House. This was the home of Washington's bride, twenty-seven-year-old Martha Dandridge Custis, whose first husband had died eighteen months earlier, leaving her with two very young children.

Reverend Mossom had been born in England and received his education at St. John's College in Cambridge University. After serving for a time at Newburyport, Massachusetts, Mossom came to Virginia and was the pastor of the young woman's parish church, St. Peter's, for four decades (1727–67). The bride's family had been active members of his congregation for years. Several of her younger siblings had been christened by Reverend Mossom, who also delivered the funeral sermon for Martha's first husband. Both her late husband, Daniel Parke Custis, and her father, John Dandridge, had served together as vestrymen and churchwardens, and at one point, they both signed an oath declaring that they did not believe in the doctrine of transubstantiation (the idea that the wine and bread used in the communion service were actually transformed into the blood and body of Christ).[2] This oath, popularly known as "the Test," was required of all officeholders, both religious and secular, in the colony of Virginia, as a means of separating Anglican beliefs about this rite from those held by the Roman Catholic Church, from which the Anglicans had broken away two centuries before. More practically, it also made it impossible for Catholics to hold political office in Virginia.[3]

Said to have been the first American-born presbyter in the Church of England, Reverend Mossom was a somewhat temperamental eccentric, who had four wives in the course of his life. According to another minister, Devereux Jarratt, an evangelical Anglican, who had been raised in this parish at the same time as Martha Washington and later "brought Methodism to Virginia in the 1770s," Mossom once got into a disagreement with his clerk, taking his subordinate to task one Sunday in his sermon, which led the clerk, later in the same service, to read out as the psalm: "With restless and ungovern'd rage,/Why do the heathen storm?/Why in such rash attempts engage/As they can ne'er perform?" The service that Sunday must have been pretty memorable; Jarratt recalled that Reverend Mossom's usual style in the pulpit was rather dull, preaching "wholly from a written sermon, keeping his eyes continually fixed on the paper, and so near that what he said seemed rather addressed to the cushion than to the congregation."[4]

Forty years after the wedding presided over by Reverend Mossom, George Washington was entombed in the old family vault at Mount Vernon on the afternoon of December 18, 1799, following Anglican and Masonic funeral rites. Four ministers (two Episcopalians and two Presbyterians) took part in that service. The lead role was taken by the Reverend Thomas Davis, rector of Christ Church in Alexandria between 1792 and 1806. Davis had been born in the colonial Chesapeake and educated at the College of William and Mary in Williamsburg. During the American Revolution, he served as a chaplain before being captured by the British in 1779.[5] He was later described as a decent man whose skills as an orator were sadly lacking. According to one clergyman who had known him, Davis "had ministered in various places in Virginia and, though a man of temperate habits and correct life by comparison with too many of our clergy, was not calculated by his preaching or conversation to promote the spiritual welfare of any people."[6]

Assisting Davis on the day of the funeral was the Reverend Walter Dulany Addison, the rector at the Episcopal Church in Oxon Hill, Maryland.[7]

Both of the Presbyterian ministers who took part in the funeral were associated with George Washington through the Alexandria Academy, a school for orphaned and needy children, to which George Washington paid an annual subscription. Born in Scotland, James Muir served as pastor of the Presbyterian Church in Alexandria for over thirty-one years, taught at a school for young ladies, held a number of local offices, and was chaplain to both the St. Andrew's Society and the Masonic Lodge in Alexandria, of which George Washington was also a member.[8] The second Presbyterian minister officiating that day was William Moffatt, a teacher at the Alexandria Academy.[9]

Stories have circulated for the past two centuries that George Washington turned from the Anglican faith and was either baptized into the Baptist Church during the American Revolution or converted to Catholicism on his deathbed. Neither of these stories can be substantiated, and their veracity is quite doubtful. In the first, Washington is said to have gone to Continental Army chaplain John Gano to request baptism by immersion. Gano, a Baptist of Huguenot descent, had been a missionary in Virginia and South Carolina before becoming a pastor to churches in North Carolina and Philadelphia and at the First Baptist Church of New York City. While New York was occupied by the British for more than seven years during the Revolution, Gano went into the army as chaplain to the Americans.

It was during the last phase of the war that George Washington is said to have approached Gano and said, "I have been investigating the Scripture, and I believe immersion to be the baptism taught in the Word of God, and I demand it at your hands. I do not wish any parade made or the army called out, but simply a quiet demonstration of the ordinance." Chaplain Gano then accompanied Washington to the Hudson River, where, in front of forty-two witnesses, he proceeded with the ceremony. Although written statements were later said to have been made by some of these witnesses, their present whereabouts are unknown and the primary evidence for this event comes from statements made by Chaplain Gano's grandchildren when they were quite elderly. Army historians investigating the case have been skeptical.[10]

According to the second tradition, within hours of Washington's death, slaves from Mount Vernon rowed over to Maryland to pick up a Jesuit priest, Leonard Neale, and bring him back to Mount Vernon, where he met alone with Washington and baptized him into the Catholic Church. Father Neale is said to have documented Washington's conversion in a letter, which was placed in a sealed packet and later sent to the Jesuit archives in Rome. A Catholic researcher relating the story in a publication in 1900 found a number of reasons to discount the legend, which was said to have been well known among both the white and African American populations in the Maryland counties immediately across from Mount Vernon.[11]

As an adult, when he could have given up activities related to the practice of religion, had he been so inclined, Washington continued to take an active part in the religious life of his family, friends, and community. He stood as godfather for at least eight children over the years: his nephews, Fielding Lewis Jr. and Charles Lewis, who were born in 1751 and 1760, respectively; Ferdinando, born in 1769, the third son of his long-time friend and hunting companion, the Reverend Bryan Fairfax; Daniel McCarty Chichester, also born in 1769, the grandson of his neighbor, Colonel Daniel McCarty; George Washington Motier Lafayette, the son born in 1779 to his friend, the Marquis de Lafayette; Catherine, a little girl born to his friend Philip Schuyler and his wife in 1781, for whom Washington "chearfully" became a sponsor; a little boy named Walter W. Buchanan, who later became a prominent doctor in New York; and Benjamin Lincoln Lear, who was the son of his long-time secretary and friend, Tobias Lear. In the case of the last of these, the minister who officiated at the ceremony recalled that both George and Martha Washington "very devoutly" attended the christening, which took place in the executive mansion in 1791.[12]

The ritual associated with christenings spelled out the very serious duties expected of godparents by Anglican, and later Episcopal, churches. If the ceremony were held at church, the minister would address the child's sponsors (the godparents) in these words:

> Dearly beloved, ye have brought *this Child* here to be baptized; ye have prayed that our Lord Jesus Christ would vouchsafe to receive *him,* to release *him* from sin, to sanctify *him* with the Holy Ghost, to give *him* the kingdom of heaven and everlasting life . . . *this Infant* must also promise by you that are *his* Sureties (until he come of age to take it upon *himself*) that *he* will renounce the devil and all his works, and constantly believe God's holy Word, and obediently keep his Commandments.[13]

The minister would then ask the godparents to answer a series of questions on behalf of the child: "Dost thou, in the Name of *this Child,* renounce the devil and all his works, the vain pomp and glory of the world . . . and the sinful desires of the flesh; so that thou wilt not follow, nor be led by them?"; "Dost thou believe all the Articles of the Christian Faith, as contained in the Apostles Creed?"; "Wilt thou be baptized in this Faith?"; and "Wilt thou then obediently keep God's holy will and commandments, and walk in the same all the days of thy life?"[14] Following the christening ceremony, the minister would make the following exhortation to the godparents:

> Forasmuch as *this child hath* promised by you *his* Sureties, to renounce the
> devil and all his works, to believe in God, and to serve him; ye must remem-
> ber, that it is your parts and duties to see, that *this Infant* be taught, so soon
> as he shall be able to learn, what a solemn vow, promise, and profession *he*
> *hath* here made by you. And that *he* may know these things the better, ye
> shall call upon *him* to hear Sermons; and chiefly ye shall provide, that *he*
> may learn the Creed, the Lord's Prayer, and the Ten Commandments, and
> all other things which a Christian ought to know and believe to his soul's
> health; and that *this Child* may be virtuously brought up to lead a godly and
> a christian life: remembering always, that Baptism doth represent unto us
> our profession; which is, to follow the example of our Saviour Christ, and to
> be made like unto him; that as he died, and rose again for us, so should we,
> who are baptized, die from sin, and rise again unto righteousness; continu-
> ally mortifying all our evil and corrupt affections, and daily proceeding in all
> virtue and godliness of living.[15]

Had Washington suffered from doubts or uncertainties concerning church doctrine, he could have declined to serve as a godfather. The necessity for sponsors to profess a belief in the Trinity, one of the tenets of the Apostles' Creed, was a primary reason behind Thomas Jefferson's refusal to stand as godfather for the children of friends.[16] As he explained to a friend in France, in 1788:

> I am not a little mortified that scruples, perhaps not well founded, forbid
> my undertaking this honourable office. The person who becomes sponsor
> for a child, according to the ritual of the church in which I was educated
> [the same Anglican Church in which Washington was raised], makes a

solemn profession, before god and the world, of faith in articles, which I had never sense enough to comprehend, and it has always appeared to me that comprehension must precede assent. The difficulty of reconciling the ideas of Unity and Trinity, have, from a very early part of my life, excluded me from the office of sponsorship, often proposed to me by my friends, who would have trusted, for the faithful discharge of it, to morality alone instead of which the church requires faith.[17]

It is certainly possible that Washington may just have been going through the motions during the christening ceremonies in which he took part, simply repeating words, without paying attention, caring about, or even believing, what they meant. But was Washington the kind of man to whom words and oaths meant nothing? As will be shown, shortly after his return from the American Revolution, Washington resigned from a long-held position at his parish church, probably because he could no longer promise to be subject to the doctrine and discipline of a church headed by the man against whom he had been fighting for eight years. Many years later, in his Farewell Address of 1796, Washington reminded his fellow citizens of the importance of religion and morality in the political life of the United States. By way of argument, he cautioned, "Let it simply be asked where is the security for property, for reputation, for life, if the sense of religious obligation *desert* the oaths, which are the instruments of investigation in Courts of Justice?"[18] These are hardly the words of a man who would take an oath or make a promise by rote.

It was not unusual for Anglican children in Virginia at this period to be christened at home, and there is evidence that members of George and Martha Washington's families observed such ceremonies. Washington noted in his diary entry for August 22, 1768, during a visit to the home of his brother, Samuel, that he was "still at my Brothers with other Company—his Child being Christned."[19] At least one christening took place in the mansion at Mount Vernon during George Washington's years as proprietor of the estate. In the spring of 1787 a son was born to Frances Bassett and George Augustine Washington, who were, respectively, the niece of Martha Washington and the nephew of George Washington. The young couple had been part of the household for several years and were proving to be a great help to the older Washingtons. After about two weeks, however, Fanny's little boy became terribly sick and his life was despaired of. On a Tuesday night, the Reverend Lee Massey, who had

Chinese export porcelain bowls, said to be the Dandridge family christening bowls. Much like weddings and funerals, christening ceremonies were often held at home in eighteenth-century Virginia. These Chinese export porcelain pieces were passed down in the family of Martha Washington, with the tradition of having been used to christen children in the Dandridge family. (Courtesy of the Mount Vernon Ladies' Association)

been the family's minister for years, was asked to come to the house, "to Christen it," and the ceremony took place in the mansion. Massey stayed the night, so that when the baby died the following day, he was present to perform the funeral rituals as well.[20]

Two men, one of whom would become an Anglican minister, while the other was ordained already, were entrusted with teaching the surviving children from Martha Washington's first marriage. The children's first tutor, a young Scotsman named Walter Magowan, arrived at Mount Vernon in the fall of 1761 to take on the education of John Parke Custis, known as Jacky, and his sister, Martha Parke Custis, called Patsy, then seven and five years old, respectively. He stayed for six years, teaching Jacky Latin and

Greek, before leaving in the fall of 1767, so that he could be ordained in England. Magowan returned to the colonies, becoming rector of St. James Parish at Herring Bay in Anne Arundel County, Maryland, and continued his friendship with the family, making frequent visits to Mount Vernon for years after leaving their employ.[21] He was described by a fellow minister—interestingly, the man who later took over Jack's schooling—as "a raw Scotchman, whom I alone got recommended & into orders. He seem'd modest, w'c is so rare a Virtue in people of his Country, that I was pleas'd w'th ye Man."[22]

Following the departure of Mr. Magowan, the Reverend Jonathan Boucher continued Jack's education. Boucher, an Englishman, had come to Virginia in 1759 as the tutor for a family on the Rappahannock River but later went back to England for his ordination in 1762. After returning to the colony in 1763, he served as the minister for at least two Virginia parishes and ran a school for boys out of his home, about six miles from Fredericksburg, Virginia. Boucher was excited about having Jack as a pupil, writing that he appreciated Washington's sense of the importance of a good education, and was especially taken with "the ardent Desire You express for the Cultiva[tio]n of his moral, as well as his intellectual Powers, I mean that He may be made a Good, as well as a learned & a sensible Man." Jack began attending Boucher's school in 1768 and stayed with the minister until 1773, even after both the master and the school moved to Annapolis, where the governor of Maryland appointed him successively to two parishes in that colony. Boucher was dismissed from his church, however, during the Revolution, because of his staunchly loyalist political views. He and George Washington grew close in the years they struggled together to get young Custis to take his studies, and life, seriously. Boucher was described as "one of the best preachers of his time" and later (1795) published a series of thirteen sermons or discourses, which he had originally given between 1763 and 1775 in Virginia. He dedicated the volume, which was published in England, to George Washington,

> not because of any concord of political sentiment between him and the
> writer, for in this respect they had been and still were wide as the poles
> asunder, but to express the hope of Mr. Boucher that the offering which he
> thus made of renewed respect and affection for that great man might be
> received and regarded as giving some promise of that perfect reconciliation

between these two countries which it was the sincere aim of his publication to promote.[23]

Many years later, after both children had died and the Washingtons were raising Martha's two youngest grandchildren, George Washington once again contemplated trusting this important task to a minister and began the process by writing to an old friend in England. Noting that the children were "promising" and that he intended especially to give the little boy "a liberal education," he indicated that he was willing to pay an annual salary of fifty to sixty pounds sterling, plus board, lodging, washing, and mending:

> How far it may command the services of a person well qualified to answer the purposes I have mentioned, is not for me to decide. To answer my purposes, the Gentleman must be a master of composition, & a good Accomptant: to answer his pupil's, he must be a classical scholar, & capable of teaching the French language grammatically: the more universal his knowledge is, the better.
>
> It sometimes happens that very worthy men of the Cloth come under this description; men who are advanced in years, & not very comfortable in their circumstances: such an one, if unencumbered with a family, would be more agreeable to me than a young man just from college—but I except none of good moral character, answering my description, if he can be well recommended. . . . In Scotland we all know that education is cheap, & wages not so high as in England: but I would prefer, on accot of the dialect, an Englishman to a Scotchman, for all the purposes I want.[24]

Where these earlier clergymen/teachers shared the Washingtons' Anglican faith, the couple would turn to a religious institution outside their denomination for the education of yet another generation of young people. Following the death of Martha Washington's favorite niece, Fanny, in 1796, the Washingtons tried to help out her widowed husband, Tobias Lear, who was overburdened with the care of his own son from a first marriage, along with the three children Fanny had had with her first husband. Fanny's daughter, Anna Maria, who was known to the family as Maria, was a particular problem, acting out her frustration and grief at the loss of both parents within just a few years of one another. After learning that she apparently had been rude to her step-grandmother, who was a dear friend, Martha Washington wrote to say that she

> was extremely sorry to be told . . . how ill she had behaved to you had I known it before I should have reprimanded her very seriously. . . . I wish something may be done with her for her advantage—I loved the childs mother and I love her it gives me pain to think that a child as circumstansed as she is should not have a disposition to make herself friends—her youth will plead for her.[25]

The Washingtons expressed great interest in having Maria attend a Moravian school for girls in Bethlehem, Pennsylvania, an intriguing choice given the decidedly evangelical and missions-oriented nature of the Moravian Church, which had been instrumental in the conversion experiences of both John and Charles Wesley many years before.[26] Although they were initially told that it would not be possible to accept the little girl because the school was filled to capacity, the Washingtons persisted, with the president himself writing to the headmaster, the Reverend Jacob Van Vleck. Upon receiving a favorable response from Van Vleck, George Washington asked if, to keep Maria from becoming too lonely, it would be possible to send along another great-niece, Mildred Thornton Ball, as well.[27] In the end, neither little girl went to the school, because Maria was showing symptoms of the tuberculosis that killed both of her parents, but George Washington wrote to express his thanks for the exception made for his young relatives: "I hope, as it always appeared to me that your consent to admit these girls at the time you did, the School being full, was [a] matter of favour, for which I felt the obligation, that no inconvenience will result from the change which has taken place."[28]

Religious books were provided for several generations of children under Washington's care. In the fall of 1761, he ordered Bibles and Anglican prayer books, "neatly bound in Turkey," with the children's names "wrote in gilt Letters on the Inside of the cover" for his wife's eight-year-old son and six-year-old daughter. Six years later, stepdaughter Patsy was given a music book containing "the New Version of Psalms and Hymns set for the Spinnet." When his stepson, Jack, was a teenager, Washington informed a prospective schoolmaster that "Master Custis" had "entered upon the Greek Testament," and that a large order for books had been placed with an English agent for the boy. Of the forty-seven titles in that order, eleven concerned the subject of religion. Many years later, in the summer of 1794, George Washington purchased a New Testament in Greek for his wife's thirteen-year-old grandson. That young man's sister, Nelly, much like her long-deceased aunt, was acquiring the musical scores for songs with a decided religious flavor, such as "Angels Ever Bright & Fair" and "Holy Holy Lord."[29]

Washington also gave personal advice of a religious or moral nature to younger members of his household. There are numerous examples of letters to various young relatives about such things as the need to provide for those less fortunate than themselves or how to dress for church. To an orphaned nephew, Washington admonished, "A good moral character is the first essential in a man. . . . It is therefore highly important that you should endeavor not only to be learned but virtuous."[30] Several years later, after receiving a letter from his step-grandson, who was away at school, Washington replied that the news that the young man seemed to be settling into his studies and was "fulfilling those obligations which are enjoined by your Creator and due to his creatures, are highly pleasing and satisfactory to me." Washington gave two reasons for his happiness on the boy's account: "first, as it is the sure means of laying the foundation of your own happiness, and rendering you, if it should please God to spare your life, a useful member of society hereafter; and secondly, that I may, if I live to enjoy the pleasure, reflect that I have been, in some degree, instrumental in effecting these purposes."[31]

Outside the circle of his family and friends, George Washington took a public role in the religious life of the local Anglican community. Following in the footsteps of his father, he was elected to serve as a vestryman for both Fairfax Parish in Alexandria (ten miles from Mount Vernon) and at Truro Parish (seven miles from Mount Vernon), an office he maintained in the latter parish between 1762 and his resignation in February 1784. He was also chosen by his fellow vestrymen to act as churchwarden for three terms.[32] The activities of each Anglican parish in Virginia at this period were overseen by a minister and a group of twelve gentlemen, known as the vestry. These men were responsible for levying taxes to pay the minister's salary and church budget, as well as upkeep and construction of church property, and care for the poor in the community. On a rotating basis, two of the vestrymen were typically asked to take on the position of churchwarden. It was these men who were responsible for the day-to-day, hands-on work of the parish:

> Churchwardens were the officers who actually saw to it that the hungry and needy were fed, clothed, and housed, that poor, orphaned, or abused children were placed in proper homes, that wrongdoers were reported to the county court, that bread and wine were provided for Holy Communion, that churches were decently furnished and kept in repair, that parish readers and sextons did their jobs, that buildings got built and renovated, and that fees and taxes were collected and salaries and reimbursements paid.[33]

There was a decided civic and/or social element to these offices, and to church attendance, as well, in the eighteenth century, but had George Washington either been plagued with reservations about Christianity or simply been tepid in his beliefs, he could have found ways to drastically limit his church activities and express his civic duty primarily through other means, especially since vestrymen were required to take what one historian has described as "formidable oaths of allegiance and of conformity to the doctrine and discipline of the Church of England."[34] He had, for example, already been serving for three years in the Virginia House of Burgesses when he became a vestryman for Truro Parish.[35]

The business of the vestry required regular meetings. Records from Truro Parish show that Washington was an active vestryman, attending twenty-three of the thirty-five meetings held between his election to the vestry and the start of the Revolution.[36] Of the twelve meetings he missed, there are no diary entries to show what was happening for three of the dates, but others show that he was conscientious and had good reasons for nonattendance: Washington was seriously ill on one occasion (March 5, 1768); in Williamsburg on three (December 1, 1769; November 20, 1772; and November 22, 1773); traveling in the Allegheny Mountains during one (November 26, 1770); in Pennsylvania on two of the dates (June 4, 1773, and September 12, 1774); at home with guests, after attending the first part of the vestry meeting the previous day for one (February 25, 1774); and presiding over a multiday sale in Loudoun County, Virginia, for one meeting (November 28, 1774).[37]

The surviving vestry book for Truro Parish shows the kinds of activities in which Washington was involved during the years he served his local church. Salaries were paid to various employees of the parish: the minister (or if he was unavailable, to either the clergymen who substituted for him or to the reader who recited the liturgy in his absence); church sextons (at least one of whom was a woman); and the parish clerks. Funds were provided for the construction and maintenance of church facilities, and in one case a man named Samuel Littlejohn was given 1,000 pounds of tobacco per year in exchange for keeping a "house fitted up . . . for Divine Worship" on his property. In addition, errors in tax assessments were rectified, money was provided to supply the elements for the communion service and to pay for digging graves, and the poor were cared for. Looking at the records of just a few meetings, it is possible to get a feel for the kinds of people the parish was helping. They included a man who needed money for his son, poor couples, and single people.

Several individuals were paid for either assisting or maintaining someone else, presumably because they were poor, disabled in some way, or elderly. A woman named Elizabeth Palmer needed help for the "support of her Idiot Son," while Elizabeth Young was given a sum of money for boarding one Charlotte Lindsay for two months. In one case, Graffton Kirk was responsible for maintaining a woman named Sarah Jackson for years; he later took on a man named Philip Bryan. A woman named Sarah Mills was given assistance for maintaining her "cripple son" until he could be bound out as an apprentice, which, the records indicated, "shd. be speedy as possible." Local doctors were reimbursed for medicines provided to several individuals. Other people were paid for supplying clothing or decent burials to those who could not otherwise afford such things. Using just one vestry meeting, on November 28, 1768, as an example; one John Berrett was given £1 5s.0d. for "burying Dorothy Chester," George Simpson received 250 pounds of tobacco "for cloathing William Burgess for 12 months from this date," and a Miss Valinda Wade was reimbursed with 600 pounds of tobacco "for taking care of Priscilla Pipsecoe in Sickness & Burying her."[38]

If his committee assignments in the House of Burgesses were any indication of his interests, then Washington's appointment to the religion committee on May 15, 1769, is telling. Granted, Washington's interest in religion may simply have been because he believed that the teachings of the Anglican Church reinforced the hierarchical nature of Virginia society at this time and were a means of exerting control over the lower classes of that society. Another possibility is that he felt more generally, as others have, that religion of any kind played "a useful role in society by promoting morality, order, and stability."[39] As one historian has phrased it, Washington, like many of the Founding Fathers, appears to have believed that: "Virtue and morality are necessary for free republican government; religion is necessary for virtue and morality; ergo, religion is necessary for republican government."[40] A more cynical person might suggest that religion could help people accept the realities of their lives without seeking to overturn them, or, looking to Karl Marx, that religion was like a drug for keeping the masses compliant. Or, like other Christians throughout the centuries, Washington may sincerely have wanted to do what he could to see that the church prospered, because he believed in its tenets and its mission.

The Religion Committee was charged with meeting and adjourning "from Day to Day, and to take under their Consideration all Matters and Things relating to Religion and Morality, and all such as shall be from Time to Time referred to them, and report their Proceedings, with their Opinions thereupon to the House: And the said Committee are to have Power to send for Persons, Papers, and Records, for their Information." Washington's initial appointment was renewed on November 7, 1769, March 3, 1772, and May 16, 1774.[41]

While perhaps not the most important committee in the House of Burgesses, the issues considered by the Religion Committee certainly touched on matters relating to the regular religious practice of many of their fellow colonists. In June of 1770, Washington was one of six committee members assigned to work on a bill for dividing the parish of Frederick, in the county of the same name, into three separate Anglican parishes.[42] Two years later, he and several others were assigned to look into the question of whether two veterans, who had been disabled during the French and Indian War, should be granted some sort of financial relief. That same year the Religion Committee took up bills "for better regulating the Election of Vestries" and for dividing parishes in Cumberland and Chesterfield Counties.[43] In 1774 the committee was again asked to ruminate on the question of dividing a parish, which at 200 miles in length and 60 in width, was thought to be too burdensome for a lone minister.[44] One historian has recently pointed out that the care taken to see that parishes were not too big, either in population or physical distance, was "most striking" for its "remarkable sense of responsibility in ensuring that Anglican worship—in form and substance—prevailed everywhere in the colony. Virginia's laity fashioned an effective establishment of the

Church of England without benefit of the Mother Church's ecclesiastical superstructure."[45]

Washington's financial records include accounts for his own parish detailing the collection of levies as well as expenditures for such things as bottles of red wine, "for administering ye Lords Supper."[46] Most Anglican churches in Virginia at this time were rather plain inside, with white walls and windows of clear, rather than stained, glass. The focal point of the space was the communion table, with the altarpiece behind it, which typically included wall tablets bearing the Ten Commandments, the Apostles' Creed, and the Lord's Prayer, as "a constant and succinct reminder of a Christian's faith and duty." One church historian, in thinking about the place of these texts on the walls of the church, has offered the opinion that they "offer compelling evidence of the austere Protestant character of eighteenth-century Anglicanism; like their co-religionists through the English-speaking world, Virginia Anglicans were people of the Word."[47]

In his capacity as a vestryman, Washington, along with his friend George William Fairfax, is known to have donated gold leaf for gilding those religious inscriptions on the altarpiece when the new church was built at Pohick in the early 1770s. Not all the gold leaf was used up on that job. In 1774 the vestry turned to William Bernard Sears, an English-born craftsman and skilled carver, who initially came to Virginia as a young indentured convict, to undertake some additional work on the church. This artisan, who was also responsible for the beautiful woodwork at several nearby plantations, was ordered to "gild the Ornaments within the Tabernacle Frames the Palm Branch and Drapery on the Front of the Pulpit/also the Eggs on the Cornices of the small Frames if the Gold will hold out/which he agrees to do for Three pounds ready Money, to be done with the Gold Leaf given to the Parish by Colo. George Washington." That same year, 1774, Washington was also charged for importing cloths and cushions of "Crimson Velvett with Gold Fring[e]," for use on the pulpit, desks, and communion table, and possibly two "Folio Prayer Books covered with blue Turkey Leather with the Name of the Parish thereon in Gold Letters," as well, for the same church.[48]

The American Revolution brought enormous change to the established church in Virginia. The fact that authorities in England had never appointed even a single bishop for the entire denomination in all of the American colonies, together with the decentralized character of the church in Virginia, where individual congregations were physically scattered and often lacked pastors, meant that when the war began, there was no one to speak with authority on behalf of the church. One church historian has written that the birth of the United States as an independent country is inextricably linked with the birth of the Episcopal Church in America, but that there were major differences between the two events:

> The independence of the State was proclaimed and triumphantly defended by the will of her people, after preparation made by long years of the assertion of popular rights and of practical self-government. When the hour of Revolution struck . . . it fell upon the ears of a people eager for the summons and of leaders trained and equipped for their welcome task of forming a free and stable government. But for the Church, the day of her liberation dawned unwelcome, and found her fearful, powerless, and unprepared. She was without organization, without leadership, and without defence. The State must speak and act in her behalf, since she had no authority and no voice of her own, and the State was of two minds in the matter, and acted inconsistently and with almost fatal hesitation.[49]

Within a year of the start of the war, Virginia adopted a Declaration of Rights, which called for the "free exercise of religion, according to the dictates of conscience." Neither that document nor the new state constitution discussed the legal status of the Anglican Church. Very soon, dissenters in Virginia were allowed to stop paying the taxes used to support the Anglican Church and pay its ministers. Not until October 1784 did the Virginia assembly give a charter of incorporation to the "Protestant Episcopal Church," which also took away the denomination's status as the state church, broke up the parish vestries, and transferred all the property of the former Anglican Church to its successor. Care of the poor, one of the primary duties of the vestries, was handed over to the counties. The turmoil, however, was not over, and would continue until the end of the century. At least one historian has suggested that Virginians' "dismantling" of their former state church was not due to a lack of faith or to weakness in the church itself, but rather to the fact that the Anglican Church, as an institution, represented a government—the British constitutional monarchy—and hierarchical social order "that no longer commanded allegiance."[50]

Despite these changes, which did have a profound influence on George Washington, his support for his local church continued until the end of his life. While he was away during the Revolution, his farm manager and cousin, Lund Washington, paid Washington's subscription to the rector at Christ Church, the Reverend Doctor David Griffith, who had been a chaplain in the Continental Army before taking over the parish in 1780. Griffith is said to have been close to Washington in camp and is credited with coming to him the night before the battle of Monmouth to warn him about General Charles Lee's scheme to make Washington look incompetent and win control of the army for himself.[51]

Following the war, George Washington continued to pay the subscription and an annual pew rent to Doctor Griffith, who is known to have visited with the family at Mount Vernon and was named the first Episcopal bishop of Virginia in 1785.[52] The little notebooks Washington kept to record various expenditures show that even while he was away from home during the presidency, he sent money to his cousin Lund, acting as his farm manager, so that his regular donations to the charity school in Alexandria and his subscription toward the salary of the Reverend Thomas Davis, Griffith's successor at Christ Church in Fairfax Parish, would be paid.[53] During the last two and a half years of his life, he made three payments toward the salary of Reverend Davis.[54]

Washington's contemporaries in his extended family also took part in the activities of their local Anglican congregations. His younger brother, Samuel, served as a vestryman for Norborne Parish, in what is now West Virginia.[55] Their brother-in-law, Fielding Lewis of Fredericksburg, Virginia, was a vestryman for two parishes (both called St. George's) over as many decades, being elected initially in the fall of 1753 and trained for the position, while serving as the junior churchwarden. He was in charge of extensive church renovations in 1757 and, the following year, was given permission to build a gallery on the west end of the Fredericksburg church. Lewis was joined on the vestry by his oldest son in 1760 and was named senior churchwarden in 1762. Eight years later, after a parish reorganization along urban/rural lines, long-time vestryman Fielding Lewis was assigned to a building committee, overseeing architectural refinements to the structure of the urban church.[56] Among his last acts on earth, Lewis began his will, which was written on October 19, 1781, with the following preamble:

> In the name of God amen I Fielding Lewis of Spotsylvania County in the parish of St. George being indisposed and knowing there is a time for

all flesh to . . . die do make and declare this my last will and testament in manner following that is to say First I bequeath my soul into the hands of Almighty God my blessed Creator hoping and believing a remission of my sins thro the merits and meditation of my Saviour Jesus Christ, my body I commit to the Earth to be intered at the discretion of my Executors here after named and as to all my worldly Estate with which it has pleased God to bless me I give and devise as follows.[57]

Later members of the Washington/Custis family would remain firmly ensconced in the Protestant Episcopal Church, but their work within that institution reflected changes that came about in the early years of the nine-teenth century. For example, following the death of Martha Washington in 1802, the Mount Vernon estate came into the hands of one of George Washington's many nephews. The new proprietor, Bushrod Washington, was a legal scholar who had served as a justice of the United States Su-preme Court since December of 1798. His surviving books testify to his interest in religion: in addition to the books, sermons, and pamphlets on that topic that had belonged to the library of his late uncle, Bushrod Washington himself owned a copy of the Bible, with the Apocrypha, plus thirteen other books on the subject of religion, and well over two hundred sermons, pamphlets, and magazines from such groups as the American Bible Society, the American Board of Commissioners for Foreign Mis-sions, various Bible Societies, the *Missionary Herald,* and the Protestant Episcopal Missionary Society.[58]

Among the objects featured in a late nineteenth-century sale of Wash-ington family memorabilia in Philadelphia was Bushrod's membership certificate from the American Sunday School Union, which was dated Jan-uary 22, 1827.[59] While Sunday schools had begun in England and America in the eighteenth century as a way of teaching young factory and mine workers to read and write, the movement was transformed by the Second Great Awakening of the late eighteenth and early nineteenth centuries. Newly energized Christians created the organizations to which Judge Washington belonged as a means of bringing an evangelical message of salvation through faith in Christ to their nation and the world.[60] Episco-pal bishop William Meade of Virginia was especially close to the family of Judge Washington's wife, of whom he wrote that they "had long been the main support of the church at Dumfries and Centreville, and their house the resort of the clergy." Meade was a frequent visitor to Mount Vernon in the years just before the War of 1812 and later left a description of Bushrod and his activities on behalf of the church:

> It is well known that Judge Bushrod Washington, the son of General Washington's brother John, inherited Mount Vernon. He was in full communion with the Church when I first became acquainted with him in 1812, having no doubt united himself with it in Philadelphia under Bishop White, while attending the Supreme Court in that place. I know that he was intimate with Bishop White and highly esteemed him. Judge Washington attended one or more of our earliest Conventions in Richmond and was a punctual member of the Standing Committee from that time until his death.[61]

Following the deaths of Bushrod Washington and his wife, Mount Vernon became the property of Bushrod's nephew, a second John Augustine Washington. He was fortunate enough to marry a most capable young woman, Jane Charlotte Blackburn, the niece of his uncle Bushrod's wife, who would own and run the estate alone for a number of years after her husband's untimely death. A very devout woman, Jane Charlotte was described by Bishop Meade of Virginia as one of "the first-fruits of my ministry" in Alexandria, indicating that she had been an early convert at his church.[62] As a widow, she shared with her teenaged son her concerns that the young man was wasting his life on things that really didn't matter:

> It is not however yet too late in life for you to regain all you have lost—provided you commence at once. . . . The consciousness of aiming alone at what is right, & pleasing in the sight of God! and continually looking to Him, for strength to persevere, will carry you thro' every difficulty, or still make you happy & respected even s[hould] you fail in achieving, what to us now seems desirable. Oh, my son, could I be assured that you were training by a course of high, honourable, pure and Holy discipline, for the performance of the duties of life, and the glory of Heaven, I should in the fullness of Maternal joy and humble gratitude to God! forget every past anxiety and care I have felt on your account, or only remember them as additional causes for thanksgiving.[63]

About a year before her own death, like earlier generations in the family, Jane Charlotte left a final testimony to her Christian faith, writing in her will that she was undertaking to write this legal document, "knowing the uncertainty of life and humbly resigned to the directing providence of God, thro faith in the all prevailing merits and atonement of my Lord and Saviour Jesus Christ."[64]

After George and Martha Washington died, her granddaughter, Nelly Custis, and her husband, Lawrence Lewis, who was George Washington's nephew, made their home at Woodlawn Plantation, about three miles from Mount Vernon, and also at a more rural plantation called Audley, near the town of Berryville, Virginia. Nelly's letters are full of references to ministers to whom she felt very close, especially Episcopal bishop William White of Pennsylvania and William Holland Wilmer, the rector at St. Paul's Church in Alexandria and later president of the College of William and Mary. Bishop White allowed Nelly's teenaged daughter, Agnes, who had died while at school in Philadelphia, to be laid to rest in his family vault. Of Mr. Wilmer, she told an old friend in Philadelphia: "My good Pastor Mr. Wilmer dined with us on Saturday. If you knew him as well as I do, I am sure you would love & respect him. I wish that you did know him. I told him that I would live in Phi[ladelphi]a if I could, some day, & that I should then insist on moving him too. He would be a great acquisition to you."[65] Some years after their own deaths, Nelly and Lawrence were described as pillars of the Episcopal congregations near their homes by a decidedly evangelical Virginia minister:

Mr. Lewis was one of the most amiable of men by nature, and became a sincere Christian, and a communicant of our Church. His person was tall and commanding, and his face full of benignity, as was his whole character. I wish some of our friends at a distance could have seen him in the position I once beheld him in the church at Berryville, when I was administering the Holy Communion. Some of his servants were members of the church in that place, and on that day one of them came up after the white members had communed. It so happened that Mr. Lewis himself had not communed, but came up and knelt by the side of his servant, feeling no doubt that one God made them and one Saviour redeemed them. Mrs. Lewis was also a zealous member of the Church, a lady of fine mind and education, and very popular in her manners. Like her grandmother, she knew the use of her hands, and few ladies in the land did more with them for all Church and charitable purposes, even to the last days of a long life.[66]

4

SUNDAYS

Public Worship and Time for Reflection

S UNDAY SERVICES in Anglican churches in eighteenth-century Virginia typically began about eleven o'clock in the morning. Once the congregation had entered the building and gotten settled, the minister and/or his clerk began reading the liturgy from the Book of Common Prayer. The "solemn, penitential mood" of the service continued as the congregation corporately confessed its sins and received absolution by the pastor. (This would not be given on days when the pastor was not present.) Psalms were recited or sung, lessons were read from both the Old and New Testaments, and there were responsive readings and additional prayers. The part of the service known as the Ante-Communion prepared the congregation for the Lord's Supper, which was typically observed about four times each year. That part of the service closed as the congregation recited the Nicene Creed; the pastor's sermon followed.

Use of the liturgy meant that services throughout the colony, and indeed the world, were largely the same, save for the sermon, no matter which Anglican congregation one joined on a given Sunday. As one historian of the church has pointed out, the emphasis on the liturgy meant that the service "was not dependent on the charisma, discernment, sensitivity, or intelligence of the parson or clerk. It was not shaped by the individual's choice of words, his theological preferences, whims or fancies, or his arbitrary selection of scripture texts. The liturgy provided a settled, coherent, and uniform context."

Evangelical descendants of the eighteenth-century Virginians who attended these services have criticized them as "a soul-deadening recitation,
a mere mouthing of words and a mindless performance of ritual actions
that obstructed genuine religious experience." That view, while it might
have been true for some individuals, ignores the fact that, for others, the
ritual proved grounding and provided comfort. Rather than being "mind-
numbing," the liturgy can help to pull a wandering mind back into the
service. Knowing that the same words have been spoken for hundreds of
years and are being recited by fellow believers throughout the world can
make a worshipper realize that God and his kingdom are bigger than just
one person and his or her little problems. This idea can, for some people,
bring a real sense of peace.

The result of the criticism, however, has been "an anti-liturgical bias
in American culture," which has "continually impeded efforts to take seriously the religious faith and practice of the colonial Chesapeake."[1] This
bias has certainly been a problem in past interpretations of the place of
religion in George Washington's life.

Over the years they lived at Mount Vernon, George and Martha Washington worshipped at Pohick Church, which he had taken a part in establishing, in Truro Parish, and later at Christ Church in Alexandria. As
they stand today, both churches were designed by a local man, Colonel
James Wren, and built about the same time, in the late 1760s and early
1770s.[2] After the original Pohick Church, which was constructed of wood
in the 1730s, on the south side of Pohick Run, became too hard to repair,
a decision was made to build a new church. Initially, there was some controversy over where to locate the new structure, with fellow-parishioner
George Mason of Gunston Hall arguing that the replacement should go
on the same site as the original church, "pleading that it was the house in
which their fathers worshipped and that the graves of many were around
it." To settle the dispute, George Washington drew up a map showing the
houses in the parish and the distance from them to various proposed sites
for the new church. That map supposedly settled the matter and a practical decision was made to locate the new church more centrally, two miles
north of the old one.[3]

Construction appears to have been completed either late in 1773 or
early in 1774.[4] Washington's financial records note a number of purchases
for the new church. In December 1773, he bought a "Latch &ca. for door
in Church."[5] Several months later, he paid for two pews, numbered 28 and

29, an acquisition that cost him almost thirty pounds.[6] In August of 1774, he spent a total of ten shillings to have William Copan put their respective ciphers or initials on the pews purchased by himself and his neighbor, George William Fairfax, for their families.[7] Sometime during that year, he also paid ten shillings to have drawers put in his pew at Pohick.[8]

Christ Church in the city of Alexandria dates from the same period as Pohick Church and also replaced an earlier structure, described as a "chapel of ease." The vestry of Fairfax Parish decided to build the new church in 1766; various problems with and changes in the builder prevented its completion until early 1773. Since part of the Mount Vernon property lay within Fairfax Parish, George Washington was entitled to buy a pew in the new building. He initially paid over thirty-six pounds for pew number 5, which remained in his possession until his death in 1799. After the formation of the Protestant Episcopal Church, which split off from the Anglican Church following the Revolution, Washington and seven other members of the congregation agreed to pay an annual rent for the use of their traditional pews, "the said sum of five pounds for each Pew for the Purpose of supporting the Ministry in the said Church."[9]

Attendance at either of these churches would have required a trip, by horseback or coach, of at least ninety minutes to two hours, each way.[10] In August of 1762, George Washington laughingly chided his brother-in-law, Burwell Bassett, for writing to him on a Sunday, "when you ought to have been at Church, praying as becomes every good Christian Man who has as much to answer for as you have; strange it is that you will be so blind to truth that the enlightening sounds of the Gospel cannot reach your Ear, nor no Examples awaken you to a sense of Goodness." He went on: "Could you but behold with what religious zeal I hye me to Church on every Lords day, it would do your heart good, and fill it I hope with equal fervency."[11] Jonathan Boucher, the Anglican clergyman who taught Martha Washington's son, knew Washington fairly well before the Revolution. Although he remained loyal to the British during the war and became highly critical of his old acquaintance, Boucher later said of Washington, "In his moral character he is regular, temperate, strictly just and honest . . . and, as I always thought, religious; having heretofore been pretty constant, and even exemplary, in his attendance on public worship in the Church of England."[12] Lee Massey, the former pastor at Pohick Church, remembered Washington in the period before the war as a regular churchgoer: "I never knew so constant an attendant at church as Washington. His behaviour in the house of God was ever so reverential that it produced the happiest effects on my congregation and greatly assisted me in my pulpit labours. No company ever kept him from church."[13]

Notwithstanding these statements, Washington was hardly at services every week. He would, in fact, have been most unusual if he had been, and the ministers quoted above were holding him to the standard of his peers. Studies of church attendance by other individuals in colonial Virginia vary from indentured servant John Harrower's average rate of 14 percent to Colonel William Byrd II's mean of about 45 to 50 percent, while a 1724 survey by the Anglican Church showed an attendance rate of 22 to 77 percent in eleven Virginia parishes. Byrd's record of church attendance is especially interesting, considering that the church in question had been built less than a half-mile from his home.[14]

Although the Washington family maintained pews in both Pohick and Christ Church, one scholar who has closely examined Washington's diaries for evidence of church attendance found that he was typically present an average of one Sunday per month (a frequency dictated in Virginia society by both custom and the law) and often spent Sundays at Mount Vernon visiting with friends, working, or foxhunting.[15] According to a former Mount Vernon slave, Washington also was known to play cards on Sunday.[16] Examination of his correspondence shows that he often wrote letters on Sundays.

The biggest problem in analyzing church attendance by members of the Mount Vernon household, based on Washington's diaries, is that these invaluable sources are not always complete. For example, while attending the Constitutional Convention in the summer of 1787, George Washington wrote in his diary on Tuesday, July 3, "Sat before the meeting of the Convention for Mr. Peale who wanted my picture to make a print or Metzotinto by. Dined at Mr. Morris's and drank Tea at Mr. Powells—after which, in Company with him, I attended the Agricultural Society at Carpenters Hall."[17] Washington did not mention his early-morning ride for exercise, perhaps because it had become routine. That same day, a man named Jacob Hiltzheimer noted in his own diary that, "On returning [before breakfast] we met his Excellency General Washington taking a ride on horseback, only his coachman Giles with him."[18] Twelve years later, in a letter to his dear friend, Bryan Fairfax, who was then traveling in England, Washington wrote that he and his wife had had dinner a few days before at Fairfax's home and could assure him that all his family were "in good health & Spirits in the afternoon." That visit was not mentioned in Washington's diary.[19]

Several other examples of this kind of omission relate directly to the question of church attendance. The first dates to 1767, when Washington's diary entries are too spotty to tell much about church attendance or anything else. A surviving letter from his cousin, Lund, who was managing the estate in his absence, related the reassuring news to George and Martha Washington, then traveling with their neighbors, George William and Sally Cary Fairfax of Belvoir, that, "The Children [John Parke and Martha Parke Custis] are very well & were Yesterday at Alexandria Church with Miss Guess who calld & carry'd them up in the Charriot."[20] Many years later, in 1797, Washington's diaries show no church attendance by anyone in the family after they returned to Mount Vernon at the end of his presidency. From a letter written by his wife's granddaughter, Nelly, later in the year, however, it can be learned that, "We have dined twice in Alexandria, & went one Sunday to Church, otherwise I have never been from Home since I returned from the Federal City."[21] The following year, when George Washington, again, said nothing about going to church in the first three months of 1798, Nelly wrote another letter, telling of how she spent several days visiting friends in Alexandria, amusing herself with balls, plays, dances, and singing. In the midst of all this, the young woman noted that, on Sunday in town, she "went to Church in the morning."[22]

My attempts to correlate such factors as weather conditions and either the presence or lack of a pastor at these churches, with Washington's known absences, to see if those might explain some of them, have proven fruitless, because of the dearth of surviving manuscripts with sufficient detail to record exactly which Sundays the pulpit for each church was covered. For example, the Truro Parish vestry book notes on June 4, 1753, that the Reverend Mr. Charles Green would preach there "every third Sunday." Evidence from Alexandria suggests that Green, who had first been recommended for the job of pastor by George Washington's father in 1736 and took over the parish the following year, was alternating his Sundays between three small congregations at Pohick, the city of Alexandria, and a third near the Falls of the Potomac.[23]

Green was an intriguing character, not just a minister, but also a practicing physician, who treated patients in both Virginia and Maryland. He had been born in Ireland and probably trained at Balliol College in Oxford before he came to Virginia about 1731. By 1733 he was serving as a minister in Cople Parish in Westmoreland County, which was the home parish of George Washington's mother, Mary Ball Washington. In the years after he moved on to Truro Parish, Green developed a close relationship with both the Fairfax family at Belvoir and with Lawrence, George Washington's older half-brother, who was living at Mount Vernon. That friendship was broken in the 1740s, however, when Lawrence accused Reverend Green of attempting to molest his wife, Ann Fairfax, the daughter of his socially prominent neighbor, Colonel William Fairfax, on several occasions before their marriage, which took place in July 1743. Lawrence's charges would lead to the only ecclesiastical trial in Virginia's history. Tried at the College of William and Mary, the case appears to have been the result of a number of misunderstandings, some admitted but hardly criminal misconduct, and perhaps some political motives. It ended in something of a draw. Green had to pay witnesses and court costs, as well as promising "to behave himself for the future with general Decency & good manners toward Fairfax, Washington & their families." He would keep his position as rector of Truro Parish, and the Fairfaxes and Lawrence Washington were told to "quash the Libel against the Defendant."

While it is unclear if the friendship between Green, William Fairfax, and Lawrence Washington ever resumed, Colonel Fairfax became a vestryman at Pohick in 1755, something that probably would not have happened without the approval of the rector. Lawrence died in 1752 and his young widow remarried within six months and moved away from the neighborhood. Whatever hard feelings remained after the case were not shared by other members of these two families. George and Martha Washington; George William and Bryan Fairfax; their sister Sally and her husband, John Carlyle; and the head of the family, Lord Fairfax, continued to socialize with Reverend and Mrs. Green and to work with him as their minister through the remainder of his life.[24]

In the mid-1760s, after the death of Reverend Green, there were several months when no minister regularly served the Pohick congregation, although the Reverend James Scott of Dettingen Parish filled in frequently (giving twenty-six sermons between November 1765 and November 1766 and another six or seven between the latter and November 1767) and the Reverend John Andrews of Cameron Parish helped out on two Sundays. Scott, who was born in Scotland, also served as a justice of the peace, was a wealthy landowner, married well to a cousin of Washington's neighbor, George Mason of Gunston Hall, and had a reputation as a truly dedicated pastor at the parish he looked after for almost forty years. Andrews, too, was born in Scotland and ministered to his parish in Loudoun County, Virginia, between 1749, when he was ordained to the priesthood, and his death in 1769.[25]

Christ Church in Alexandria was going through a number of problems with its minister about this time. Serving the congregation between 1765 and 1778 was a man named Townshend Dade Jr., who seems to have been a rather disreputable individual. In papers submitted to a court in England by several of Dade's parishioners, the young minister was described as a "Person of ill Fame dissolute manners Lewd Conversation [illegible] Lascivious Disposition." Apparently, he had wooed and won the favors of the wife of an Alexandria merchant, which led to a request that the court take action against him. No evidence of a trial or other disposition of the case has been found, but Dade was forced to resign during the Revolution.[26]

The journal kept by a young Englishman traveling in America in the mid-1770s provides a snapshot of the problems Christ Church was having with its minister at that point. Several days after his arrival at Alexandria in the fall of 1774, Nicholas Cresswell noted that he had gone to church, where he "heard a very indifferent Sermon." Things were much the same the following week, when he recorded that the church building was "pretty," with a "large congregation, but an indifferent Parson." When the young man returned on Sunday, January 1, he found that, "The Parson is drunk and can't perform the duties of his office." Two months later, "The Parson is too lazy to preach." After attending a Methodist service in Leesburg, Cresswell even attributed the growth of the Methodists in Virginia to "the great negligence of the [Anglican] Church Parsons."[27] Things deteriorated even more once the Revolution started. After being in America for about two years, Cresswell wrote in disgust about the state of the Anglican Church in the fall of 1776 and predicted that it would be superseded by other denominations:

No service at Church to-day. Religion is almost forgotten or most basely neglected. In short, the Parsons are not willing to expound the Gospel to people without being paid for it, and there is no provision made for the Episcopal Clergy by this new code of Laws, therefore Religion as well as Commerce is at a stand. Indeed, the few that pretend to preach are mere retailers of politics, sowers of sedition and rebellion, serve to blow the cole of discord and excite the people to arms. The Presbyterian Clergy are particu-

larly active in supporting the measures of Congress from the Rostrum, gain-
ing proselytes, persecuting the unbelievers, preaching up the righteousness
of their cause and persuading the unthinking populace of the infallibility
of success. Some of these religious rascals assert that the Lord will send his
Angels to assist the injured Americans. They gain great numbers of converts
and I am convinced if they establish their Independence that Presbyty [Pres-
byterianism] will be the established religion on this Continent.[28]

During the Revolution, ill-health or the diminishing size of his congregation seems to have caused Reverend Green's successor at Pohick, Lee
Massey, to stop officiating regularly at services. Massey, a native Virginian,
had been educated at the College of William and Mary in Williamsburg
and trained as both a lawyer and a physician. His membership in the Fairfax County Committee of Safety indicates that his political sympathies
were similar to those of George Washington.[29] According to a younger,
evangelical Episcopal clergyman, his sermons were said to "evince talent
and are sound in doctrine, but, like most of that day, want evangelical life
and spirit, and would never rouse sinners to a sense of their condition. He
was a man of great wit and humour, the indulgence of which was the fault
of many of the clergy of that day."[30] After the 1780s, the pulpit at Pohick,
when filled at all, was manned by itinerant preachers.[31] A description of
the city of Alexandria in 1795 by a European visitor suggests that, even in
that urban setting and at such a late date, Christ Church was still holding services only once a month.[32] The decline evident in the churches
near Mount Vernon was symptomatic of problems throughout Virginia.
According to one church historian, there had been ninety-one Anglican
clergymen in Virginia before the Revolution, serving in 164 churches and
chapels; following the war, there were only twenty-eight "found labouring
in the less desolate parishes of the State."[33]

The uncertainty of services at such times as these undoubtedly dimin-
ished the Mount Vernon family's church attendance, a response that was
hardly unusual in Virginia at this period. Although it was typical to have
the parish clerk read the liturgy on Sundays when ministers were serving their other churches, many colonists chose not to attend when they
knew their ministers were away. A study of church attendance by Colonel
William Byrd II, for example, indicates that, in one three-year period, he
only went to church on one occasion when the minister was not present.
Since only ordained ministers in the Anglican Church were permitted to

give sermons, it was probably the absence of a sermon that kept Colonel Byrd—and others—from services on those Sundays.³⁴ At other times, the Washington household are known to have absented themselves from church: when someone in the family was sick; when the weather was bad; when the family's vehicle had been used to take a guest to their home and had not returned in time to go to church; when George Washington was traveling; when the minister scheduled to preach was sick; and when the chariot broke on the way to church.³⁵ Especially between the mid-1760s and the summer of 1773, when Martha Washington's daughter died suddenly during an epileptic seizure, the chronic illness of this one frail family member, who sometimes suffered from as many as two seizures a day, undoubtedly affected the family's church attendance for the worse.³⁶

There is also evidence that, as he aged, Washington found the distance from church and the resulting long carriage ride more than he could manage and spent the day quietly at home answering letters. Following the decline of Pohick Church after the Revolution and his own retirement from the presidency, he wrote a friend to apologize for not writing more often:

> Six days do I labour, or, in other words, take exercise and devote my time to various occupations in Husbandry, and about my Mansion. On the seventh, now called the first day, for want of a place of Worship (within less than nine miles) such letters as do not require immediate acknowledgment I give answers to (Mr. Lear [his secretary] being sick and absent). But it hath so happened, that on the two last Sundays, call them the first or seventh day as you please, I have been unable to perform the latter duty [writing letters], on account of visits from Strangers, with whom I could not use the freedom to leave, or recommend to the care of each other, for their amusement.³⁷

This level of church attendance does not mean that Washington considered it unimportant. Before the Revolution, as he was looking into the possibility of sending his stepson to the Reverend Jonathan Boucher's school in Annapolis, Washington informed the teacher that, if young Jack did come to the school, he would be sent off with a number of amenities, including "two Horses, to furnish him with the means of getting to Church and elsewhere as you may permit."³⁸ Twenty years later, Washington found himself responsible for the upbringing of two other young men, his orphaned nephews, Lawrence Augustine and George Steptoe Washington, the sons of his younger brother, Samuel. The boys were sent to study in Alexandria, where they lodged with a Col. Samuel Hanson, but Washington was surprised one night in the summer of 1788 to find Lawrence at Mount Vernon, after an altercation with the colonel. Equally disappointing was the fact that the boy's older brother had attempted to physically intervene, when Hanson tried to punish Lawrence, a punishment that George Washington felt was deserved. A series of letters ensued between the various parties, giving everyone a chance to vent their emotions. According to George Steptoe, the original offense, which precipitated the entire incident, was Lawrence Augustine's perceived truancy from church:

> Whither my conduct was justifiable in doing what I have, I am not a judge, but with pleasure leave it to be determin'd by you when made acquainted with the circumstances of the case. You have been informed that Laurence has attended divine servise but once or twice, if the information was received from Col. Hanson I wish not to contradict him, but of late he has attended pretty constant, and the reason of his absence from Church that day, was on account of his coat, but of this also I am not to judge if Col. Hanson thinks proper to correct him I acknolidge it is not my business to interfere, neither would I have had the least idea of doing it if it had been done in an orderly manner, especially since I know it to be your desire.[39]

George Washington's church-going habits were noticeably more regular during the presidency. A French acquaintance from that period in his life noted that, "On Sundays, he never fails, with his family, to attend divine service," while one of his pastors recalled the president's "constant attendance on Christian worship."[40] Washington's efforts to set an example as president were certainly a consideration, a fact he admitted in a letter written at the close of his presidency to the officials of the churches he attended in Philadelphia, acknowledging that his attendance "on public worship" was "prompted by a high sense of duty" and his subsequent gratitude for "the liberal and interesting discourses which have been delivered" by them. His more frequent church attendance in those years might also be attributable to a more mundane reason, such as the better roads and shorter distance needed to travel to church in the cities of New York and Philadelphia. As president, Washington attended first Saint Paul's Church and later Trinity Church in New York and both Saint Peter's Church and Christ Church in Philadelphia.[41]

Washington probably wore some of his best clothing to church. In a letter to a teenaged nephew, in which he offered advice on many aspects of life, Washington advised the young man to eschew dandyism and to keep his clothing budget under control. In addition, he suggested that his nephew "always keep some clothes to wear to Church, or on particular occasions, which should not be worne every day; this can be done without any additional expense; for whenever it is necessary to get new Clothes, those which have been kept for particular occasions will then come in as every day ones, unless they should be of a superior quality to the new."[42]

On at least one occasion, George Washington indicated his belief that Sunday should be a time of rest, but that the press of various duties tended to get in the way. Writing to his longtime secretary from Mount Vernon on his way back to Philadelphia following his 1791 southern tour, Washington noted:

> This is the eve of my departure for George town, & being Sunday, ought to have been a day of rest; but it is not so with me, either from company, or business; the latter, occasioned by a constant succession of company during the whole of last week: wch obliged me to postpone many matters until this day, which ought, & but for that reason, would have been done in the course of it—Such time as I have been able to spend in my study to day, has been employed in sorting of the Letters & Papers which have been recd since I left Charleston—part of which I enclose, because my travelling writing desk will not contain them.[43]

According to the two grandchildren from his wife's first marriage, who were raised by the Washingtons, both making visits and receiving visitors were generally prohibited by the family on Sundays during Washington's presidency, and the president would often read aloud "sermons and other sacred writings" to his family on that day.[44] The papers of Tobias Lear, Washington's secretary and a member of the household for many years, reinforce the children's memories of the quiet and reflective nature of Sundays in the executive mansion:

> While President, Washington followed an invariable routine on Sundays. The day was passed very quietly, no company being invited to the house. After breakfast, the President read aloud a chapter from the Bible, then the whole family attended church together. Washington spent the afternoon

writing personal letters, never neglecting his weekly instructions to his manager at Mount Vernon, while Mrs. Washington frequently went to church again, often taking the children with her. In the evening, Lear read aloud to the family some sermon or extracts from a book of a religious nature and everyone went to bed at an early hour.[45]

The 1772 purchase of a book entitled *Sermons on the Lord's Prayer* suggests that the habit of reading sermons aloud in the Washington household may have predated the grandchildren by a number of years.[46]

A houseguest who spent ten days, including two Sundays, at Mount Vernon in 1798 kept a journal that gives credence to the grandchildren's and Lear's memories of life in the Washington household. On the first Sunday, he noted that George Washington "retired to write letters, this day being set aside for this activity," while another family member accompanied the guest on a walk around the grounds. The visitor commented rather morosely that, in contrast to other evenings, the family enjoyed "no music, not even a game of chess," and, by way of explanation, wrote, "It was Sunday; everyone retired at nine o'clock." The next Sunday must have been spent in a similarly quiet manner, for the usually dedicated, and detailed, diarist wrote simply, "10 [June] Sunday, cool weather, I caught a river turtle weighing at least 12 pounds. We retired at 9 o'clock."[47]

Among the books acquired by Martha Washington over the years were a number that could have provided appropriate amusement on a Sunday. There was, for example, a volume of psalms and hymns by English minister Isaac Watts, ordered during one winter at her husband's Revolutionary War headquarters in Newburgh, New York.[48] At least two collections of sermons were purchased during George Washington's presidency, quite likely the very ones her grandchildren later remembered. The presidential years also saw the purchase of other religious works for the first lady, including several books of prophecies, one of which dealt specifically with "Prophetic Conjectures on the French Revolution."[49] Among the other books was a commentary on the Psalms by George Horne, the Lord Bishop of Norwich and president of Magdalen College, which was acquired by Martha Washington in 1793 and given to one of her nieces in 1800.[50] Another piece dating to this period was recorded in the family's financial records as "Jenning's Evidence of the Chr Religion," probably a reference to *A View of the Internal Evidence of the Christian Religion* by Soame Jenyns, the sixth edition of which was published in Hartford,

Connecticut, in 1789.[51] One of the most interesting books acquired at this time was *Klopstock's Messiah,* a romantic treatment of the life of Christ written by the German poet Friedrich Gottlieb Klopstock between 1749 and 1773, which was translated into seventeen languages.[52]

The inventory done shortly after George Washington's death in 1799 shows that the family library at Mount Vernon contained approximately thirty-five titles relating to religion, a bit less than 7 percent of the total.[53] Actually, this figure is somewhat misleading, however, because it is often difficult to tell the subject of a book from the cryptic titles mentioned by the appraisers who did the inventory. An examination of the surviving books from George Washington's library, which are now at the Boston Athenaeum, indicates that there were roughly fifty volumes on various aspects of religion and philosophy, of which most dealt with religion. Subjects included Arminianism; the Quaker sect; an explanation of the Thirty-Nine Articles of the Church of England and elaboration on the Book of Common Prayer; several Bibles, concordances, and prayer books; Moravian missionary work among Native Americans; the theology of the ancient Persians; prophecy and revelation; appropriate prayers for the sick; Universalism; Swedenborgianism; and church history. In addition, there were about 170 sermons, discourses, and other short works, often bound together in volumes entitled, simply, "Sermons," "Masonic Sermons," or "Political Sermons." Many of these pamphlets were gifts to Washington from their authors, but the fact that he kept them, took the time and expense to have them bound, and often wrote his name on them, suggests that they were important to him and that these may also have been some of the texts the grandchildren remembered hearing Washington read aloud on Sundays.[54]

On days when the family couldn't make it to church, and throughout the rest of the week, there was artwork in their home that would have brought to mind stories and characters from the Bible, as well as principles based on Christian religious beliefs. It is true that many of these were the work of popular artists and engravers and that they may simply have been acquired for their artistic value, rather than their religious content.[55] The possibility that they were there because they spoke to something in the Washingtons' souls should not, however, be overlooked. The fact that a number of these pieces refer to incidents that depended on revelation, rather than reason, is perhaps also telling, especially given George

Washington's statement that, among the many blessings that had accrued to society by the time of the American founding, he counted, "above all, the pure and benign light of Revelation."[56]

At the time of George Washington's death, pastels depicting the Virgin Mary and Saint John the Evangelist were hanging in the large dining room.[57] The pair remained at Mount Vernon for several decades after coming into the possession of later members of the Washington family, specifically Bushrod Washington, John Augustine Washington II, and John Augustine Washington III. The pastels probably left Mount Vernon when the house was sold to the Mount Vernon Ladies' Association, just' before the Civil War, and were eventually sold by Washington heirs at a Philadelphia auction in 1891. After an absence of almost 150 years, the lovely painting of the Virgin was returned to Mount Vernon in 2003. Recent examination suggests that it is probably an eighteenth-century copy of a work by Rosalba Carriera of Venice, an extremely popular artist best known for her pastels, which were much sought-after by English visitors to the continent. At this point, there is no indication how the Washingtons came to own the painting, but the fact that it and its companion piece were hung in the most prominent room in their home might suggest that the subjects were very special to them.[58] St. John, for example, was not only described in Christian writings as "the Beloved Apostle," and considered one of the great messengers of the gospel, he was also one of the patron saints of the Freemasons, a group to which George Washington belonged for most of his life which traditionally celebrated St. John's feast day on December 27.[59] In addition to these New Testament figures, an engraving entitled *The Flight,* illustrating a famous scene from the life of Jesus, hung in one of the bedrooms on the second floor. Published in London by John Boydell in 1783, after a painting by Claude le Lorraine, it depicted the escape to Egypt by Joseph and Mary in order to protect the infant Jesus from the wrath of King Herod the Great.[60]

Two of the engravings on the walls of the small dining room in 1799 suggest religious themes. The first, published in London in 1782 by John Boydell, after a painting by Benjamin West, records a scene from the life of the Saxon king, Alfred the Great, who made attempts to establish both a monastery and convent and was noted for encouraging learning within his kingdom, with the goal that his subjects would increase in wisdom and live according to divine will. Entitled *Alfred the Great Dividing His*

Pastel of *The Virgin Mary*, after Rosalba Carriera. This lovely depiction of the Virgin Mary was placed by George Washington in the most splendid room at Mount Vernon, where it was treasured by several later generations of his family. (Courtesy of the Mount Vernon Ladies' Association)

Loaf with the Pilgrim, the engraving illustrates a legend dating to a desperate period in Alfred's life, the year 878, when he had retreated to the island of Athelney to devise a means of defeating his Viking enemies. While there, one of his patron saints, Cuthbert of Lindisfarne, came to Alfred in the guise of a pilgrim, asking for food. Although he and his family had only one loaf of bread, Alfred set aside half to share with the poor traveler. Saint Cuthbert later appeared to the king in a vision, giving advice on how to defeat the Danes and promising both victory and prosperity in the future.[61] While the Washingtons may not have known the details of the incident depicted in this engraving, its subject, a Christian ruler sharing with someone less fortunate and thus helping another person along their spiritual journey, may well have resonated with them.

Also in the dining room where the Washington family took their everyday meals was another Boydell engraving, this one also after a Benjamin West painting, which depicts William Penn, the founder of the colony of Pennsylvania, in the process of making a treaty with a group of Native Americans in order to acquire the land for his new settlement. This was an extremely popular engraving that struck an emotional cord with the

American public and that has been widely reproduced in the centuries following its publication by Boydell in 1775.[62]

Raised as an Anglican, Penn had been educated at Oxford, where he came under the influence of a prominent Puritan scholar during the years of Oliver Cromwell's governance. Following the restoration of the king in 1660, and the subsequent resurgence of the Anglican Church, Penn became uncomfortable with the ritual and trappings of the church in which he had been brought up, and later became a Quaker. Despised at the time, the sect was pacifistic and sought to replace the traditional elements of a Christian worship service with an emphasis on the promptings and insights provided by the inner light of the Holy Spirit within each believer. Penn's conversion led to a period of estrangement from his family (his father was an admiral in the British navy), as well as imprisonment in the Tower of London at the hands of the government. His eventual reconcilia-

Engraving of *The Flight,* by John Boydell, after Claude le Lorraine, London, 1783. This scene from the early life of Jesus was hung by the Washingtons in one of the second-floor bedrooms at Mount Vernon. Like several of the pieces of religious art in the household, it related to an episode in which revelation from God, rather than reason, was a key element. (Courtesy of the Mount Vernon Ladies' Association)

Engraving of *Alfred the Great Dividing His Loaf with the Pilgrim,* by John Boydell, after Benjamin West, London, 1782. Throughout their lives, both George and Martha Washington actively cared for and supported those less fortunate than themselves. The subject of this engraving, an incident in the life of Alfred the Great, would have reinforced biblical teachings on the need for, and importance of, charity. (Courtesy of the Mount Vernon Ladies' Association)

tion with his father left him the heir to a fortune, and a large debt owed to the estate by the Crown was paid off by making William Penn the proprietary governor of a tract of land in the American colonies, which Charles II named Pennsylvania. Here Penn was able to create a society based on an idea that had become very important to him, freedom of religion. In the charter of the colony, he acknowledged that "the happiness of Mankind Depends So much upon the Enjoying of Libertie of theire Consciences." He invited persecuted religious groups from throughout Europe to settle in Pennsylvania, which, as a result, grew faster than the other colonies. Acting on his belief that everyone should be treated justly, Penn insisted on purchasing land from the Indians and concluding each of these transactions with a treaty, even though he could simply have claimed the territory on the basis of the royal charter. Penn's actions led to many years of peace with the native peoples, undoubtedly another factor in the rapid growth of the colony.[63]

There were several elements in Penn's personal story, as well as in the scene shown in the engraving, which would have made it meaningful to Americans in general, and to Washington in particular. Freedom of conscience was central to Washington's concept of American life. As president, in a letter to a group of Quakers, he noted that in the United States people "remain[ed] responsible only to their Maker for the Religion or modes of faith which they may prefer or profess."[64] The idea of treating everyone fairly was important to Washington, and the fact that Penn's efforts to treat the native peoples justly and with dignity resulted in a long period of peace would have appealed to the old general and statesman, who, upon his retirement from the presidency, advised his countrymen: "Observe good faith and justice towds. all Nations. Cultivate peace and harmony with all. Religion and morality enjoin this conduct;

Engraving of *William Penn's Treaty with the Indians*, John Boydell, after Benjamin West, London, 1775. Widely copied in the eighteenth and nineteenth centuries, this engraved depiction of the treaty negotiations at the time of the founding of the colony of Pennsylvania sent a message to viewers about fairness, justice, and brotherly love. (Courtesy of the Mount Vernon Ladies' Association)

and can it be that good policy does not equally enjoin it?"[65] The theme of brotherly love embodied by Penn's treaty so touched the family at Mount Vernon that Martha Washington even made a patchwork quilt featuring that motif. In the center of the bedcover she placed a large square of linen printed with an image based on the West/Boydell engraving, which was taken from an imported European fabric being sold in Philadelphia in 1788.[66]

Finally, in the bedroom they shared for so many years, George and Martha Washington had hung two engravings with religious subjects.[67] The first was described by the executors conducting the inventory after George Washington's death as a picture of "A Parson." This particular entry probably relates to an engraving that descended in the Washington family and was returned to Mount Vernon several decades ago. Seemingly done by engraver John Ogborne of London about 1786, this small round piece illustrates a scene from a popular novel, *The Sufferings [or Sorrows] of Werther,* by Johann Wolfgang von Goethe, in which the protagonist accompanies his friend, and unrequited love interest, Lotte, as she visits an aged parson and his wife in a neighboring village. In beginning this section of the novel, Goethe has Werther write of Lotte, a warm, caring person, who routinely visits the sick and aged in her community: "What Lotte must mean to a sick man I feel in my poor heart. . . . She will spend a few days in town at the bedside of some good woman who, in the view of the doctors, is approaching her end and wishes to have Lotte beside her in her last moments."[68]

The second engraving in the Washingtons' bedroom to relate to the Christian religion was a portrait of Selina Shirley Hastings, Countess of Huntingdon. The countess had initially been a very devout and active member of the Anglican Church, but she became an early convert to Methodism in 1739, after becoming convinced that the only way to salvation was not through doing good works but through faith in Jesus as her savior. For the rest of her long life, she was considered to be one of Britain's leading evangelical figures. She also associated with other leaders of the evangelical movement: John Wesley, the founder of the Methodist denomination; the authors of some of the most popular hymns in the modern Christian repertoire, including Wesley's younger brother Charles ("Love Divine, All Loves Excelling," "Hark, the Herald Angels Sing," "Christ the Lord Is Ris'n Today"), Isaac Watts, who is known as the father of English hymnody ("When I Survey the Wondrous Cross,"

Engraving of *The Aged Parson*, from Goethe's *The Sorrows of Werther*, by engraver John Ogborne, London, ca. 1786. A scene from Goethe's sad, romantic tale, *The Sorrows of Werther*, which hung originally in the Washingtons' bedchamber. Lotte, the young woman paying a call on an aged minister, exhibited the qualities of benevolence and caring which were so often linked to Martha Washington in descriptions by her contemporaries. (Courtesy of the Mount Vernon Ladies' Association)

"Oh God Our Help in Ages Past," and "Jesus Shall Reign Where'er the Sun"), John Newton ("Amazing Grace," "How Sweet the Name of Jesus Sounds," "Glorious Things of Thee are Spoken"), William Cowper ("There is a Fountain Filled with Blood"), William Williams ("Guide Me, O Thou Great Jehovah"), and Augustus Toplady ("Rock of Ages"); and the evangelist George Whitefield, whose charitable works in America were continued by the countess after his death.[69] She was also associated with the enslaved African-born writer Phillis Wheatley, who dedicated a poem on the death of Whitefield and a volume of poetry to the countess, who, in turn, insisted that the work bear a portrait of the author on the frontispiece.[70]

Engraving of *The Right Honble. Selina Countess Dowager of Huntingdon,* by J. Fittler, after R. Bowyer, ca. 1791. One of the leading figures in the British evangelical movement in the eighteenth century, the countess corresponded with George Washington with a plan for missions to Native Americans. Her portrait was an interesting choice for the walls of the Washingtons' bedchamber. (Courtesy of National Museum of American History, Smithsonian Institution)

A formidable woman, the countess encouraged thousands of young evangelical ministers, began a seminary in Wales to train still others, supported chapels, wrote hymns herself, and spent most of her long life trying to bring the gospel, in the form of evangelical Protestantism, to both the British aristocracy and the lower classes throughout the country. George III once said of her that he wished he had "a Lady Huntingdon in every diocese in my kingdom." He continued:

> There is something so noble, so commanding, and withal so engaging about her, that I am quite captivated with her Ladyship. She appears to possess talents of a very superior order—is clever, well-informed and has all the ease and politeness belonging to her rank . . . she is an honour to her sex and the nation.[71]

During the first half of the 1780s, the Countess of Huntingdon began a correspondence with George Washington, described in greater detail elsewhere in this work, concerning a scheme she had for settling the American frontier with "good, religious people," with the intention that they would both proselytize among and raise the living standards of "those poor Savages," their Native American neighbors. Although the plan eventually came to naught, Washington did write to Congress on behalf of the countess, who may have been a very distant relation, to express his support for it.[72] Her engraved portrait descended in the family of Martha Washington's granddaughter Nelly, with the story that it had been a gift to George Washington from the countess herself. However, it was actually sent to Washington in June of 1791 by the artist, Robert Bowyer, a miniaturist to King George III. Bowyer wrote at the time to notify Washington of the countess's recent demise, "an event which must be regretted by every friend to real religion upon the face of the earth."[73] Washington wrote back to Bowyer early in 1792:

> Although I had not the satisfaction of knowing the late Countess personally, yet having been honored with her correspondence, and learning from others the amiable and benevolent character which she sustained, I have respected her virtues, and am pleased with having in my possession the picture which you have been so polite as to send me, and for which I must beg you to accept my best thanks.[74]

The placement of this engraving, whose subject was not an especially attractive woman physically, in the room to which Martha Washington retreated each day for her morning and evening devotions, may have indicated that the countess was a special heroine of Mount Vernon's mistress. Throughout the mansion, these graphic images would have reminded those who saw them of events in the Bible, served as examples of how later Christian heroes lived out their faith, and reinforced the duties of benevolence and spreading the Gospel.

There is also a suggestion that the Washington family may have prepared their hearts for the coming Sunday service by practicing the custom of fasting one day per week, although the evidence is slim and the reasons for it unclear. Archibald Robertson, a Scottish artist who came to America in 1791, described a visit with the Washington family in Philadelphia, during which they ate fish, rather than meat, because it was Saturday. Whether the Washingtons abstained from meat on Saturdays for religious reasons, which appears to be Robertson's inference, or because of their well-documented love of fish and seafood, we can't say. Information from another source describes George Washington's typical Saturday "salt fish dinner," as consisting of boiled beets, potatoes, onions, and fish, garnished with egg sauce and fried pork scraps. The presence of the last ingredient might negate religious reasons for the family's practice of eating fish on Saturday.[75]

At least in New England, the Puritans, an offshoot of the Anglican Church, are known to have practiced the custom of eating fish on Saturday to continue the religious tradition of fasting one day a week, while distancing themselves from the Roman Catholic practice of fasting on Friday. It was not unusual in that part of the country, however, to dress up the fish with salt pork scraps and fat or rich butter and egg sauces. It may be that the Washingtons became aware of this custom during the Revolutionary War and continued it later, either because of its religious associations, for the memories it evoked of friends and times past, or simply because they enjoyed this combination of flavors.[76]

According to the step-granddaughter he raised, George Washington was attentive and respectful during church services. As she put it, "No one in church attended to the services with more reverential respect." Noting, by way of contrast, that her grandmother, "who was eminently pious, never deviated from her early habits" and "always knelt" during the service, Nelly recalled that Washington, "as was then the custom, stood during the devotional parts of the service."[77] Nelly's statements are supported by those of Bishop William White of Philadelphia, who wrote many years later about his long association with Washington and the latter's attitude during services:

> The father of our country, whenever in this city [Philadelphia], as well during the revolutionary war as in his Presidency, attended divine service in Christ Church of this city; except during one winter; when, being here for the taking of measures with Congress towards the opening of the next campaign, he rented a house near to St Peter's Church. . . . During that season, he attended regularly at St Peter's. His behaviour was always serious and attentive; but as your letter seems to intend an inquiry on the point of kneeling during the service, I owe it to truth to declare, that I never saw him in the said attitude. During his Presidency, our vestry provided him with a pew, ten yards in front of the reading desk. It was habitually occupied by himself, by Mrs Washington, who was regularly a communicant, and by his secretaries.[78]

A woman identified as "Mrs. M.," who had seen Washington at a service at Alexandria's Christ Church during the summer of 1799, later wrote down her impressions of his demeanor:

> I was in Alexandria, on a visit. . . . Whilst there, I expressed a wish to see General Washington, as I had never enjoyed that pleasure. My friend, Mrs. H., observed, "You will certainly see him on Sunday, as he is never absent from church when he can get there; and as he often dines with us, we will ask him on that day, when you will have a better opportunity of seeing him." Accordingly, we all repaired to church on Sunday, and seated in Mr. H.'s large double pew, I kept my eyes upon the door, looking for the venerable form of him I had so long desired to see. . . . He walked to his pew, at the upper part of the church, and demeaned himself throughout the services of the day with that gravity and propriety becoming the place and his own high character. After the services were concluded we waited for him at the door, for his pew being near the pulpit he was among the last that came out—when Mrs. H. invited him to dine with us. He declined, however, the invitation, observing, as he looked at the skey, that he thought there were appearances of a thunderstorm in the afternoon, and he believed he would return home to dinner.[79]

Washington has been criticized by those writing about his faith for not kneeling during portions of the Sunday church services he attended. In the first half of the twentieth century, Franklin Steiner asked the question, "Can there be found any evidence that Washington was a 'praying man?'" He then answered his own query: "Bishop White, whose church he [Washington] attended on and off for 25 years in Philadelphia, says he never saw him on his knees in church. That ought to settle the question."[80] The careful reader will note, however, that Bishop White did not say that Washington did not pray, only that he did not kneel.

More recently, David Holmes offered the following opinion on this subject:

> Many who have left descriptions of Washington at worship specifically note that he insisted on standing in his pew for prayers, instead of (as was usual for Anglicans) kneeling. Washington's choice of posture represents a puzzling idiosyncrasy, unless it stemmed from childhood upbringing, from

a knowledge that Christians (like Jews) originally stood for prayer, or from his field experience on Sundays in the English Army.[81]

Once again, however, family testimony has been ignored. In her recollections of her step-grandfather's customary practices in church, Nelly Custis Lewis stated that at that time and place (the Protestant Episcopal churches of New York and Philadelphia in the late 1780s and 1790s), it was customary to stand during prayers. It was her grandmother's practice of kneeling, in fact, that might have been viewed as old-fashioned.

5

CONFIRMATION
AND COMMUNION

Questions about a Rite and Sacrament of the Church

W HILE HOLY COMMUNION is a prominent feature of modern
Anglican/Episcopal church services, this was not the case during George Washington's lifetime. Typically, communion was
offered only three or four times a year. Communicants would come forward to receive the elements of bread or wine at the altar rail and usually
knelt, but those who had scruples against taking that posture (for fear that
they would appear to be worshipping either the elements themselves, the
altar, or the act of consecration) were allowed to stand. Unlike their Roman Catholic brethren, Anglicans did not believe in transubstantiation,
the idea that the bread and wine were transformed into the actual body
and blood of Jesus. Officeholders in Virginia were required to swear to
this Anglican tenet as a means of keeping Catholics out of the political life
of the colony.[1]

One historian who has examined religious practices in eighteenth-
century Virginia has noted what he interpreted as the secular nature of
that society, quoting, by way of example, an Anglican minister who recorded that "generally speaking, none went to the table [for communion],
except a few of the more aged." A study of church practice in America,
undertaken by the Anglican Church in 1724, indicated that perhaps 15
percent of adult Anglicans in the southern colonies were regular communicants at the handful of communion services typically held each year,
in comparison with a rate of 5 percent to 30 percent of those eligible to

receive communion in England in the first half of the eighteenth century.[2] Records for Oxfordshire in England show that between 1738 and 1811, only 5 percent of the population took communion.[3]

Several reasons have been suggested for this low rate of participation in such a fundamental Christian rite. Perhaps the most prevalent thought of later historians of this period is that the rationalism of the educated classes led them to reject anything that smacked of mystery and the supernatural. Still others—Deists or skeptics—may have stayed away from the communion table because of their lack of belief. At least one historian has pointed out, however, that the most important factor keeping people from participating in communion was "scrupulousness," the feeling on the part of the worshipper that he or she was either not worthy to take part or had not properly prepared beforehand.[4]

In theory, a prerequisite for taking communion in an Anglican church was that a young person be confirmed. This typically meant proving to a bishop or his representative, in front of the entire congregation, that he or she knew such basics as the Lord's Prayer, the Apostles' Creed, and the Ten Commandments, thus fulfilling a promise made for them by their godparents at the time of their christening. In preparation for the rite of confirmation, young people would be catechized, or taught the essentials of the Christian faith and how to apply them in the course of their lives, by either their parents, their pastor, or some combination of the two.

The catch for Anglicans living in Virginia and the other American colonies was that the British church never appointed a bishop for them before the Revolutionary War. Without a bishop, no one could be confirmed. Colonial Anglicans were not barred from the communion table, however, because the prayer book noted that anyone could take part in this rite who was "ready and desirous to be confirmed."[5]

After the war, when the Anglican Church in America became the Protestant Episcopal Church, bishops were appointed, and it finally became possible for young people to be confirmed. At that point, after the 1780s, certain older, especially devout members of these new Episcopal congregations took the opportunity to at last be confirmed themselves. The mother of future president James Madison was eighty-four years old in 1816, when her parish was first visited by an Episcopal bishop in an official capacity and she was confirmed, although she had been taking communion since the age of twenty.

There is no evidence that George Washington ever took advantage of the opportunity offered by the creation of American bishops to undergo confirmation, which one historian has described as "an active affirmation of Christian belief." This omission on Washington's part leads this historian to say that Washington seemed "indifferent" to this particular rite, failed to provide a good example to other members of his denomination, and was heavily influenced by deism. But there is no evidence for the confirmation of Martha Washington either, a woman he considers an "orthodox Anglican."[6]

The Washingtons' home parishes in Virginia did not have a bishop until 1790, when James Madison, a second cousin of the future president, was appointed to that position, at a time when George Washington was serving as president and the couple was, as a consequence, living in New York and Philadelphia. Bishop Madison was only able to make a few "partial visitations of the Diocese," as his duties as president of the College of William and Mary seem to have taken much of his attention (he had become a professor there in 1774 and was made president of the school in 1777), so much so that he ordained relatively few pastors and, seemingly, confirmed few congregants, before his death in 1812.[7] Perhaps the Washingtons had no desire to be confirmed, either because of their age and the fact that they had managed quite well without it for so long, or because one or both of them no longer believed. But they may well have had no opportunity to undergo confirmation in the last decade or so of their lives, when it would, theoretically, have been possible. It is possible that the Washingtons could have been confirmed by the bishops in either New York or Philadelphia, but, as we will see in more detail, there are suggestions that George Washington had a problem with at least one of the new bishops in the Episcopal Church and may have not trusted that any of them had the best interests of the United States at heart. Such doubts could easily have kept him from seeking confirmation at their hands.

George Washington's relationship with the ordinance or sacrament of communion is complicated, but it certainly fits the eighteenth-century norm for Virginia. As was shown earlier, Washington supplied his local congregation with wine for the communion service before the Revolution. According to a letter written by Martha Washington's granddaughter Nelly, based on conversations with her mother, Eleanor Calvert Custis Stuart, who was a member of the Mount Vernon household for years, George Washington regularly took communion with his wife before taking command of the Continental Army; after that time, he, and the majority of the congregation, would exit the church building after the blessing but before the start of the communion service, leaving those who were partaking in the ceremony, including Mrs. Washington, inside. Nelly recalled that, during the presidency, she would generally leave the church with her step-grandfather, and the two would go home, sending the carriage back for Martha Washington, who was a regular communicant, at the close of the service.[8]

While Nelly wrote these recollections many years after her step-grandfather's death, the subject probably came up a number of times during her childhood. Given the natural curiosity of children and their interest in how and why certain things are done or not done, the difference in practice between her grandparents was probably something she had questioned her mother about on a number of occasions as she grew up at Mount Vernon.[9]

Nelly's statements about Washington's behavior in regard to communion during the presidency are confirmed by one of the ministers whose services he attended in Philadelphia. Col. Hugh Mercer of Fredericksburg, Virginia, had written Bishop William White to ask "whether General Washington was a *regular communicant* in the Episcopal Church in Philadelphia, or whether he *occasionally* went to the communion only, *if he ever did at all.*" Mercer went on to say that, "The whole country knows that he was a religious man, and served his God with humility and reverence. No authority can be more complete and authentic than yours, on this point, as he was, I believe, a regular attendant on your ministry in Christ Church." In response, Bishop White noted, "Truth requires me to say, that General Washington never received the communion, in the churches of which I am parochial minister," even though "Mrs. Washington was an habitual communicant."[10]

It appears from another source, however, that the change in George Washington's religious practices may not have been as abrupt or complete as Nelly and others in the family believed. According to one clergyman who knew him well, while at Morristown, New Jersey, during the Revolution, George Washington was "at his particular request, admitted to commune at the Lord's Table, with the Presbyterian church of that place, then under the pastoral care of the Revd Dr. Timothy Jones." The minister went on to note that, "I believe there still are, living, eyewitnesses of this fact."[11]

On at least one occasion during his presidency, Washington's practice of leaving church before communion earned him a rebuke from a clergyman. Dr. James Abercrombie, assistant rector of Christ Church in Philadelphia, one Sunday from the pulpit chastised Washington and others who set a bad example by turning "their backs upon the celebration of the Lord's Supper." Later in the week, he learned in a conversation with a senator that the president had mentioned the reproof at dinner: "that he honored the preacher for his integrity and candour; that he had never considered the influence of his example; and that, as he had never been a communicant, were he to become one of them, it would be imputed to an ostentatious display of religious zeal arising altogether from his elevated station."

After this incident, Washington stopped attending church on days when communion services were held, although his attendance was regular on other Sundays.[12] While the words "he had never been a communicant" might be understood to mean that Washington had absolutely never taken communion, it must be taken into account that this statement was being repeated third hand (from Washington, to the senator, to Reverend Abercrombie), and that, given testimony by Washington's step-granddaughter that he had been a communicant before the Revolution, the president might have simply been saying that he had never taken communion at that particular church, or in that city.

The reason for the change noted by the family in George Washington's customary practice is not recorded by them or in his surviving writings, but scrupulousness may well have been the cause. One of Washington's earliest biographers has suggested that "after he took command of the army, finding his thoughts and attention necessarily engrossed by the business that devolved upon him, in which frequently little distinction could be observed between Sunday and other days, he may have believed it improper publicly to partake of an ordinance, which, according to the ideas he entertained of it, imposed severe restrictions on outward conduct, and a sacred pledge to perform duties impracticable in his situation."[13]

A nineteenth-century Episcopal bishop, with close ties to the later generations at Mount Vernon, suggested a similar reason for Washington's behavior:

> If it be asked how we can reconcile this leaving of the church at any time of the celebration of the Lord's Supper with a religious character, we reply by stating a well-known fact . . . that in former days there was a most mistaken

notion, too prevalent both in England and America, that it was not so neces-sary in the professors of religion to communicate at all times, but that in this respect persons might be regulated by their feelings, and perhaps by the circumstances in which they were placed. I have had occasion to see much of this in my researches into the habits of the members of the old Church of Virginia. Into this error of opinion and practice General Washington may have fallen, especially at a time when he was peculiarly engaged with the cares of government and a multiplicity of engagements, and when his piety may have suffered some loss thereby.[14]

To understand the change in George Washington's communion hab-its after the American Revolution, consider the state of the denomina-tion in which he had grown up. As the war approached, Anglicans in the Middle Colonies (New York, New Jersey, Delaware, and Pennsylvania) called on their spiritual leaders in England to provide them with a bishop and, in their arguments, took care to link the interests of the church and the British monarchy. As one wrote in 1767, "Episcopacy and Monarchy are, in their Frame and Constitution best suited to each other. Episcopacy can never thrive in a Republican Government, nor Republican Principles in an Episcopal Church."[15] Just two months after Washington's return to Mount Vernon at the close of the war, and ten months before the Protes-tant Episcopal Church was first chartered in Virginia, he resigned his po-sition on the vestry at Truro Parish, an office he had held for twenty-two years.[16] Although he offered no reason for this action, it is quite likely related to the fact that, as a vestryman, he had to pledge loyalty and obedi-ence to the "doctrine and discipline of the Church of England," an institu-tion headed by the king of England. After eight years of war fought to win independence from the British monarchy, Washington could not in good conscience adhere to those oaths and thus submit to the Crown.

At this point, Anglican clergymen in the various states were trying to reorganize the American branch of the church into the Protestant Episco-pal Church, but it would be several years before the change was complete, and there was controversy about some of the ensuing changes in both personnel and liturgy. The first bishop of the church in America, elected by the Connecticut clergy in March 1783, was Samuel Seabury, a minister who had written pamphlets espousing the Loyalist cause before the Revo-lution and who served during the war as both a guide for British troops on Long Island and in Westchester County, in New York, and as a chaplain, first on a British man-of-war, and later with the King's American Regiment. When the British prime minister would not allow English bishops to consecrate Seabury as a bishop in the new church, he went to Scotland, where the rites were performed by several bishops of the breakaway Scottish branch of the Anglican Church.

Both Seabury's political views during the war and his consecration in Scotland, which was not viewed as valid by many church members, made him a controversial choice for bishop.[17] When a young clergyman, who had served as a tutor at the home of Washington's brother, John Augustine, came to Mount Vernon in the fall of 1785 to ask for a reference to Bishop Seabury, with the hopes that he could be ordained, Washington noted in his diary that he "could not give him more than a general certificate, founded on information, respecting his character; having no acquaintance with him, nor any desire to open a Corrispondence with the *new* ordained Bishop."[18]

This last comment, and especially Washington's emphasis on the word "new," suggests that he might have had a problem with Seabury and the subsequent organization of the Episcopal Church, which affected his religious practice in the last fifteen years of his life. It may well be, too, that those earlier arguments about the link between the Anglican Church and the British monarchy had resonated with him and that he was having trouble reconciling how the new Episcopal Church was going to work with this new form of government, or how supportive it might be. Bishop Seabury was hardly the only Anglican minister to remain loyal to the Crown during the Revolution. Of the 218 men known to have served as chaplains with the American army during the war, only about 10 percent are identified in the records as Anglican/Episcopalian.[19] Washington could have had considerable doubts that the "new" bishop, and the pastors over whom he presided, would be any better for a republic than one of the old ones back in England. In a similar vein, one student of Washington's life has written about another early leader of the Episcopal Church in the United States: "Bishop White had been ordained after the Revolution in England or Scotland. GW may have felt that to accept communion at his hand would have been an improper acknowledgement of the authority of a foreign hierarchy."[20]

Another factor in Washington's change in practice regarding communion is the American Revolution itself, which greatly broadened his horizons in several areas of his life. For example, as will be examined in greater detail below, his ideas about slavery changed dramatically, from unthinking acceptance of that institution to a desire for its abolition.[21] According to one Washington historian, the wartime years he spent in Pennsylvania, New Jersey, and New York exposed Washington to a different type of economy and agriculture than were practiced in Virginia before the war and led him to share the views of the inhabitants of those mid-Atlantic, rather than Southern, states about slavery.[22]

Similarly, before the war, most of Washington's experiences with the church had been in Virginia, a colony where the Anglican Church was a very strong state institution and where those with dissenting beliefs had been persecuted to varying degrees in the decade before the Revolution. Among the teachings of certain Anglican churchmen on the eve of the war were the idea that the Church of England was the only true church; that no one could become a Christian or be ordained to the ministry outside of the Church of England; that marriages could be legitimate only if performed by an Anglican minister; that the English king ruled by divine right; that a believer's duties as a Christian included loyalty to the king and government; that an established national church was essential for every nation; that the continued supremacy of the Church of England and the retention of the American colonies were necessary for the preservation of the empire; that "Independence in Religion will naturally produce Republicans in the State and from their Principles, too prevalent already, the greatest evils may justly be apprehended"; and that dissenters had no inherent rights, but were tolerated as a necessary evil until they could be persuaded, or coerced, into conforming with the Anglican church.[23] These views were very conservative, and Washington had quite obviously, and publicly, disagreed with the more politically oriented of them during the war. They were also very much out of line with the Latitudinarian beliefs that had shaped Washington's youth.

During the Revolution, George Washington not only traveled to colonies where there was greater political toleration of dissenters, but he also served in the army with men whose religious beliefs and practices were not Anglican. Furthermore, the spiritual needs of the Continental Army were met by chaplains who represented a variety of Christian denominations: Congregationalist, Presbyterian, Anglican, German Reformed, Lutheran, French Reformed, Baptist, Roman Catholic, and Universalist.[24] Washington came to trust these men. He showed considerable faith in one, Baptist chaplain David Jones of Pennsylvania, whose distinguished career included training as a doctor and undertaking two missions to the Indians on the Ohio before settling down to a pastorate, which he left to join the army in 1776. As a chaplain, Jones took part in the battles at Ticonderoga, Morristown, Brandywine, and Yorktown; was almost killed at Paoli; and was considered so valuable that the British General Howe is said to have offered a reward for his capture.[25]

It was during the winter at Valley Forge that Washington confided to Jones that if the chaplain ever had "anything private to communicate" to him, that he should "never do it before my family" (using the term "family" for his military staff), perhaps indicating that he had some doubts about their loyalty, but not that of Chaplain Jones.[26] After the war, Jones, then serving as pastor of the Great Valley Baptist Church in Chester County, Pennsylvania, would visit his old commander at Mount Vernon and spend the night.[27]

Jones was one of many ardent patriots serving as chaplains to the Continental Army. Congregationalist Samuel West of Massachusetts is credited with breaking a code used by Dr. Benjamin Church, who was an agent for the British. Another New England Congregationalist, Abner Benedict from Connecticut, helped to develop a primitive torpedo. A Presbyterian from New Jersey named James Caldwell, who was also a deputy quartermaster and assistant commissary general, may have managed spies on Staten Island and gained fame at the battle of Springfield. There, noticing that the American forces were slackening their fire because of a lack of wadding for their muskets, he ran to a nearby Presbyterian church, grabbed as many Watts hymnals as he could, and handed them out so that the pages could be torn out and used in the guns. Traditionally, he is said to have encouraged the soldiers with the words: "Give them Watts, boys, give them Watts!"

Chaplain Caldwell paid a terrible price for his loyalty. In 1780 the British took revenge on his family.[28] Upon learning that the British were nearing his home, Chaplain Caldwell "retired into the country, leaving his lady with the care of the family, supposing that the customary respect for the female character would be a pledge for her safety." A fellow officer described "the horrid and barbarous deeds of the enemy," which he said would "be an everlasting stigma on the British character":

> Mrs. Caldwell . . . and a young woman, having Mrs. Caldwell's infant in
> her arms, seated themselves on the bed, when a British soldier came to the

house, and putting his gun to the window of the room, shot her through the breast, and she instantly expired. Soon after, an officer with two Hessian soldiers came and ordered a hole to be dug, the body to be thrown in, and the house to be set on fire. Thus was murdered an amiable and excellent lady, and the worthy husband left with nine children, destitute of even a change of clothes, or any thing to render them comfortable. The house and every article belonging to this respectable family were consumed, together with the church and thirteen dwelling-houses.[29]

Caldwell was shot to death in 1781 by an off-duty sentry, who was later executed for the murder. Washington himself contributed to the support of the Caldwells' children after the deaths of their parents, and the Marquis de Lafayette even sent one of the children to his wife in France to be educated.[30] It may be that those wartime relationships with colleagues and ministers of other denominations led Washington to a broader definition of what it meant to be Christian, taking him outside the prevailing Anglican model (which, in turn, had moved away from the teachings of the church in which he had been raised), and also gave him an unconcern with labels and the form of specific rituals.[31]

Like many others before and after him, Washington may also have stopped taking communion out of a sense that he was involved in an ongoing sin.[32] The most obvious possibility has to do with Washington's continued participation in the institution of slavery, even though, as was mentioned earlier, he had come to believe it was wrong over the course of the American Revolution. During the conflict, his views on slavery were radically altered, evidence that he truly believed the wartime rhetoric about freedom and liberty. He wrote a few years after the conflict, "Liberty, when it begins to take root, is a plant of rapid growth," which was certainly true of his views on slavery.[33] Within three years of the start of the war, Washington, then forty-six years old and a slaveowner for thirty-five years, confided in a cousin back in Virginia that he longed "every day . . . more and more to get clear of" the ownership of slaves.[34]

Following the Revolution, Washington looked into a variety of ways to manumit his slaves. His protégé, the Marquis de Lafayette, was an ardent abolitionist, and the two men discussed, in letters and in person, an experiment to prove that a plantation could be operated using free labor. In the last days of the Revolution, Lafayette wrote his old commander, suggesting an experiment in which the two would purchase some land, which Washington's slaves would then work as tenants. Lafayette believed that Washington's participation in the project would help to "render it a general practice." The young man hoped, if his plan proved successful in the United States, to then spread out to the West Indies. He expressed the passionate sentiment that, "If it be a wild scheme, I had rather be mad in this way, than to be thought wise in the other task."[35] Washington responded warmly to the idea, but preferred to discuss the details in person:

> The scheme . . . which you propose as a precedent, to encourage the emancipation of the black people of this Country from that state of Bondage in wch. they are held, is a striking evidence of the benevolence of your Heart. I shall be happy to join you in so laudable a work; but will defer going into a detail of the business, 'till I have the pleasure of seeing you.[36]

Not long after the close of the war, Lafayette finally came to Mount Vernon, where he and Washington continued their long-standing discussion about the experiment, perhaps getting into those deferred details. Another houseguest at that same time was quite taken with the conversation, later writing to his host in continuation:

> You wished to get rid of all your Negroes, & the Marquis wisht that an end might be put to the slavery of all of them. I should rejoice beyond measure could your joint counsels & influence produce it, & thereby give the finishing stroke & the last polish to your political characters. Could it not be contrived that the industrious among them might be turned into copyholders on the lands of their present masters, & by having a special interest in the produce of their labors be made [mutilated] more profit than at present? A[nd c]ould not this in its consequences excite the lazy to exertions [tha]t might prove highly beneficial? I am not for letting them all loose upon the public; but am for gradually releasing them & their posterity from bonds, & incorporating them so in the states, that they may be a defence & not a danger upon any extraordinary occurrence.[37]

By 1785 Lafayette was ready to begin the experiment. In June of that year, he ordered his attorney to purchase a plantation for him in French Guinea, with the proviso that none of the slaves on the plantation be sold or exchanged. He informed Washington in February 1786 that he had secretly acquired an estate, "and am going to free my Negroes in order to Make that Experiment which you know is my Hobby Horse."[38] Upon learning of this move, Washington responded:

> The benevolence of your heart my D[ea]r Marq[ui]s is so conspicuous upon all occasions, that I never wonder at any fresh proofs of it; but your late purchase of an Estate in the Colony of Cayenne with a view of emancipating the slaves on it, is a generous and noble proof of your humanity. Would to God a like spirit would diffuse itself generally into the minds of the people of this country.[39]

Washington himself made a start at a similar experiment at Mount Vernon. In the last six years of his life, he advertised to rent the four outlying farms of his plantation, if he could find "good farmers" from England or Scotland willing to take on the project. This scheme would relieve Washington of the burden of managing this land, while at the same time ensuring a stable income. In correspondence, he also wrote that "many of the Negroes, male and female, might be hired by the year as labourers," if the tenants chose to use them, instead of bringing in workmen from their own country.[40] Unfortunately, although he corresponded with a number of prospective tenants, none of the negotiations proved fruitful.

It was also in the period between the end of the war and the start of his presidency that abolitionists began approaching Washington to seek his support for their cause. At least one challenged him on this issue, specifically citing religious reasons for Washington to take the step of emancipating his slaves. Robert Pleasants was a Quaker whose plantation-owning father had tried to free his own slaves in his 1781 will. Even before the law in Virginia was changed in 1782, making it possible for individual owners to liberate their slaves without a special act of the legislature, the younger Pleasants had been giving his slaves their own farms; after that year, he emancipated eighty of them.

Pleasants, who was a leader of the Virginia abolition movement and would go on to encourage the education of both slaves and freed blacks, contacted Washington in December of 1785. He began with his concerns for Washington's reputation and went on to the thought that it was strange that Washington, "who could forego all the Sweets of domestic felicity

... & expose thy Person to the greatest fatigue & dangers in that cause, should now withhold that inestimable blessing from any who are absolutely in thy power, & after the Right of freedom, is acknowledg'd to be the natural & unalienable Right of all mankind." Knowing Washington to be a generous man, Pleasants felt that Washington's hesitation in this instance was not the result of "interested motives," but perhaps of "long custom, the prejudices of education towards a black skin, or that some other important concerns may have hitherto diverted thy attention from a Subject so Noble and interesting, as well to thy own Peace & reputation, as the general good of that People, and the community at large." Pleasants offered the opinion that Washington should not delay in freeing his slaves, because it was "a Sacrifise which I fully beli[e]ve the Lord is requiring of this Generation." He went on to say that he wished "that thou may not loose the opertunity of Crowning the great Actions of thy Life, with the sattisfaction of, 'doing to Others as thou would (in the like Situation) be done by,' and finally transmit to future ages a Character, equally famous for thy Christian Virtues, as thy worldly achievements."

He reminded Washington of a coming day of judgment: "For notwithstanding thou art now receiving the tribute of praise from a grateful people, the time is coming when all actions will be weighed in an equal ballance, and undergo an impartial examination." Pleasants closed by hoping Washington would not think him presumptuous, stating that he had no selfish motives for "offering these hints to his serious consideration," other than "what may arise from the pleasure of hearing he had done those things—which belong to his present & future happiness, and the good of those over whom Providence hath placed him."[41]

Over and over again, Washington responded to conversations and letters on this subject with his conviction that the best way to effect the elimination of slavery was through the legislature, which he hoped would set up a program of gradual emancipation, and for which he would gladly give his vote. As he assured his friend Robert Morris in 1786, he hoped that no one would read his opposition to the methods of certain abolitionists, in this case, the Quakers, as opposition to abolition as a concept:

I hope it will not be conceived from these observations, that it is my wish to hold the unhappy people, who are the subject of this letter, in slavery. I can only say that there is not a man living who wishes more sincerely than I do, to see a plan adopted for the abolition of it; but there is only one proper and effectual mode by which it can be accomplished, and that is by Legislative authority; and this, as far as my suffrage will go, shall never be wanting.[42]

He admitted to Lafayette, however, that he "despaired" of seeing an abolitionist spirit sweep the country. He confided to the younger man in 1786: "Some petitions were presented to the Assembly at its last Session, for the abolition of slavery, but they could scarcely obtain a reading. To set them [the slaves] afloat at once would, I really believe, be productive of much inconvenience & mischief; but by degrees it certainly might, & assuredly ought to be effected & that too by Legislative authority."[43] To another correspondent about this same time, Washington wrote that it was "among my first wishes to see some plan adopted, by which slavery in this country may be abolished by slow, sure, and imperceptible degrees."[44]

In a fervor of emotion sparked by the Revolution, three New England states (Vermont, New Hampshire, and Massachusetts) appear to have abolished slavery outright during the war, while legislatures in the upper South (Virginia, Maryland, and Delaware) made it easier for slave owners to free their slaves, something which had been impossible for a private individual to do in Virginia between 1723 and 1782. There was even a precedent for the type of gradual process of emancipation that Washington favored. Pennsylvania had passed a law in 1780 that all slaves born in the future would become free when they reached the age of twenty-eight. Other Northern states followed suit. In the year Washington died, for example, the New York legislature agreed to free future-born slave men at twenty-eight and women at twenty-five years old. New Jersey, Connecticut, and Rhode Island instituted similar plans. As a result of these laws, about 75 percent of African Americans in the Northern states were free by 1810.[45]

While he could never bring himself to publicly lead the effort to abolish slavery, probably for fear of tearing apart the country he had worked so hard to build, Washington could, and did, try to lead by setting an example.[46] In his will, written several months before his death in December 1799, Washington left directions for the emancipation, after Martha Washington died, of all the slaves who belonged to him. Washington was not the only Virginian to free his slaves at this period. Toward the end of the American Revolution, in 1782, the Virginia legislature had made it legal for masters to manumit their slaves without a special action of the governor and council, which had been necessary before, and a number of people took advantage of this new law, including one large slaveholder who, alone, freed more than five hundred people during the 1790s.[47]

Of the 318 slaves at Mount Vernon in 1799, fewer than half, 123 individuals, belonged to George Washington and would go free. When her first husband, Daniel Parke Custis, died without a will, Mrs. Washington had received a life interest in one-third of his estate, including the slaves (the other two-thirds of the estate went to their children). For all intents and purposes, neither George nor Martha Washington could free these slaves and, upon her death, they reverted to the Custis estate and were divided among her grandchildren. By 1799, 153 slaves at Mount Vernon were part of this dower property. It was largely because of the Custis estate that George Washington waited as long as he did to free his own slaves. Over the forty years since George Washington and Martha Dandridge Custis were married, his slaves had intermarried with hers, leading to a heartbreaking situation in which families would be broken up when the Washington slaves were emancipated. George Washington was trying to put off that terrible consequence for as long as possible.[48]

The one slave Mrs. Washington owned outright and could have manumitted, a man named Elish, who had been purchased by her from a Washington relative, she bequeathed to her grandson, George Washington Parke Custis.[49] Forty more slaves were rented from a neighbor, while another man, Peter Hardiman, was rented from the widow of Mrs. Washington's son. All these people would eventually return to their owners. In accordance with state law, George Washington stipulated that elderly slaves or those who were too sick to work were to be supported throughout their lives by his estate. Children without parents, or those whose families were too poor or indifferent to see to their education, were to be bound out to masters and mistresses who would teach them reading, writing, and a useful trade, until they were ultimately freed at the age of twenty-five. Washington stated quite strongly that he took these charges to his executors very seriously:

> And I do moreover most pointedly, and most solemnly enjoin it upon my Executors . . . to see that this clause respecting Slaves, and every part thereof be religiously fulfilled at the Epoch at which it is directed to take place; without evasion, neglect or delay, after the Crops which may then be on the ground are harvested, particularly as it respects the aged and infirm.[50]

In December 1800, Martha Washington signed a deed of manumission for her deceased husband's slaves, a transaction that is recorded in the abstracts of the Fairfax County, Virginia, Court Records. They would become free on January 1, 1801.

Slavery was the primary issue leading to inner conflict in the last decades of Washington's life. It may well be that feelings of shame or inadequacy, stemming from a belief that slavery was wrong, while being largely unable to eradicate it, or even to extricate himself from his own direct involvement with it, led him to feel that he was unworthy of taking communion. Toward the end of his life, he looked back reflectively on his years as a slaveowner and allowed some of the guilt he evidently felt to show just a little:

> The unfortunate condition of the persons, whose labour in part I employed, has been the only unavoidable subject of regret. To make the Adults among them as easy & as comfortable in their circumstances as their actual state of ignorance & improvidence would admit; & to lay a foundation to prepare the rising generation for a destiny different from that in which they were born; afforded some satisfaction to my mind, & could not I hoped be displeasing to the justice of the Creator.[51]

6

PRAYER

Private Devotions

THERE ARE A number of highly romanticized—and highly suspect—
stories about George Washington praying, most, if not all, of which
probably date to the nineteenth or twentieth centuries. The earliest
version of a typical example dates to 1808 and the publication of the sixth
edition of Parson Weems's biography of Washington, which told the story
of a Quaker farmer named Potts, who came across Washington praying
on his knees in the woods near his Valley Forge headquarters.[1]

By 1860 the story had been changed a bit, the farmer had become
anonymous, and the location for the incident had been moved from
Pennsylvania to New York. Published in 1860 by the fundraising newslet-
ter of the Mount Vernon Ladies' Association, it was written by an octo-
genarian in New Haven, Connecticut, named Grant Thorburn Sr. The
author related that in 1796, when he was twenty-four years old, he heard
a Quaker farmer tell how, during the Revolution, near West Point, New
York, he went out early one morning to round up some of his cows. As
he walked past a "clump of brushwood," he heard what he described as "a
moaning sound, like a person in distress." As he got closer, he could hear
someone praying and hid behind a tree, until the speaker came into the
open, and the farmer recognized him as "George Washington, the captain
of the Lord's host in North America." The farmer's religious and political
beliefs caused him to oppose the war, but when he returned home, he
told his wife, "We must not oppose this war any longer; this morning I

heard the man George Washington send up a prayer to heaven for his country, and I know it will be heard." From that day on, the farmer is said to have passed on intelligence concerning the British to Washington. The article then went on to suggest that, "From this incident we may infer that Washington rose with the sun to pray for his country; he fought for her at meridian, and watched for her in the silent hours of midnight."[2]

In addition to these rather fanciful stories, a collection of prayers, which have been attributed to Washington, has often been used as evidence for his deep religious convictions. Based in large part on the Anglican/Episcopal prayer book, these handwritten prayers for morning and evening devotions were found among other Washington objects being offered for sale from the collections of several collateral descendants in 1891. While their authenticity has been questioned over the years, with various Washington "authorities" weighing in on one side or the other, the most recent consensus seems to be that these prayers are not in George Washington's handwriting.[3]

Several officers who served with Washington during the Revolution would later recall that their commander had a regular time for private prayers, but their testimony has largely been discounted, because they told, rather than wrote, their stories to others, who then published the information many years later. Some of these stories had been through several hands before they were finally published and so, unfortunately, should be handled as hearsay. For example, according to Gen. David Cobb from Washington's staff, "Throughout the war, as it was understood in his [Washington's] military family, he gave a part of every day to private prayer and devotion."[4]

In another case, Gen. Robert Porterfield, who had been a young officer with two Virginia regiments during the Revolution, would later relate that, as part of his duties, he often came into contact with George Washington: "Upon one occasion, some emergency . . . induced him to dispense with the usual formality, and he went directly to General Washington's apartment, where he found him on his knees, engaged in his morning's devotions. He said that he mentioned the circumstance to General [Alexander] Hamilton, who replied that such was his constant habit."[5]

There is, however, stronger evidence that Washington probably engaged in private prayer. The recollections of Cobb and Porterfield, above, fit rather neatly with a statement, published in 1801 by a Frenchman who knew Washington both during the Revolution and the presidency, that

"Every day of the year, he rises at five in the morning; as soon as he is up, he dresses, then prays reverently to God."[6] Lending credence to these stories, perhaps, is a surviving order, dating to a few years before the start of the Revolution, showing that Washington was looking to buy "A Pray[e]r Book with the New Version of Psalms & good plain Type—cov[ere]d with red Moroco—to be 7 Inch[e]s long 4 ½ wide, & as thin as possible for the great[e]r ease of carry[in]g in the Pocket."[7] If Washington took a prayer book with him to the war, it was very likely this one.

In a general order given after the battle at Brandywine, Washington himself commented on the importance of prayer to the American cause in the Revolution. After noting that the outcome of the latest encounter with the British was not as positive as he had hoped, Washington assured his army that the enemy's losses had been considerable and even larger than their own, and that he "had full confidence that in another Appeal to Heaven (with the blessing of providence, which it becomes every officer and soldier humbly to supplicate), we shall prove successful."[8]

Several members of Washington's family have left remarks on the subject of George Washington and daily prayer, which should not be easily dismissed. Mrs. Washington's youngest granddaughter, Nelly, admitted to a Washington biographer that she had always assumed that at least some of the time Washington spent alone each day in his study before breakfast and then later in the evening was spent in prayer:

> It was his custom to retire to his library at nine or ten o'clock, where he remained an hour before he went to his chamber. He always rose before the sun, and remained in his library until called to breakfast. I never *witnessed* his private devotions. I never *inquired* about them. I should have thought it the greatest heresy to doubt his firm belief in Christianity. His life, his writings, prove that he was a Christian. He was not one of those, who act or pray, "That they may be seen of men." He communed with his God in secret.[9]

George Washington's nephew Maj. George Lewis, who served with his uncle's bodyguard during the Revolution, later related overhearing Washington's early morning prayers as he came to deliver some newly arrived dispatches to his room; the young man then went to another part of the house for a short while until those morning devotions had been completed.[10] His younger brother, Robert Lewis, who lived with their uncle's family in the early months of the presidency, claimed to have inadvertently walked in on Washington, who was involved in prayer and Bible reading in his study, early in the morning and also in the evening. According to this account, recorded by Washington biographer Jared Sparks:

> It seems proper to subjoin to this letter what was told to me by Mr. Robert Lewis, at Fredericksburg, in the year 1827. Being a nephew of Washington, and his private secretary during the first part of his presidency, Mr. Lewis lived with him on terms of intimacy, and had the best opportunity for observing his habits. Mr. Lewis said he had accidentally witnessed his private devotions in his library both morning and evening; that on those occasions he had seen him in a kneeling position with a Bible open before him, and that he believed such to have been his daily practice. Mr. Lewis is since dead, but he was a gentleman esteemed for his private worth and respectability. I relate the anecdote as he told it to me, understanding at the time that he was willing it should be made public on his authority. He added, that it was the President's custom to go to his library in the morning at four o'clock, and that, after his devotions, he usually spent his time till breakfast in writing letters.[11]

Lending credence to the statements by these family members is information provided by a visitor to Mount Vernon. Polish nobleman Julian Ursyn Niemcewicz spent considerable time with the Washingtons, both in the new federal city and at Mount Vernon in 1798. In the biography he wrote of George Washington, which was first published in 1803, Niemcewicz provided numerous intimate details about life on the Virginia estate, including Washington's daily schedule, which began with rising at five in the morning, after which he noted that the former president "dresses himself and prays with great piety."[12]

Other relatives remembered desperate prayers on the occasion of a sudden death in the family. Washington's sister-in-law, Hannah Bushrod Washington, and others informed Martha Washington's granddaughter, Nelly, that Washington had prayed "most fervently, most affectingly" at the side of the girl's aunt, Martha Parke Custis, as the young woman lay dying in 1773; another witness to this same scene, probably Martha Washington's daughter-in-law, Eleanor Calvert Custis Stuart, described him kneeling by the girl's bed as he "solemnly recited the prayers for the dying—while tears rolled down his cheeks, & his voice was often broken by sobs."[13]

From these descriptions, it sounds as if Washington's entreaties in this case were a mix of spontaneous pleas for help and more formal examples from the prayer book. Among the prayers in one of the Anglican prayer books in the Mount Vernon collection are two that might have been spoken in this instance. The first, "A Prayer for a sick person, when there appeareth small hope of Recovery," reads:

> Father of mercies, and God of all comfort, our only help in time of need; We fly unto thee for succour in behalf of this thy servant, here lying under thy hand in great weakness of body. Look graciously upon [her], O Lord; and the more the outward man decayeth, strengthen [her], we beseech thee, so much the more continually with thy grace and holy Spirit, in the inner-man. Give [her] unfeigned repentance for all the errors of [her] life past, and stedfast faith in thy Son Jesus, that [her] sins may be done away by thy mercy, and [her] pardon sealed in heaven, before [she] go hence, and be no more seen. We know, O Lord, that there is no word impossible with thee; and that if thou wilt, thou canst even yet raise [her] up, and grant [her] a longer continuance amongst us. Yet, forasmuch as in all appearance the time of [her] dissolution draweth near, so fit and prepare [her], we beseech thee, against the hour of death, that, after [her] departure hence in peace and in thy favour, [her] soul may be received into thine everlasting kingdom, thro' the merits and meditation of Jesus Christ thine only Son our Lord and Saviour. *Amen.*[14]

In the second, "A Commendatory Prayer for a sick Person at the point of Departure," the person making the prayer asks:

> O Almighty God, with whom do live the spirits of just men made perfect, after they are delivered from their earthly prisons; We humbly commend the soul of this thy servant, our dear [sister], into thy hands, as into the hands of a faithful Creator, and most merciful Saviour; most humbly beseeching thee that it may be precious in thy sight. Wash it, we pray thee, in the blood of that immaculate Lamb that was slain to take away the sins of the world; that whatsoever defilements it may have contracted in the midst of this miserable and naughty world, through the lusts of the flesh, or the wiles of Satan, being purged and done away, it may be presented pure and without spot before thee. And teach us who survive, in this and other like daily spectacles of mortality, to see how frail and uncertain our own condition is,

and so to number our days, that we may seriously apply our hearts to that holy and heavenly wisdom, whilst we live here, which may in the end bring us to life everlasting, through the merits of Jesus Christ thine only Son our Lord. *Amen.*[15]

Statements by Martha Washington's former maid that she never heard the General pray, "and does not believe that he was accustomed to," must be viewed in the light of another statement she made, recalling that "Mrs. Washington used to read prayers, but I don't call that praying." These remarks probably speak more, however, to the differences between the formality of the Washingtons' eighteenth-century Anglican faith and the less formal and more participatory services of the nineteenth-century evangelical denominations, with which this former slave was probably accustomed, than they do to the daily practice of religion in the Washington household.[16]

Mrs. Washington regularly retired to her room between 9 and 10 o'clock in the morning "for an hour of meditation reading & prayer and *that* hour no one was ever allowed to interfere with." She and Nelly, the granddaughter she raised, also prayed, read the Bible, and sang hymns in the evening, in preparation for bed. Among the books surviving in the collections at Mount Vernon is a book of common prayer, authorized by the Protestant Episcopal Church of America, bearing an inscription by Martha Washington's great-grandson Lorenzo Lewis, which records that Mrs. Washington read from this particular book twice a day from the time it came into her possession until her death in 1802. In addition to the prayer book, a large Bible was purchased for Martha Washington in New York at the start of her husband's first term as president. She also saw that other members of the family, not just those in her immediate household, were provided with similar devotional materials. About the same time she acquired the Bible, Mrs. Washington sent four prayer books to Mount Vernon, one each for her niece, Fanny Bassett Washington, her husband's niece, Harriot Washington, and her two oldest granddaughters, Eliza Parke Custis and Martha Parke Custis.[17] Following George Washington's retirement from the presidency, ten shillings, six pence were used to purchase an additional prayer book and three testaments for Mrs. Washington,[18] although the recipients are unknown.

In regard to prayers at mealtimes, surviving descriptions by guests of the Washingtons indicate that sometimes prayers were offered and other times they were not. It was not unusual at this period for people to say prayers at both the beginning and end of a meal. For example, a tutor at one Virginia plantation recorded that during dinner at the home of a local minister, he, as the guest, was asked to "'say Grace' as they call it; which is always express'd . . . in the following words, 'God bless us in what we are to receive'—& after Dinner, 'God make us thankful for his mercies.'"[19]

One guest at Mount Vernon, Amariah Frost, made a point of mentioning that no prayers were offered at dinner on the day he ate with the Washington family.[20] Another guest, however, the Reverend John Latta, a former Presbyterian chaplain from Pennsylvania, recorded that George Washington asked him to "officiate in [his] clerical character" at both the beginning and end of the meal. Whether this was done out of deference to, or affection for, a guest is impossible to say, but, according to another minister's recollection of the executive mansion during Washington's administration, George Washington himself generally stood and said grace before congressional dinners, unless there was a clergyman present who could be asked to say prayers before and after the meal.[21]

This memory squares neatly with dinner descriptions from both the Revolution and Washington's presidency. In a journal kept by Frenchman Claude Blanchard, who served with the Comte de Rochambeau during the Revolution, the writer noted that, during dinner at Washington's military headquarters in the summer of 1781, a clergyman said grace at the conclusion of the meal, "after they had done eating and had brought on the wine." He was informed that it was the General's habit to offer the blessing if no clergyman was present, "as fathers of a family do in America." He recalled that the "first time that I dined with him there was no clergyman and I did not perceive that he made this prayer; yet I remember that, on taking his place at table, he made a gesture and said a word which I took for a piece of politeness, and which perhaps was a religious action. In this case, his prayer must have been short; the clergyman made use of more forms."[22] Several years later, Sen. Paine Wingate of New Hampshire left a description of the first official dinner the Washingtons hosted in the executive mansion in New York. That day, according to Wingate, "As there was no clergyman present, Washington himself said grace on taking his seat."[23] However George Washington may have felt about these rituals, a letter to Martha Washington from her son, who was away at college, assuring her that he offered thanks to God at the end of his breakfast, certainly suggests that such prayers were important to Mrs. Washington.[24]

On at least one occasion, it was not whatever prayers may have started and ended the meal at Mount Vernon, but a misunderstood conversation at the dinner table that led a visiting clergyman to be momentarily taken aback. In closing a letter to George Washington, an Anglican clergyman, who had been a strong supporter of the American cause during the war and later visited the estate to gather material for a history of the Revolution, sent best wishes to several members of the extended Washington household, including a nephew, described as "the young Washington who startled me at the table, before I had time for recollection, by saying that he loved the devil." The boy, probably one of the orphaned sons of Samuel Washington, had been talking about a particular spicy, or "deviled," dish. In his letter to the young man's uncle, the minister expressed the hope that the teenager would "hate all that goes under that name, except the broiled & peppered gizzard or what is equally innocent."[25]

There is evidence from the other members of the Washington and Custis families that prayer had a regular place in their lives, especially in the nineteenth century. Among the surviving papers of Judge Bushrod Washington, the proprietor of Mount Vernon from 1802 until his death in 1829, was a collection of private prayers, as well as others for use in a family setting.[25] Martha Washington's great-granddaughter Mary Anna Randolph Custis kept a prayer journal for several years, beginning with her conversion, about the time of her engagement to Robert E. Lee, in the summer of 1830. In it she recorded her one-sided conversations with and musings to God, her delight in feeling like "a new being" and having "a new spirit within me," although these "mercies seem so unmerited I scarcely comprehend them as yet." Mary Custis was confirmed at Christ Church in Alexandria, Virginia, on October 5, 1830. In the years to come, she would ask God for help in raising her children, confide her concerns for the spiritual welfare of "those most dear to me," and ask for help in conquering fatigue and physical illness.[27]

Family prayer was a feature of life at both Hayfield, the nearby home of George Washington's distant cousin Lund Washington and at Arlington, the beautiful mansion built by Mary Custis's father, George Washington Parke Custis, who was Martha Washington's grandson. At both homes, family members and domestic slaves attended these daily private services together, although at Hayfield, the differing religious beliefs of the enslaved members of the household eventually led them to balk at the prepared Episcopal prayers being offered. In her prayer journal, Lund's wife sadly wrote in the summer of 1792:

> My family is got so Baptistical in their notions, as to think they commit a crime to join with me in Prayer morning & evening . . . so that I am oblig'd to give out having Prayers—in my family,—which has given me great concern—but I trust as my gracious God knows the desire I had to serve him daily in my family—that I shall not be answerable for not having family Prayers—I persever'd in it as long as I could—until it was a mere farce to attempt it any longer . . . a master or mistress of a family, ought to have daily Prayer in their family—but when their Servants will go out of the way at the time they are going to be call'd to Prayer—it is impossible for them to have it, & then if they are made to come—they appear quite angry—which must be extremely wrong—therefore I think it must be best let alone."[28]

Family prayers at Arlington seem to have gone more smoothly. Two years after Martha Washington's death, the grandson she had raised married a devout young woman named Mary Lee Fitzhugh. Young Custis appears to have used considerable good sense in choosing his bride. She was a cousin of Bishop William Meade of Virginia, who wrote after her death that she "was to me as sister, mother, and faithful monitor. . . . Scarcely is there a Christian lady in our land more honoured than she was, and none more loved and esteemed. For good sense, prudence, sincerity, benevolence, unaffected piety, disinterested zeal in every good work, deep humility and retiring modesty . . . I never knew her superior."[29] In addition to teaching the slaves in her household to read and write, the newest Mrs. Custis also held a weekly Sunday School lesson to teach them about Christianity, and led morning and evening devotions for all members of the household, including slaves and houseguests, with the help of her Bible and prayer book.[30] The author Benson Lossing described her, at the age of sixty, still playing a leading role in the religious life of her family, as

> a charming woman, Christlike in character and disposition, and saintlike in her works of benevolence and her perennial goodness, then presided over the household at Arlington. She was like a mother and a guardian angel in her care for the physical and spiritual comfort of their slaves, and was a blessing to the poor far and near. She was a most gentle creature. . . .

Her piety was fervid but unostentatious. . . . She conducted family worship morning and evening, while her husband, standing, invoked a blessing at every meal.[31]

As Mrs. Custis aged, some of the teaching was taken over by her grand-daughters, and arrangements were occasionally made to have a student from the nearby (it was only three miles away) Episcopal Seminary in Alexandria in to preach to the enslaved community, sometime after that institution was founded in 1823.[32]

7

EVIDENCE OF BELIEF

Contemporary Statements

I T IS POSSIBLE to learn something about the religious beliefs behind the practices previously discussed, although it is clear from his statements on the subject that the reticent George Washington was a military man, not a theologian or philosopher. There was an assurance and a practical bent to his faith, rather than continued questioning or a need to search deeper for answers. While some of this might be the reflection of a mind satisfied with the religious answers it got from the established church at a fairly young age, it might also be a result of Washington's early frontier experiences, in which he faced death a number of times while in his early twenties. Like frontline soldiers throughout history, he had to come to grips with the possibility of his own imminent mortality and make his peace with his God. Then, having settled these weighty questions to his own satisfaction and in accordance with his own practical personality, there was no need for continued searching and questioning.

Washington's writings indicate certain basic elements of his faith, which fall well within the bounds of Christian orthodoxy. Many of those who question Washington's adherence to Christianity point to the paucity of his references to Jesus as one of their prime arguments.[1] In the thousands of pages of Washington's surviving papers, there appear to be two references to Jesus. The first, from a speech to the Delaware nation during the Revolution, tells them that, "You do well to wish to learn our arts and ways of life, and above all, the religion of Jesus Christ. These will make you a greater and happier people than you are."[2] The second reference is from Washington's Circular to the States, written in the last months of the Revolution, in which he asks that God "would most graciously be pleased to dispose us all, to do Justice, to love mercy, and to demean ourselves with that Charity, humility and pacific temper of mind, which were the Characteristicks of the Divine Author of our blessed Religion, and without an humble imitation of whose example in these things, we can never hope to be a happy nation."[3] Both of these would fall into the category of public statements rather than personal correspondence, a classification about which one of Washington's premier biographers has written:

> The tone of Washington's addresses and circulars was distinctly more fervent, to be sure, [at the end of the Revolution] than in 1775, if the theme touched religion, but this change had not become marked until Jonathan Trumbull, Jr., had joined the staff and had begun to write Washington's public papers of this type. Trumbull's alternate and successor in this capacity was David Humphreys, who, like the Connecticut Governor's son, was of theologically minded New England believers. The part these two men played in accentuating and enlarging with their pens the place that Providence had in the mind of Washington probably was among the most extraordinary and least considered influences of Puritanism on the thought of the young nation.[4]

During both the Revolution and the presidency, Washington's public statements concerning religion were often drafted by a variety of other people, who, in addition to the two men mentioned above, included Joseph Reed, Tench Tilghman, David Cobb, James Madison, and Alexander Hamilton. It has been noted that all of these statements were written under Washington's direction and approved by him and that, while some of these documents might have been "expressed with more positive religious feeling than Washington himself habitually displayed . . . none of them was inconsonant with his conviction that religion was one of the 'firmest props of the duties of Men & citizens' and important for the well-being of his soldiers."[5] Several historians who have delved into the issue of the influence of his aides and secretaries on Washington's correspondence have concluded that he kept a close eye on the words that went out over his signature. According to one, the changes found in drafts of correspondence prepared by the aides were often the result of trying to "clearly express Washington's thought, and that distinct changes of that thought usually emanated from Washington himself."[6] In other words, it is not likely that aides were slipping comments about Jesus or other aspects of religion into the official correspondence without Washington's knowledge and approval.

An examination of statements by other members of the Washington family and by their friends in the eighteenth century suggests, however, that references to Jesus by Anglicans/Episcopalians of George and Martha Washington's generation and later were not common until after the turn of the century and that Washington was not vastly different in this usage from his contemporaries. Often friends or family members with whom Washington was close did seem to speak easily of their religious beliefs, suggesting both that he was hardly put off by such language and perhaps that he shared the beliefs of his correspondents. During a serious illness in the fall of 1757, Washington received a letter from Dr. James Craik, with whom he had served in the army for the previous three years. In this long letter, the doctor advised his friend on building up his strength, and closed with the thought that, since reading and writing were probably too strenuous for Washington at that point, he would "only Pray God, who is the best of all Physicians, that he in his infinite mercy, may restore you, to your wonted health."[7] Over twenty years later, after warning Washington about the "Conway Cabal," a plot to remove him from command of the army, Craik expressed the prayer that, "God, of his infinite mercy Protect & Defend you from all your open and Secret Enemies, and Continue you in health to finish the Glorious undertaking."[8] The two would remain close until Washington's death twenty-one years later.

Looking at the next two generations of the family, Martha Washington's niece, Frances Bassett Washington, closed a letter to her uncle with "devout prayers to the bestower of all blessings, long to continue to you health & happiness."[9] George Washington's step-grandson, George Washington Parke Custis, then sixteen years old, referred not to Jesus but to "God," "that Providence which has preserved me," and a desire that "That great Parent of the Universe prolong your days."[10] The widow of one of Washington's brothers concluded a letter to George Washington with the "ardent" prayer that he and Martha Washington would "long injoy every gift of bountious Heaven."[11]

The primary exception to the rule that Washington's friends and family did not generally mention Jesus is an eighteenth-century family member who wrote extensively about her religious beliefs. Elizabeth Foote

Washington, the wife of Washington's cousin Lund, kept a spiritual diary for many years, which is now in the collection of the Library of Congress. Elizabeth began keeping the journal as she was preparing to be married. In its first pages, she asks for a "Blessing of the almighty," and that "my gracious God" will "direct & influence my heart & its affections, that I may make it my study to please my husband in every thing that is not against the divine Laws, & as there is a probability of my living in Houses not my own for some time [she and Lund would live at Mount Vernon until after the end of the Revolution]—may the divine goodness assist me, so that I may study to live in peace & friendship with the family where I live." The diary goes on:

> I hope I have prepared myself for the worst that may happen—that is—if my marriage should prove a unhappy one—I trust I have so sincere a desire to please my Saviour, that I hope I shall be enabled to bear with whatever is the divine will,—& as I believe nothing happens by chance, so it is my duty to bear with what the almighty permits . . . but as my gracious God has been infinitely merciful to me, so I humbly hope my marriage may be an happy one—& tha[t] my husband may never be against my being as religious as my inclination may lead me.[12]

As she wrote periodically in her journal over the next seventeen years, Elizabeth Foote Washington revealed herself to be a woman of strong faith, an evangelical Anglican, who wrote out morning and evening prayers "for use in my family," but who also composed others, "for a person in private, for I think it is the duty of every creature to pray in private as well as publick, & not only of a morning & evening, but through the day they ought every now & then [to] send up a devout thought to heaven which no doubt the divine goodness will except as a continual prayer, though a person is not always on their knees."[13]

Over the years, she wrote of her relationship with and feelings about her slaves, to whom she gave reading lessons and Bibles.[14] Upon losing the second of her two children, she asked her "gracious Redeemer" to "support my Spirits while under the rod of affliction," and wrote that, "My greatest comfort is—that the almighty knows it was my sincere intention to bring my children up to glorify him in all their actions—blessed—be the divine goodness—that I can take comfort in thinking that their Redeemer should think them worthy to enjoy heaven, without experiencing any of the troubles that attends mankind in passing through this vale of misery,—my gracious God—thou hast confer'd great honour on me—that thou shouldest think me worthy to bring children who thou has thought was only fit to live with thee."[15] In July of 1792 she lamented the hypocrisy of those who "talk everlastingly about religion & to see their actions not corresponding to it," but worried that, "altho' my heart has been much taken up with religion, yet very little have I talked about it—perhaps I may have erred on the other side, & not vindicated religion when I ought to have done it—but I always found myself not competent to speak of it as I would wish, therefore thought it best to say but little, & endeavour to attain the practicle part."

She was also bothered by the fact that she was not able to attend church, probably because of the distance of her plantation from Alexandria, and soundly criticized those who "say, they can read their Bible they can read a sermon at home & that is as well as if they went to church, & they often say it is better, because they may read a better Sermon then they might hear preached at church."[16] In her journal, Elizabeth wrote of her sins, for which she believed Jesus's blood and advocacy on her behalf before God were the only answers.[17]

This little work, written in secret and never intended for eyes other than those of the author, is the most outspokenly Christian manuscript to survive from the extended Washington family in the eighteenth century. Elizabeth Foote Washington's faith would remain strong until her death, many years after she stopped writing in her journal. Among the books she owned was a collection of sermons entitled *The Backslider,* which was written by the Reverend Andrew Fuller, a Baptist minister, and published in Boston in 1802. In her will, dated 1810, she left the following bequest and testimony:

> To the Washington Society of Alexandria 10 shares of the same [Potomac Bank stock] and also my shares in the Potomac Company . . . to apply to the education of such poor girls as they think proper; nor can I forbear on this solemn occasion to greet them in the name of our Holy Father and invoke his benediction upon their efforts to rescue from poverty and the sinks of shameless immorality those sweet . . . blossoms which under their fostering care and virtuous inculcation may add much to the store of human

happiness; I confine this my donation to my own sex, because I believe
that human happiness has material dependence upon our moral and religious worth.[18]

By the nineteenth century, as the influence of the Second Great Awakening led the Episcopal Church in the United States to become more
evangelical, and consequently to stress the need for each believer to make
a personal commitment to God, other members of the Washington and
Custis families spoke more easily of Jesus. For example, in a long letter
on the subject of religion, Martha Washington's eldest granddaughter expounded to her grandson in 1831:

> Man was created superior to all other beings on Earth—he was told his duty
> but disobey'd God's will, & so wicked was the human race—that all were
> destroy'd by a vast deluge, except one family, who loved & served God. The
> world was peopled from them & again was much wickedness, till Jesus christ
> the Son of God came down from heaven, to teach us the sure road to heaven,
> & to offer himself as an atonement for our Sins—Those who believe in him,
> & obey the laws & commandments of God, will possess the joys of heaven;
> those who reject the mercy held out to them will suffer eternal misery.[19]

In a similar vein, nine years later, Jane Charlotte Blackburn Washington,
who was mistress of Mount Vernon between roughly 1829 and 1843, closed
a letter to a correspondent, "In strong faith that all will be restored—and
humble hope, that thro' the merits and atonement of our blessed Redeemer, we shall All meet in his glorious presence."[20]

In making such strong statements on the need for conversion, and in
emphasizing the "atonement of our blessed Redeemer," Eliza and Jane
Charlotte were reflecting profound changes in both the church and their
society. As the historian Jan Lewis has written, Virginians in the early
nineteenth century did not necessarily become more religious, but "they
became religious in a different way." Where before they "were taught that
an all-wise dispenser planned things for the best," and that a person had a
"duty . . . to do his best and trust in God," without a lot of reflection, which
was to be avoided, Virginians now turned inward:

> In the decades following the American Revolution, genteel Virginians would
> abandon the religious style of their ancestors. . . . Not only would men and

women openly avow their faith in God and Christ, but they would do so in a certain manner: They accepted Christ into their hearts. A devotion to God and to Christ and, more especially, a particular way of expressing that devotion and thinking and feeling about matters of faith became socially preferable and personally necessary even to the offspring of Deists.[21]

Religion would become more personal and more emotional in the nineteenth century.[22] Perhaps the best illustration of these changes in the Washington/Custis family can be found in the conversion story of Agnes Lee, one of the seven children born to Martha Washington's great-granddaughter, Mary Anna Randolph Custis, and Robert E. Lee. The journal Agnes kept as a teenager documents her growing attraction to religious matters and an ever-increasing sense of her own unworthiness, beginning in the spring of 1856. She recorded that she had been raised to believe that the only way she would ever find true satisfaction and peace was "in the bosom of my Saviour & only there." She noted that she had "often determined to try to be a christian" but was troubled by "the awful thought" that she was "one of the doomed." After about a year of questioning, Agnes finally found peace. She wrote in August of 1857, after examining her diary entries from the previous year: "I have been reading over a burst of sorrow at my own wickedness, written last summer. As I feared, that passed away . . . adoring thanks I trust I will ever render to my Father in Heaven that He did not leave me to sin & death as I richly deserved. In his great mercy His spirit again came to me. & in His love He called me to himself."[23] Very few Anglicans could have written such words one hundred years earlier.

In the eighteenth century, George Washington and other members of the family sometimes addressed people as fellow believers, challenging them as Christians to live up to their beliefs or to use their faith to overcome a difficulty, something that might seem strange or out of character if it had come from someone who was not himself a Christian, which Washington seemed to acknowledge in a letter written in 1763. When an old friend asked him for a substantial loan, Washington sent the man his regrets, along with a copy of his account with an English firm, which, he stated, "Upon my honr and the faith of a Christian is a true one," to show that he simply didn't have the wherewithal to help at that point.[24] A decade later, upon learning of the death of his younger sister, Martha Washington's son, John Parke Custis, wrote a long letter to his mother, closing with the words, "I will no longer detain you on a subject which is painful to us both but conclude with beging you to remember you are a Christian and that we ought to submit with Patience to the divine Will."[25]

Many years after that, when the gardener at Mount Vernon was having problems with drinking, George Washington wrote to him from the executive mansion in Philadelphia, first outlining the dangers of alcoholism and then closing with the words, "Don't let this be your case. Shew yourself more of a man, and a Christian, than to yield to so intolerable a vice. . . . I am Your friend."[26] Washington wrote in a similar vein to a friend who had just lost his wife, expressing his sympathy and then continuing, "Remembring that all must die, and that she had lived to an honourable age, I hope you will bear the misfortune with that fortitude and complacency of mind, that become a Man and a Christian."[27] Likewise, in his orders to his soldiers in May of 1778, Washington exhorted them with the words, "While we are zealously performing the duties of good Citizens and soldiers we certainly ought not to be inattentive to the higher duties of Religion. To the distinguished Character of Patriot, it should be our highest Glory to add the more distinguished Character of Christian."[28] Given statements such as these, and the positive evidence for Washington's religious practices and his statements about the deity, as well as his actions outside a strictly religious context, it seems that those who doubt Washington's Christianity must come up with stronger examples than simply arguing lack of evidence.

Foremost among the religious elements exhibited in Washington's writings was a belief in the existence of a Supreme Being or God. He typically referred to this being as "Providence," which has led one Washington biographer to comment that Washington "seems to have lacked a personal religious faith; when he referred to a force that initiated and controlled life, he always vaguely called it Providence or another unrevealing term."[29]

The use of the word "Providence," however, seems to put Washington squarely into common religious usage during his lifetime. "Providence" was often used in the seventeenth, eighteenth, and nineteenth centuries as a substitute for the term "God," and it "applied to the Deity as exercising prescient and beneficent power and direction."[30] What has been termed "providentialist" theology or doctrine was fundamental to European Protestantism, which was brought to America with the English colonists. It held that "all events in the world were controlled directly by God and expressed his omnipotent will," and that "men and women should submit to divine providence." Central, as well, were the beliefs that wondrous events were a sign of the approbation or disapproval of the deity; that suffering came about as a judgment from God, to which the believer must respond with repentance; and that "God was inherently mysterious and his will utterly impenetrable."[31]

Several examples of the use of the word "Providence" by some of Washington's contemporaries are useful at this point. A 1752 sermon on gambling by Anglican minister William Stith, president of the College of William and Mary in Williamsburg, contended that gambling pulled people away from their primary occupations, robbed "their Country of the Profit and Advantage of their Labours" and ran "counter to GOD's Providence," and contradicted "his divine Will in allotting them their Rank and Condition in the World." Among the other problems inherent in this pastime was the fact that "every puny Mortal, that has lost a Sum of Money, thinks himself authorized to call Divine Providence to an Account." Contrarily, "however Divine Providence may be rated for their Losses, and it's Justice questioned, yet the Case is quite altered, when they happen to win."[32] Some years later, as tension grew between the American colonies and England, John Dickinson, a lawyer from Pennsylvania, wrote about the freedoms he cherished: "We claim them from a higher source, from the King of Kings and Lord of all earth. They are not annexed to us by parchments and seals. They are created in us by a decree of Providence which established the laws of our nature. . . . They are founded in the immutable maxims of reason and justice."[33] Not quite two months before the writing of the Declaration of Independence, Presbyterian leader John Witherspoon of Princeton University preached a sermon taken from Psalm 76:10. He began by noting, "The doctrine of divine providence extends not only to things which we may think of great moment, and therefore worthy of notice, but to things the most indifferent and inconsiderable." He then reminded his listeners that, "It would be a criminal inattention not to observe the singular interposition of Providence hitherto, in behalf of the American colonies."[34] Two years later, in another sermon, given at Valley Forge on May 6, 1778, Anglican chaplain John Hurt of Virginia reminded his congregants that, "The more we do for ourselves the more reason we have to expect the smiles of Providence." He encouraged them to "exert ourselves from the highest to the lowest, to deserve the great and wonderful deliverance which Providence hath manifested toward this infant land!"[35]

Not long after the war, Washington received a letter from an Episcopal minister in New Jersey, enclosing two of the writer's sermons as well as his congratulations "on the Establishment of Peace and Independence to these States." The clergyman also wanted to "mention that I feel Sensations of Gratitude to those, who, under Providence, have been instrumental in obtaining these invaluable Blessings."[36] A few months later, another minister, who had been corresponding with Washington for several years while working on a history of the late war, wrote to thank him for a box of shrubs from Mount Vernon, which had just arrived. He indicated that he might try to take some of the plants to London, and that "should Providence fix me in that spot or neighbourhood," he would try to send Washington some examples of English varieties.[37]

Others who were very close to Washington, and who were known to be devoutly Christian, used this same terminology, clearly referring to God. One example, taken from a letter to a friend, also shows Martha Washington's playful, and little known, sense of humor. Writing from Valley Forge, the wife of the American commander indicated her "unspeakable pleasure" upon learning that British general John Burgoyne and his army were being held prisoner in Massachusetts since the Battle of Saratoga the previous year. "Would bountifull providence aim a like stroke at Genl Howe, the measure of my happyness would be compleat."[38] About a decade later, in his funeral sermon for the Reverend David Griffith, the former minister of Christ Church in Alexandria, the Reverend Bryan Fairfax reminded his listeners that when someone very dear dies unexpectedly, "What shall we say as to the dispensation of Providence, but that his ways are past finding out."[39]

Four years into George Washington's presidency, shortly after the death of his nephew George Augustine Washington, the young man's widow, Fanny Bassett Washington, acknowledged, "It has been the will of God to visit me with heavy causes of sorrow, & not to receive them as such, woud argue an insensibility to his [God's] dispensations." After detailing her ideas about how she and her children would live in the future, she closed with the "fervent prayer" that "it may be the will of providence, long to continue every blessing to you."[40] A few weeks later, as she worked out the details of life without the husband she had loved so dearly, Fanny offered to send her eldest son to the president, who would oversee his education, "whenever you think proper," noting that "I trust & hope Providence will reward your generous care of him, by bestowing on him every virtuous disposition."[41] In a letter to her aunt the following year, Fanny confided that "the little experience I have had" had taught her "not to look for happiness in the world." Admittedly "deprest" at the thought of raising her three children alone, the young widow said that she was trying to "banish every murmering reflection & trust to the Providence that has hitherto conducted me through life, for assistance in the discharge of duties which his will has evidently lain on me."[42]

In George Washington's worldview, Providence was good and guided or directed events on earth. Following a disastrous battle during the French and Indian War, for example, he informed his brother, "I now exist and appear in the land of the living by the miraculous care of Providence, that protected me beyond all human expectation; I had 4 Bullets through my Coat, and two Horses shot under me, and escaped unhurt."[43] Many years later, in the early days of another war, Washington confided to a friend: "For more than two months past, I have scarcely immerged from one difficulty before I [have] been plunged into another. How it will end, God in his great goodness will direct."[44] Still at war five years later, Washington acknowledged to one minister: "We have . . . abundant reason to thank providence for its many favourable interpositions in our behalf. It has, at times been my only dependence for all other resources seemed to have fail'd us."[45] By 1790, during the first term of his presidency, he had added another blessing to the list, giving credit now to "the Almighty" for both the success of the American cause in the Revolution and "the establishment of our present equal government."[46]

Washington was not the only one of his contemporaries to see the hand of God working directly in the formation of the United States. His dear comrade, Gen. Nathanael Greene, wrote to a ministerial friend at the close of military action in 1778, to let him know that he had survived the latest campaign. He mentioned the battle at Monmouth and an action in Rhode Island, commenting that, "To behold our fellows, chasing the British off the field of battle, afforded a pleasure which you can better conceive that I describe." He continued, "If . . . I had before been an unbeliever, I have had sufficient evidence of the intervention of Divine Providence to reclaim me from infidelity: my heart, I do assure you, overflows with gratitude to Him whose arm is mightier than all the Princes of the earth."[47]

Samuel Langdon, a Congregationalist minister who had served as a chaplain in both King George's War and the Revolutionary War and headed Harvard University between 1774 and 1780, wrote to Washington early in his presidency to send a sermon he had given the year before.[48] Langdon started out by acknowledging his realization, "with pleasing astonishment & religious gratitude that the american States have been favored with such signal interpositions of Providence as fall little short of real miracles, & that the King of Heaven hath given them a great Charter of Liberty." He saw this not as partiality on God's part toward their countrymen, "who, like Israel, have shewed ourselves an unworthy people, by growing more regardless of his gospel in the enjoyment of the multitude of his mercies." Instead, Langdon speculated that the formation of the United States was a step in bringing "forward some grand revolutions in the civil & ecclesiastical polity of the nations, agreable to the Prophecies of the new Testament, which now approach their fulfilment."

Langdon also gave God the credit for having put Washington in charge of the army. He recalled that when he had met Washington for the first time at Cambridge, early in the Revolution, "I was ready to look up to heaven & say, 'Blessed be God; who hath given us a General who will not rashly throw away the lives of his Soldiers, or hazard the fate of his Country unnecessarily upon a single Battle, but will proceed with all wisdom & caution!'" Langdon had been an unofficial part of Washington's military household for several months, and recalled that he could "never forget the high satisfaction I then enjoyed, in observing your religious as well as military character." He noted that, from the beginning, Washington had "directed your eye to the great Lord of the Universe, implored his help, acted as his servant, & found him present to support you under, & carry you through the most pressing & discouraging difficulties. He has made good his word in your great Success & universal fame, 'Them that honour me I will honour.'" After listing all the reasons why Washington had earned the admiration of people, even outside the United States, he noted that "all good men love & honour you most of all, because you so constantly ascribe the glory of the great Events in America to him that rules over the kingdoms of the world, & orders all things for the accomplishment of his wise & holy purposes." Langdon closed by commending Washington for the care he had taken "to pay your acknowledgements to the supreme Lord of heaven and earth for the great things he hath done for us." He also encouraged him, in "the prevailing infidelity of the present degenerate times," to continue "to give glory to the most High." Reminding him that "your conversation and Example may have great influence in your high Station, let all men know that you are not ashamed to be a disciple of the

Lord Jesus Christ, & are seeking the honors of that kingdom which he has prepared for his faithful Servants." The minister ended with the hope that Washington would receive the letter as "an unaffected testimony not only of the most honorable esteem, but likewise of [Langdon's] characteristic Christian Love."[49]

The press of his duties prevented Washington from responding until several months later, when he wrote to thank Reverend Langdon for the sermon, as well as for "the friendly expressions contained in your letter." He then went on to offer the opinion that,

> The man must be bad indeed who can look upon the events of the American Revolution without feeling the warmest gratitude towards the great Author of the Universe whose divine interposition was so frequently manifested in our behalf—And it is my earnest prayer that we may so conduct ourselves as to merit a continuance of those blessings with which we have hitherto been favoured.[50]

Washington also believed that Providence was wiser than any human and that it was up to each person to trust the final outcome of any situation to the Deity. One of the severest, but hardly unexpected, blows to the Washington family came with the death of nephew George Augustine Washington from tuberculosis in 1793. Upon learning of the young man's demise, George Washington's long-time friend, neighbor, and foxhunting companion, Bryan Fairfax, who was also a minister in the Episcopal Church, wrote to offer his condolences. Washington responded that the death of his nephew was something "I sincerely regret"; however, since it was "the will of Heaven, whose decrees are always just & wise, I submit to it without a murmur." Fairfax then wrote that he was "pleased at Your entire submission to the will of Heaven in Your late afflictive Loss," but added that "it was no more than I expected." He went on to say that, "having encountered & surmounted many & various Difficulties & disappointments, and believing in a superintending Providence," he knew that Washington would "also bear with Patience those Afflictions which his Wisdom shall direct."[51] A few days later, in a letter to a friend on the issue of the rapid spread of democratic ideas in Europe, Washington noted that "the great ruler of events" was the only one who knew how the political situation there would resolve. People had to confide "in his wisdom and goodness" and "safely trust the issue to him, without perplexing ourselves to seek for that, which is beyond human ken; only taking care to perform the parts assigned us, in a way that reason and our own consciences approve of."[52]

Washington's views in this regard were shared by his wife and the younger members of the family. Shortly after receiving a condolence letter from the Marquis de Lafayette upon the death of her husband, the widowed Martha Washington wrote that her only consolation for her "irreparable loss" was to be found in "that source of infinite wisdom and good help which alone can mitigate our grief and lessen the poignancy of the keenest affliction." She closed this section of the letter, "To his [God's] will do I resign my self for the few remaining days of my life."[53] In a similar fashion, nephew William Augustine Washington wrote, after losing his young son and daughter, that the "mysteries and decrees of an allwise Providence, are unsearchable to short sighted Mortals," and that it was a "duty" of humankind "to be resigned to the Divine Will." The grieving father confessed that he had always found consolation in that duty, noting that his "remaining children are a great comfort to me, and I am sincerely thankful to Almighty God for that Blesing."[54]

Even when faced with serious illness and possibly imminent death, George Washington's faith in Providence never wavered. During a life-threatening illness shortly after he became president, Washington assured the attending physician, Dr. Samuel Bard of New York, that "I am not afraid to die and therefore can bear the worst. . . . Whether tonight or twenty years hence makes no difference. I know I am in the hands of a good Providence."[55] Washington suffered from several serious medical conditions during his presidency. During a bout with one of them, Washington had a similar conversation with a former military aide, expressing his great doubts about "whether ever I shall rise from this bed, & God knows it is perfectly indifferent to me whether I do or not." His longtime friend reportedly responded, "If, Sir, it is indifferent to you, it is far from being so to your friends and your Country. For they believe it has still great need of your services."[56]

There is also evidence in Washington's writings about the relationship between Providence and human beings. In a letter to a friend who had just lost his father, Washington sought to comfort him with the reminder, "As an inexhaustible subject of consolation, that there is a good Providence which will never fail to take care of his Children."[57] Christianity is the only religion that I am aware of that turns to the relationship between a father and his children as a metaphor for the relationship between the deity and human beings, a practice that devolves from the words of Jesus in the New Testament.[58] It is clear from his correspondence that Washington thought that the behavior of a person or group of people could have a strong influence on whether Providence would bless them and their endeavors. During the early stages of the Revolution, as commander in chief of the Continental Army, Washington informed his soldiers of the possible consequences of their actions on those of Providence:

> That the Troops may have an opportunity of attending public worship, as well as take some rest after the great fatigue they have gone through: The General in future excuses them from fatigue duty on Sundays (except at the Ship Yards, or special occasions) until further orders. The General is sorry to be informed that the foolish, and wicked practice, of profane cursing and swearing (a Vice heretofore little known in an American Army) is growing into fashion; he hopes the officers will, by example, as well as influence, endeavour to check it, and that both they, and the men will reflect, that we can have little hopes of the blessing of Heaven on our Arms, if we insult it by our impiety, and folly.[59]

Twenty years later, on the verge of retiring from the presidency, Washington advised his countrymen about their behavior toward other peoples and nations in the future, and closed with the question, "Can it be, that Providence has not connected the permanent felicity of a Nation with its virtue?"[60]

Washington appears to have believed that, while God/Providence directed the course of events on earth, human beings could not always understand why certain things occurred and simply had to turn to their reasoning powers and their religious beliefs in order to make sense of it all, and, in the end, come to acceptance of God's will. Upon learning of the death of a young niece in the spring of 1773, he wrote to the girl's grieving father with the following advice:

> That we sympathize in the misfortune, and lament the decree which has deprivd you of so dutiful a Child, & the World of so promising a young Lady, stands in no need, I hope, of argument to proove; but the ways of Providence being inscrutable, and the justice of it not to be scannd by the shallow eye of humanity, nor to be counteracted by the utmost efforts of human

Power, or Wisdom; resignation, &, as far as the strength of our reason &
religion can carry us, a chearful acquessence to the d[iv]ine will is what we
are to aim at.[61]

There is evidence that Washington himself knew how difficult it could
be to put this advice into practice. A foreign visitor who met him shortly
after the death of Martha Washington's son in 1781 noted that the demise
of this promising twenty-seven-year-old, who had been raised by George
Washington from the time he was only five, had left the young man's step-
father in an uncharacteristically emotional state, something that does not
come across in the laconic Washington's writings: "The general was un-
commonly affected at his death, insomuch that many of his friends imag-
ined they perceived some change in his equanimity of temper subsequent
to that event. It is certain that they were upon terms of the most affectionate and manly friendship."[62]

In at least two surviving letters, George Washington hinted at a belief
that Providence/God had a plan in mind for his life and that it was up
to him as an individual, with divine assistance, to discern what that plan
was. In December of 1788, as he was trying to decide whether or not to
accept the presidency of the United States if it were offered to him, Washington wrote an old friend: "How can I know what is best, or on what
I shall determine? May Heaven assist me in forming a judgment: for at
present I see nothing but clouds and darkness before me."[63] Four years
later, in response to a colleague who urged him to take on a second term
as president, Washington wrote back:

> I can express but one sentiment at this time, and that is a wish, a devout one,
> that whatever my ultimate determination shall be, it may be for the best. . . .
> But as the allwise disposer of events has hitherto watched over my steps, I
> trust that in the important one I may soon be called upon to take, he will
> mark the course so plainly, as that I cannot mistake the way. In full hope of
> this, I will take no measure, yet a while, that will not leave me at liberty to
> decide from circumstances, and the best lights, I can obtain on the Subject.[64]

Martha Washington expressed a similar view of the way Providence
worked in the life of an individual when she responded to a widowed
niece who was contemplating remarriage, "I really dont know what to

say to you on the subject; you must be governed by your own judgement, and I trust providence will derect you for the best."[65] A few years later, her sister-in-law Hannah Bushrod Washington, the widow of George Washington's younger brother, mused in a rather sad letter that in caring for all the sick and dying members of her family over the years, her grief was "in some degree mitigated by reflecting that I have been & still am useful to those I love and (perhaps) am answering the purpose for which I was made."[66]

There is considerable evidence from Washington's writings that he would not have quarreled with the concept of original sin, the idea that, as a direct result of Adam and Eve's disobedience in the Garden of Eden, all human beings are born with a sinful nature and have a tendency to do that which is wrong. Over and over again, his mistrust of people comes through, as the following example will show. In a letter to his cousin Lund, written during the Revolution, Washington wrote a long passage about a land transaction, which then reminded him that his stepson, John Parke Custis, was becoming involved in some undesirable transactions of his own, "in spite of all the admonition and advice I gave him against selling faster than he bought." Custis had sold off some land to buy an estate, not far from Mount Vernon, from the Alexander family, without benefit of a written contract. Washington hoped there would not be a problem, noting "the many proofs we dayly see of the folly of leaving bargains unbound by solemn covenants. I see so many instances of the rascallity of Mankind, that I am almost out of conceit of my own species; and am convinced that the only way to make men honest, is to prevent their being otherwise, by tying them firmly to the accomplishm[en]t. of their contracts."[67]

Less than a year later, Washington wrote in connection with someone who was suspected of being a double agent, that, "We must endeavour to make it his interest to be faithful . . . we must take care if possible not to let motives of interest on the other side bear down his integrity and inclination to serve us. Few men have virtue to withstand the highest bidder."[68] During the long months between the writing of the Constitution and its adoption, Washington noted to another friend that, "The various passions and motives, by which men are influenced are concomitants of fallibility— engrafted into our nature for the purposes of [the] unerring wisdom."[69]

George Washington also believed in the existence of an afterlife of some kind. In an unusually emotional letter, written shortly after the death of his young stepdaughter following several years of illness, Washington tried to let Patsy's extended family know what had happened, and to express his certainty of the girl's continued existence in another life: "It is an easier matter to conceive, than to describe the distress of this Family . . . when I inform you that yesterday . . . the Sweet Innocent Girl Entered into a more happy and peaceful abode than any she has met with in the afflicted Path she hitherto has trod."[70] Many years later, during his presidency, when a favorite nephew died, Washington wrote the young man's widow that "Reason and resignation to the divine will, which is just, and wise in all its dispensations, cannot, in such a mind as yours, fail to produce this effect [abating her sorrow]." Newly remarried, the young widow herself died in 1796, prompting Washington to write his former secretary and longtime friend, the husband she left behind: "To say how much we loved, and esteemed our departed friend, is unnecessary. She is now no more! but she must be happy, because her virtue has a claim to it."[71]

Washington's reaction to the death of another relative has led one historian to see skepticism about the nature of the afterlife as Washington saw it.[72] Just a few months into his first term as president, a letter arrived informing Washington of his mother's death after a long struggle with breast cancer. In the letter, Burgess Ball noted that Mary Ball Washington had "lived a good Age &, I hope, is gone to a happier place than we at present live in."[73] In a letter to his sister about the death of this significant figure in his life, Washington reiterated that same hope:

> Awful, and affecting as the death of a Parent is, there is consolation in knowing, that Heaven has spared ours to an age, beyond which few attain, and favored her with the full enjoyment of her mental faculties, and as much bodily strength as usually falls to the lot of fourscore. Under these considerations and a hope that she is translated to a happier place, it is the duty of her relatives to yield due submission to the decrees of the Creator.[74]

In this case, Washington expresses no more skepticism than did Burgess Ball. Why might the two have referred to hope in regard to Mary Ball Washington when Washington had earlier expressed certainty about the fate of Patsy Custis? Perhaps Washington's actions in another context could explain some of the discrepancy. Shortly after returning from the Revolution, Washington tried to regain some control over the western lands on which he had tenants who had not paid the rent owed to him in years. As he was making a tour of the properties, he wrote in his diary on September 19, 1784, "Being Sunday, and the People living on my Land, apparently very religious, it was thought best to postpone going among them till tomorrow."[75] Washington's skepticism about the sincerity of his tenants' religious beliefs here seems to hinge on the difference between their observance of religious tradition or ritual, when they were not doing their duty, to either God or him, by paying their rents. Over a year later, in a discussion of evicting some of these tenants, Washington noted that, "I never should have thought of this mode of punishment, had I not viewed the defendants as willful and obstinate Sinners—persevering after timely & repeated admonition, in a design to injure me."[76]

Similarly, Washington's mother, despite her reputation as a godly woman, had plagued her son for years and had publicly embarrassed him with charges that he did not properly take care of his aged and widowed parent. Upon learning during the Revolution that Virginia was thinking of setting up a pension for Mary Ball Washington, her son wrote that he and his siblings "would feel much hurt, at having our mother a pensioner, while we had the means of supporting her; but in fact she has an ample income of her own."[77] Six years later, when she conveyed her "want of money" to him through another relative, Washington sent a small amount to her, but went on to say that he was then in tight financial circumstances and reminded her that she had, over the years, kept all the proceeds of the farm he had inherited from his deceased father:

> I am willing, however unable, to pay to the utmost farthing; but it is re-
> ally hard upon me when you have taken every thing you wanted from the
> Plantation by which money could be raised, when I have not received one
> farthing, directly or indirectly from the place for more than twelve years, if
> ever, and when, in that time I have paid, as appears by Mr. Lund Washing-
> ton's accounts against me (during my absence) Two hundred and sixty odd
> pounds, and by my own account Fifty odd pounds out of my own Pocket to
> you, besides (if I am rightly informed) every thing that has been raised by
> the Crops on the Plantation. . . . I do not mean by this declaration to with-
> hold any aid or support I can give from you; for whilst I have a shilling left,
> you shall have part, if it is wanted, whatever my own distresses may be . . .
> tho' I have received nothing from your Quarter, and am told that every far-

thing goes to you, and have moreover paid between 3 and 4 hundred pounds besides out of my own pocket, I am viewed as a delinquent, and considered perhaps by the world as [an] unjust and undutiful son.[78]

Perhaps any skepticism about where his mother was spending eternity, if there were any such doubts, might go back to Washington's perception that his mother's lack of fairness in her treatment of him, her failure to give him the just profits he had earned on the farm that was his, or even to acknowledge that he had been caring for her, conflicted with her reputation for piety. If his response about the tenants is any indication, he may well have viewed his mother's actions in regard to himself as obstinate and sinful. As he once wrote as a young man, "Nothing is a greater stranger to my Breast, or a Sin that my Soul abhors [more], than that black and detestable one Ingratitude."[79]

Washington did not limit his expressions about the possibility of an afterlife to relatives, but also spoke of the subject in letters to friends. When congratulating his old comrade, Gen. Henry Knox, who had just named a newborn son after him, Washington wrote: "I pray you to accept the acknowledgment of my sense of the honor you have conferred on me by giving him my name. I hope he will live to enjoy it long after I have taken my departure for the world of spirits."[80] And Washington's friends also wrote to him about a life beyond this earthly one. About two years after the end of the Revolution, Caleb Gibbs, who had been an important part of Washington's military household for four years, wrote his old commander that his "love and regard for you and Mrs. Washington" had prompted him to visit them in Virginia, but that his financial situation had made it impossible for him to undertake the trip. The best he could offer, under the circumstances, was to "offer you to heaven for the best of protections in this life, and the full enjoyment and fruition of Happiness in that which is to come."[81] It would hardly make sense for Gibbs to say such a thing unless he knew that it would be meaningful to his correspondent.

Other members of the family, including Martha Washington, her son John Parke Custis, and his youngest daughter Nelly, both of whom were raised by the Washingtons at Mount Vernon, shared George Washington's belief in an afterlife. Martha Washington, however, expressed not only some understandable doubts about the nature of this new life, but also some poignant comments on the present one. When the sister she considered "the greatest favorite I had in the world" died in 1777, she sought to console her newly widowed brother-in-law, Burwell Bassett, reminding him that "She has I hope made a happy exchange—and only gon a little before us," and expressing the wish that, "The time grows near when I hope we shall meet never more to part." At that point, Martha was forty-six, had already lost her father, four siblings, her first husband, and three of her four children, and her second husband was then at war, facing death at the head of Britain's rebellious American colonies. She went on to say, wistfully: "If to meet our departed Friends and know them was scertain we could have very little reason to desire to stay in this world where if we are at ease one hour we are in affliction days."[82] When his own sister died in the summer of 1773, John Parke Custis wrote to comfort his mother, reminding her that Patsy was now with God: "Her case is more to be envied than pitied, for if we mortals can distinguish between those who are deserveing of grace & who are not, I am confident she enjoys that Bliss prepar'd only for the good & virtuous, let these considerations, My dear Mother have their due weight with you and comfort yourself with reflecting that she now enjoys in substance what we in this world enjoy in imagination & that there is no real Happiness on this side of the grave."[83]

Regarding her grandparents' faith, Nelly wrote that Martha Washington had no doubts about her husband's immortality: "After forty years of devoted affection and uninterrupted happiness, she resigned him without a murmur into the arms of his Savior and his God, with the assured hope of his eternal felicity."[84] Backing up Nelly's recollections is a letter written by a newly widowed Martha Washington, in which she confided to a friend her hopes of being reunited with her late husband: "For myself I have only to bow with humble submission to the will of that God who giveth and who taketh away looking forward with faith and hope to the moment when I shall be again united with the Partner of my life."[85]

Several years earlier, as Nelly was working through her own grief at the death of a cousin, Frances Bassett Washington Lear, she drew on her skills as an artist to produce a small watercolor that portrayed a young woman dressed in a black high-waisted dress weeping over a funeral monument, with a small, dejected-looking spaniel at her feet (undoubtedly Nelly and her little dog, both of whom were depicted by other artists of the period). In the midst of this sadness, a few comforting words were inscribed on the monument, expressing hope in a future reunion with this much-loved member of the family: "She is not lost!/Blest thought!/But gone before/me."[86] Nelly's older sister, Eliza, writing not quite a year be-

Mourning picture for Frances Bassett Washington Lear, by Eleanor Parke Custis, ca. 1796. Martha Washington's youngest granddaughter, Nelly, was about fifteen years old when she worked out her grief at the death of a young relative, using ink and watercolor. She also left there a testimony to her belief in an afterlife. (Courtesy of the Mount Vernon Ladies' Association)

fore her own death, expressed her belief in an afterlife as well, challenging her young grandson to always remember "as a stimulous to virtue—our Grandmother [Martha Washington] sits in the highest heaven, among God's chosen spirits—for, she loved & served him all her days, & went on her way rejoicing to her Lord & Master."[87]

Evidence that George Washington probably believed that one element of the afterlife included a time of judgment before God might be found in comments he made to an early biographer, and quoted earlier in reference to his concerns about slavery. The closing phrase, "Could not I hoped be displeasing to the justice of the Creator," indicates both a wish to please and, perhaps, an uncertainty about the outcome of a coming judgment.[88]

That concept of a future judgment before God was also expressed by his step-granddaughter, Eliza, many years later, when she assured a young grandson:

> Those who do right, are sure of a reward far more precious, than all this world can bestow—the blessing of God, whom no artifice can blind, no earthly vice or cunning deceive. . . . He sits on the eternal tribunal, where all must appear—the secrets of all be disclosed & his fist must seal our doom— that doom is for eternal punishment, or for eternal joy.[89]

8

OUTWARD ACTIONS

Charity and Toleration

THERE IS ABUNDANT evidence that both George and Martha Washington took concrete steps to care for those less fortunate than themselves by giving money and food to the poor. Such charities, which to a certain extent were probably expected from members of their social class, may also have been a way of expressing religious beliefs through action. During the Revolution, when he was away from home and his wife spent many months each year at his headquarters, George Washington instructed his farm manager:

> Let the Hospitality of the House, with respect to the poor, be kept up; Let no one go hungry away. If any of these kind of People should be in want of Corn, supply their necessities, provided it does not encourage them in idleness; and I have no objection to your giving my Money in Charity, to the Amount of forty or fifty Pounds a Year, when you think it well bestowed. What I mean, by having no objection, is, that it is my desire that it should be done. You are to consider that neither myself or Wife are now in the way to do these good Offices.[1]

This same manager once remarked that, "Mrs. Washington's charitable disposition increases in the same proportion with her meat house."[2] An example of her "charitable disposition" can be seen in a letter she wrote at the beginning of the Revolution, when she directed that a Mrs. Boyly be given "corn or wheat as she may want it, while her husband is ill and unable to provide for her . . . let her have a barrel of corn and half a barrel of wheat as [she] sends for it and give her a fat hog."[3] Many years after their deaths, Mrs. Washington's youngest granddaughter remembered: "He [George Washington] would have blush'd to find such trifles fame, (as giving *fish* to the poor). . . . Many were an[nually] fed & clothed from his and Grandmama's hands, besides the charity almost daily bestowed on wayfaring persons. But it was their aim to conceal from the *left* hand, what the *right* performed, & accident only discover'd their good deeds."[4]

One example of the way the Washingtons tried to keep these deeds confidential can be seen in a letter written by George Washington to the Reverend William White in 1793, when the president noted that he intended to make a donation for the poorest inhabitants of Philadelphia. Not being a part of the community, however, he was concerned, both about how to proceed with making such a gift and how to ensure that it got to the people who really needed it, and "therefore have taken the liberty of asking your advice." He went on to confide: "I persuade myself justice will be done my motives for giving you this trouble. To obtain information, and to render the little I can afford without ostentation or mention of my name are the sole objects of these enquiries."[5]

In addition to food and clothing, the Washingtons also gave money for charitable causes. As George Washington exhorted one of his young nephews: "Let your *heart* feel for the affliction, and distresses of every one, and let your *hand* give in proportion to your purse; remembering always, the estimation of the Widows mite." He went on to caution, however, that "not every one who asketh . . . deserveth charity; all however are worthy of the enquiry, or the deserving may suffer."[6]

Family financial records from before George Washington's election to the presidency contain numerous references to contributions for "charity" but do not generally spell out the beneficiary of those gifts.[7] That situation changed after the inauguration, when Washington's secretaries kept the financial records and frequently took care to say something about who the recipients were and why they needed the money. They recorded, for example, that Martha Washington provided $8 to aid a number of poor families who were presumably hurt and made homeless by a fire in Philadelphia in May of 1791. The range of people assisted by the president and first lady is rather impressive: "a poor woman who brought a recommendation from Dr. Rogers," a Presbyterian minister; "an old soldier, to help defray the cost of his passage to England"; another "poor old Soldier"; "a poor woman by the name of Eleanor Low who brot. a petition to the President"; "a poor woman . . . to relieve her husband from Prison"; "Mrs. Weizenfels for the relief of herself & children"; "a poor man who came to make enquiery about his Son"; "4 poor widows," each given a load of wood; another "poor Widow" named Mary Brasher, who was supplied with money for "a load of wood"; "a woman by the name of Johnson, to enable her to get to Norfolk"; "a poor woman, daughter to a Clergyman in Maryland"; "a poor woman who brot. a petition"; "a poor man who had his house burnt"; "a man who had his house burnt on Shippen's farm"; "a poor woman towards paying her passage to N. York"; "an old man"; "a Mrs. Konig who brot. a recommendation from the minister of the Dutch Church"; "a man by the name of Caleb bull who had lost his leg"; "Jacob Issacs the salt fish waterman—to enable him to go home"; "a poor woman who had been a Nurse in an Hospital"; "a negro who brot. a sub[scriptio]n paper with many respectable names, towards purchasing his freedom"; "a poor woman nam'd Eleanor Haily"; "a poor woman with 6 children going from N. York to Baltim[or]e"; "a man by the name of Jenkins who says he was a Lieut. in Genl. Braddock's trooops"; "a poor woman whose husband was wounded at Stoney Point & recommended by Dr. Shippen & others"; "a poor man to enable him to pay his passage to Rhode Island"; "an old German Doctor in great distress who served under Genl. Lincoln to the Southward"; "an insane woman"; a woman who couldn't pay her "house rent"; "a poor blind man"; "a poor woman who has come from the Western Country to get the pay of her husband—in great distress"; "a negro who calls himself Prince Achmet"; "a poor woman who brought a crippled child to be put in the Hospital"; "two distressed French women at New Castle"; "Pothe, a poor old man"; "a poor french woman"; one James Allen, "who had his brew house burnt"; "a poor Mason"; "a poor girl," for whom Mrs. Washington paid "three months schooling"; "a distressed woman from Charleston"; "a distressed Frenchman"; "a poor widow who's daughter was blind"; "a distressed negro sailor"; and "a distressed soldier & wife."[8] Following his retirement, during the last year of his life, Washington made at least one large donation of $100 for "the poor."[9]

Not just individuals, but also more organized causes drew the attention of the Washingtons. Offering money was contributed at church, and both clergymen and churches were helped with a number of worthy projects. For example, Mrs. Washington gave her grandchildren two guineas "for the contribution at Church at the Mason's Sermon" on July 5, 1789, and put two shillings into the collection plate on November 29th. Money was given to an "Irish clergyman"; a Dr. Rogers from the Presbyterian Church received ten pounds to help the poor members of his congregation in November 1789. Three days before his birthday in 1791, the president gave $5.34 to a minister from New Jersey "towards establishing a school." The following May, during a "charity sermon" at Christ Church, the president contributed $4 for the orphan school of the parish. The next year, he gave $8 for another charity sermon at the same church. When Dr. William White, one of the chaplains of Congress and the first bishop of the Protestant Episcopal Church in Pennsylvania, needed funds to establish a dispensary in 1792, George Washington donated $46 for that cause; several years later, he gave Dr. White another $250 "to be distributed among the Poor" of Philadelphia. In addition to these charities, which were either church related or sponsored by clergymen, another group benefited from its association with the Washingtons. Early in 1790, George Washington made a very large donation of fifty guineas or £93 6s.8d. to "the Society for relieving distressed debtors." This was not the first time Washington had helped out this particular group of prisoners; he had arranged to have "provisions & beer" sent to them just a few months before. One of the most generous donations ever made by George Washington was a gift of $250 to a committee organized to help French colonists in Haiti after a violent slave uprising there during his presidency. He presented a like sum shortly before his retirement from the presidency to a group helping the survivors of a severe fire in the city of Savannah.[10]

George Washington was personally tolerant of religious beliefs and practices that differed from his own, which would have been consistent with his upbringing. Although he had been raised and lived much of his life in a colony where Anglicanism dominated as the state religion, Virginia had a largely "live and let live" attitude toward religious differences before the 1760s. An example of this can be seen in a list of titheables for Fairfax County, Virginia, which was drawn up by the Reverend Charles Green of Truro Parish in 1749, five years before George Washington took over management of Mount Vernon. This manuscript shows that of the 2,035 individuals to be taxed, quite a few belonged to denominations other than Anglican. There were at least forty-eight households containing people described as "Papist," thirty-two with Presbyterians, seventy-four with Quakers, and five with Anabaptists, while three contained people listed as

"In the Hands of a Good Providence"

"Sectarys." Despite their religious differences with the Anglicans, a number of these people were said to "sometimes come to Church," presumably because of difficulties in attending churches of their own denominations. There were other men with the name "Preacher" written in the notes beside their names, one specifically described as "Quakr Preachr," and another of whom it was noted, "his wife a Preacher." Not having grown up in the Anglican Church did not prevent a person from serving in the parish: there were several men on Rev. Green's list described as "formerly Papist, Lately Vestryman."[11]

Washington's tolerance was clearly stated in a letter written to a friend after the Revolution: "Being no bigot myself to any mode of worship, I am disposed to indulge the professors of Christianity in the church, that road to Heaven, which to them shall seem the most direct plainest easiest and least liable to exception."[12] One reason for this was his belief that, throughout history, religion had been a particularly divisive issue. In a letter to a correspondent in Ireland, a country already torn by religious wars, he wrote of his hopes that the time in which the two of them lived would be different:

> Of all the animosities which have existed among mankind, those which
> are caused by a difference of sentiments in religion appear to be the most
> inveterate and distressing, and ought most to be deprecated. I was in hopes,
> that the enlightened and liberal policy, which has marked the present age,
> would at least have reconciled Christians of every denomination so far, that
> we should never again see their religious disputes carried to such a pitch as
> to endanger the peace of Society.[13]

According to one historian, Washington was "never deeply impressed by doctrinal arguments" and, when traveling, was known to "attend the services of any other denomination with equal cheerfulness."[14] Others in his social and political milieu were known to do the same thing, however, including even those who might have expressed greater interest in doctrinal issues. During the first Continental Congress, John Adams could not find a Congregational church in Philadelphia, so he not only attended Anglican services at Christ Church, but also worshipped with Methodists, Baptists, Presbyterians, Quakers, and German Moravians.[15]

While he may not have put much stock in doctrinal issues, there is evidence that Washington had some interest in them. A friend, Alexandria merchant Samuel Hanson, wrote to him in January 1786 to say that the last time he had visited at Mount Vernon, Washington had "expressed an inclination to peruse the Pamphlets of the Revd Messrs Wharton & Carroll, upon the subject of their religious Controversy."[16] Hanson was enclosing the pieces written by the first author but had not yet been able to procure the work of the second, both of whom were Maryland natives. Several years earlier, Charles Henry Wharton, who had been raised in the Roman Catholic Church, had authored a pamphlet in order to raise money to relieve American prisoners being held in British jails. Originally published in Annapolis in 1779, and a year later in London, the work praised Washington as someone who was

> strictly just, vigilant, and generous; an affectionate husband, a faithful friend, a father to the deserving soldier; gentle in his manners, in temper rather reserved; a total stranger to religious prejudices, which have so excited Christians of one denomination to cut the throats of those of another; in his morals irreproachable; he was never known to exceed the bounds of the most rigid temperance; in a word, all his friends and acquaintance universally allow, that no man ever united in his own person a more perfect alliance of the virtues of a philosopher with the talents of a general. Candour, sincerity, affability, and simplicity, seem to be the striking features of his character, till an occasion offers of displaying the most determined bravery and independence of spirit.[17]

Wharton eventually left the church, while serving as a chaplain to a Catholic congregation in Worcester, England. He came back to America in 1783 and would go on to become a clergyman in the Episcopal Church. In 1784 Wharton tried to explain the reasons for this conversion to his former congregation in a pamphlet entitled *A Letter to the Roman Catholics of the City of Worcester*. The Reverend John Carroll, who had studied with the Jesuits in France and would later become the first Roman Catholic bishop in the United States and the first archbishop of Baltimore, responded by composing *An Address to the Roman Catholics of the United States of America* that same year. Wharton, in turn, published *A Reply to an Address to the Roman Catholics of the United States of America* in 1785.[18] There is no evidence that Washington ever met Charles Henry Wharton; however, a gentleman identified only as "a Mr. Wharton," who visited him briefly at Mount Vernon in February 1773, might have been the Maryland pamphleteer who wrote so flatteringly, and knowingly, about him during the war. Many years later, Washington would get to know Bishop Carroll, who corresponded with him during the presidency about the need for missions to the Indians and once came to dinner at Mount Vernon in June of 1799, along with several other members of the prominent—and Catholic—Carroll and Digges families of Maryland.[19]

Washington's attendance at Presbyterian services in Morristown during the Revolution was mentioned earlier. Other denominations with which he is known to have worshipped include Quakers, Roman Catholics, Congregationalists, Baptists, and Dutch Reformed. Washington once humorously noted in his diary that he had gone to the Dutch church in York, Pennsylvania, in the summer of 1791, because there was "no Episcopal Minister present in the place." The service, however, was conducted completely in German, "not a word of which I understood," and the president recorded that he was, therefore, "in no danger of becoming a proselyte to its religion by the eloquence of the Preacher."[20]

Washington's comment about the Dutch service was unusual, because he rarely recorded either his thoughts about, or his reactions to, the religious gatherings he attended. For example, on Sunday, October 9, 1774, while serving as delegates to the First Continental Congress in Philadelphia, both he and John Adams visited the First Presbyterian Church on Market Street in the morning and St. Mary's Catholic Church, which was located at Fourth and Spruce Streets, in the afternoon. In his usual laconic manner, Washington's diary simply stated, "Went to the Presbyterian Meeting in the forenoon and Romish Church in the Afternoon. Dind at Bevan's."[21] Adams, a Congregationalist, always more descriptive and revealing than his colleague from Virginia, recorded the day in his diary. Of the Protestant minister, he noted that the elderly gentleman was "a Man of Abilities and Worth," but, like most of the ministers in Philadelphia, was inferior to those in Boston. Turning to the Catholic service, Adams wrote:

> Went in the Afternoon to the Romish Chappell and heard a good discourse upon the Duty of Parents to their Children, founded in Justice and Charity. The Scenery and the Musick is so callculated to take in Mankind that I wonder, the Reformation ever succeeded. The Paintings, the Bells, the Candles, the Gold and Silver. Our Saviour on the Cross, over the Altar, at full Length, and all his Wounds a bleeding. The Chanting is exquisitely soft and sweet.[22]

Adams was even more expansive about these new experiences in a letter to his wife, Abigail, who was back home in Braintree, Massachusetts. Writing her later that same day, he confided his reactions to these different modes of worship, giving us a flavor of what Washington would have seen there, as well:

> This afternoon, led by Curiosity and good Company I strolled away to Mother Church, or rather Grandmother Church, I mean the Romish Chappell. Heard a good, short, moral Essay upon the Duty of Parents to their Children. . . . This afternoons Entertainment was to me, most awfull and affecting. The poor Wretches, fingering, their Pater Nosters and Ave Maria's. Their holy Water—their Crossing themselves perpetually—their Bowing to the Name of Jesus, wherever they hear it—their Bowings, and Kneelings, and Genuflections before the Altar. The Dress of the Priest was rich with Lace—his Pulpit was Velvet and Gold. The Altar Piece was very rich—little Images and Crucifixes about—Wax Candles lighted up. But how shall I describe the Pictures of our Saviour in a Frame of Marble over the Altar at full Length upon the Cross, in the Agonies, and the Blood dropping and streaming from his Wounds.
>
> The Musick consisting of an organ, and a Choir of singers, went all the Afternoon, excepting sermon Time, and the Assembly chanted—most sweetly and exquisitely.
>
> Here is every Thing which can lay hold of the Eye, Ear, and Imagination. Every Thing which can charm and bewitch the simple and ignorant. I wonder how Luther ever broke the spell.[23]

At one point, early in the Revolution, Washington took a very public stance in support of a prospective army chaplain, a controversial man, who has been called the "founder of Universalism in America."[24] Just months into his command of the Continental Army, Washington faced a situation in which three Rhode Island regiments had chosen as their chaplain a man named John Murray, an English immigrant then living in Massachusetts, whose views on heaven and hell differed from those of his more orthodox (that is, Calvinist) brethren in the clergy. The Universalists shared the Calvinist belief in doctrines such as original sin (that all humans, through the sin of Adam and Eve, were born with the inclination to sin), predestination (that God had decided at the beginning of the world which people were saved and which would be damned), and the idea that all humans, because of their sin, deserved damnation for eternity. The two groups broke ranks, however, over the limits Calvinism placed on who would or would not get into heaven. Universalism espoused the belief that, because Christ had died for the sins of everyone, then salvation must be open to everyone, not just the few who were "the elect," or, as Murray put it, "that *every* individual shall in due time be separated from sin, and rendered fit to associate with the denizens of heaven."[25] Reverend Murray was offered the position as chaplain to Nathanael Greene's brigade in May of 1775:

> Amidst that concurrence of events which the great Creator in infinite wisdom directs, for the accomplishment of his own purposes, a British armament hath set hostile foot upon American ground. What the design of the Almighty may be, we cannot at present absolutely determine. One thing we know, *our cause is just,* and also that the Parent of the universe can do no wrong . . . it is requisite, propriety of manners, regularity of conduct, and a due reliance upon the Almighty controller of events, should be cultivated and enforced. . . . We have, therefore, selected you, as a Chaplain to our Brigade, well convinced that your extensive benevolence, and abilities, will justify our choice. We cannot, without doing violence to the opinion we have formed of your character, doubt of your ready compliance with our united request.[26]

Unfortunately, Reverend Murray, who accepted the position almost immediately, had made some enemies among the clergy, both because of his religious views and because he had once reportedly offered to administer communion at a dinner party, as the guests were drinking wine and talking after the meal.[27] When other chaplains complained about Murray's appointment, the Englishman and General Greene had dinner with the commanding general to discuss the situation.[28] Greene, who was very close to Washington, had heard Murray preach several years before, and described him as "a Gentleman of Elevated Faculties, a fine Speaker, and appears by his Language to be a Lover of Mankind."[29] Seven days after this meeting, Washington declared in a general order that, "The Revd Mr. John Murray is appointed Chaplain to the Rhode-Island Regiments and is to be respected as such."[30] Murray would serve as a chaplain until the end of that same year, when he was forced to resign for health reasons. Several years later, General Greene wrote of Murray's time in the Army:

Mr. John Murray was appointed Chaplain to Colonel Varnum's Regiment by his Excellency General Washington during the Army's lying before Boston; and during his officiating in that capacity his Conduct was regulated by the Laws of virtue and propriety. His actions were such as to make him respected as an honest man and a good Christian. He liv'd belov'd and left the Army esteemed by all his connection and Patrons.[31]

Washington's relationship with Reverend Murray and his wife would continue for many years. In 1788 Murray married a well-educated young widow, whose prominent Massachusetts family had been converted to Universalism through his preaching.[32] In the first year of the presidency, Reverend Murray and his wife had the opportunity to socialize several times with the Washingtons, during the course of a long journey that brought them to New York City. The women in George Washington's family appear to have been particularly drawn to Judith Sargent Murray, a gifted poet and writer, who used her talents to promote both Universalism (she wrote a catechism for children in 1782) and feminism. Martha Washington felt comfortable enough with the younger woman to confide her fears about her husband's health, after his recovery from a serious illness. Granddaughter Nelly Custis, then just eleven years old, created a floral painting for Mrs. Murray, who in turn thanked the little girl with a poem. Both Martha Washington and Nelly Custis would later correspond with Mrs. Murray.[33]

In the autumn after his retirement from the presidency, George Washington subscribed to two copies—one for himself and one for Mrs. Washington—of Judith Sargent Murray's most renowned work, *The Gleaner,* a three-volume compilation of her poetry, plays, and essays. One of those essays, entitled "Necessity of Religion, Especially in Adversity," began with the words, "No—Atheism will never do," pointed out the benefits of the separation of church and state, and went on to illustrate the integral role of religion in the life of an individual community and its inhabitants. In another, "Spirit Independent of Matter," the author turned "with disgust and horror," from the beliefs of those who believed that man would never break "his sepulchral enclosure" after death and expounded on the immortality of the soul. In his thank-you letter, Washington noted that the books had "been read with very great pleasure."[34]

In addition to the Murrays, George and Martha Washington welcomed a number of dissenting (non-Anglican) ministers to their home over the years. For example, in the spring of 1785, two Methodist bishops, Thomas Coke and Francis Asbury, arrived at Mount Vernon with the intention of persuading George Washington to sign an antislavery petition for presentation to the Virginia legislature. The two men had been sent by John Wesley to oversee and guide the Methodist movement in America. Asbury had been in the country since before the Revolution, while Coke made the journey in 1784. The bishops had with them a letter of introduction from Gen. Daniel Roberdeau, a longtime friend of George Washington and strong supporter of the patriot cause during the late war. Roberdeau, who was of Huguenot descent and a practicing Presbyterian, had been a friend of evangelist George Whitefield, which was the likely source of his interest in Methodism. Unfortunately, Roberdeau was unable to make the trip to Mount Vernon that day because of an illness in his family.[35]

While Washington, Asbury, and Coke all recorded the meeting in their diaries, it was Coke who left the best description of the events and conversation that day:

> Thursday [May] 26. Mr. *Asbury* and I set off for General *Washington's*. We were engaged to dine there the day before. . . . He received us very politely, and was very open to access. . . . After dinner we desired a private interview, and opened to him the grand business on which we came, presenting to him our petition for the emancipation of the Negroes, and intreating his signature, if the eminence of his station did not render it inexpedient for him to sign any petition. He informed us that he was of our sentiments, and had signified his thoughts on the subject to most of the great men of the State: that he did not see it proper to sign the petition, but if the Assembly took it into consideration, would signify his sentiments to the Assembly by a letter. He asked us to spend the evening and lodge at his house, but our engagement at *Annapolis* the following day would not admit of it.[36]

About a year after this visit, Asbury sent Washington a copy of the Methodist prayer book, along with a second, for "your Lady," and a collection of sermons, "as a small token of my great respect and veneration for your Person."[37] Among the Methodist writings in George Washington's library at the time of his death were an ordination sermon delivered by Thomas Coke in Baltimore in December of 1784; a 1787 address by both Coke and Asbury *"To the Annual Subscribers for the Support of Cokesbury-College, and to the Members of the Methodist Society*"; and six sermons or pamphlets by John Wesley published between 1774 and 1784.[38]

More controversial than the Methodists was Joseph Priestley, a scientist, political thinker, and Unitarian theologian, who had been forced to move with his wife to the United States in 1794, after his religious views led to riots in his native England. Priestley had been raised in a dissenting household—his family were Congregationalists—and was educated at a "four-year Dissenter's college," but he soon moved away from their strict form of Calvinism and rejected orthodox Christian teachings on the Trinity, the identity of Jesus, the soul, the spirit, and divine intervention in the playing out of history. He identified with the Socinians, a heretical sect that espoused the beliefs that Christianity was

> a practice of moral conduct based on the teachings of Jesus, which were attested by miracles, interpreted by human reason (reason and revelation coincided), and issued in eternal life; God was one person, revealed by a divinely inspired but human Jesus . . . ; people were not born with original sin; adult baptism by immersion was a rite of initiation into a church; the Lord's Supper was purely a memorial celebration; churches cared for their poor; and each church was supervised by chosen elders.[39]

Washington might have become familiar with Priestley's work through colleagues, friends, and acquaintances, like Benjamin Franklin, Thomas Jefferson, John Adams, and Benjamin Rush, who, while they may not have always agreed with Priestley, attended his lectures, read his works, and promoted their publication. In addition, Washington had the opportunity to read Priestley for himself. Early in Washington's presidency, an English friend, merchant Samuel Vaughan, who had been an ardent supporter of the American cause during the Revolution, sent him a collection of pamphlets written by British supporters of the French Revolution. Among these works were two speeches by Priestley, who had tutored two of Vaughan's sons, as well as a pamphlet entitled *Unitarian Society*, which had recently been published in London by the Unitarian Society for Promoting Christian Knowledge and the Practice of Virtue.[40] The talks by Priestley—one a funeral sermon or eulogy, the second a discourse on *The Proper Objects of Education in the Present State of the World*—were still in Washington's library, bound with other pamphlets in a volume entitled *Sermons,* at the time of his death in 1799.[41]

During a visit to friends in Philadelphia in 1796, Priestley's hosts took him along when they called on the American president for tea. Priestley later wrote that they "spent two hours as in any private family. He [Washington] invited me to come at any time, without ceremony." Washington read one of Priestley's books and invited the Englishman for a longer visit at Mount Vernon, which never seems to have taken place.[42] The relationship between the two men would continue for several years. Within two months of their initial meeting, Priestley, in his role as a scientist, appears to have contacted Washington with some concerns about American patent laws, which allowed patents to be granted only to American citizens. In response, a letter from someone on Washington's staff noted that the president had looked into the matter and that he could see no reason for the restriction, but would "take occasion to enquire into the cause of this limitation, and if it should not appear improper, to relinquish it."[43] Upon his retirement from the presidency in March of 1797, Washington asked that "one of those Thermometers that tells the state of the Mercury within the 24 hours" be sent to him at Mount Vernon. In his instructions, Washington suggested that "Doctor Priestley or Mr. Madison can tell where it is to be had."[44] Later that year, George Washington Parke Custis reported to his step-grandfather that he was studying "the principles and uses of History . . . in a course of lectures by Priestley" at Princeton.[45] By the time of Washington's death, the retired president had added several additional works by Priestley to his library.[46]

The actions of both George and Martha Washington indicate that their toleration was not limited simply to other varieties of Christians. In the early months of his presidency, George Washington wrote: "I trust the people of every denomination, who demean themselves as good citizens, will have occasion to be convinced that I shall always strive to prove a faithful and impartial Patron of genuine, vital religion."[47] He would, however, also support those who did not believe in God at all. In a letter concerning his need to find skilled workmen for his Mount Vernon estate, Washington remarked that he was primarily interested in their work skills, not their religion: "If they are good workmen, they may be of Asia, Africa, or Europe. They may be Mahometans, Jews, or Christian of any Sect, or they may be Atheists."[48] These were not just empty words. Among the many doctors entrusted with the care of Martha Washington's daughter, Patsy, as the young woman struggled with epilepsy, was John de Sequeyra of Williamsburg, the son of a prominent Sephardic Jewish family in London, who came to Virginia in 1745 after receiving his medical training at the University of Leyden. The doctor must have been esteemed in Williamsburg; he was called in to treat Governor Botetourt in his final illness and was named the first visiting physician at the city's new hospital for the insane in 1773.

Sequeyra saw Patsy Custis on at least eight occasions in the fall of 1769.[49] According to one student of the Jewish community in the early United States, George Washington's relationship with Dr. Sequeyra was his "first and only known and documented direct personal and professional contact with a colonial Jew."[50] Many years after the death of her daughter, Martha Washington is known to have patronized at least one Jewish business in New York as first lady. In June of 1790, she purchased twenty pounds of cotton from Solomon Levy, whose father, Hayman Levy, was a supporter of the American Revolution and a prominent member of the Jewish community in New York, where he was president of Shearith Israel, that city's synagogue.[51]

The Washingtons are known to have supported the religious beliefs and practices of their hired servants, even when the denominations of the latter differed from their own. A devotional book entitled *The Whole Duty of Man* was purchased on behalf of an employee named Sarah Harle, in 1766. Many years later, shortly after hiring a group of German servants to work in the executive mansion in Philadelphia, the Washingtons paid $3 "for a bible and prayer book for the Dutch woman."[52] Over a period of about thirty years, George Washington's instructions to his overseers indicated that they were expected to remain with the slaves they supervised during work hours, with the exception of mealtimes, and that the overseers were not to leave their respective farms without permission, with two exceptions: times when they had "unavoidable business," or "on Sundays," in order "to attend Divine Worship."[53] Research into the religious beliefs and practices of the slaves at Mount Vernon indicates that the enslaved residents of the plantation included not only Christians—of both Anglican and dissenting denominations such as Baptists, Methodists, and Quakers—but perhaps also Muslims, and believers in traditional African religions. There is no evidence that the Washingtons interfered in any way—either positively or negatively—with the religious lives of their slaves, beyond giving them Sundays and three religious holidays off each year (four days at Christmas, and the Mondays after both Easter and Pentecost).[54]

This toleration even included younger members of the extended Mount Vernon household, who were certainly free to express their feelings on the practice of organized religion. Not so for her youngest granddaughter, Nelly. Martha Washington also found reason for concern about the girl's older sister, Eliza Parke Custis, who had been raised by their mother on a different plantation. When Eliza came to stay at the presidential mansion for a prolonged visit, Martha confided to another relative that Eliza seemed to be a rather withdrawn young woman who was happiest being alone. Among the symptoms her grandmother found worrisome was that "she dont like to go to church every Sunday thinks it too fatiguing."[55] Her grandmother would have been delighted to learn that Eliza would later make some profound statements about the importance of the Christian faith in her life.

Surviving financial records show that George Washington gave money to a number of religious groups over the years. During the first months of his presidency, he made a donation to help reconstruct the Reformed Church in Harlem, which had been destroyed during the Revolution and was now being rebuilt. In March of 1790, he gave a little over $5 for the building fund of a church near Albany, New York. Ten months later, he subscribed $10 for the purchase of an organ for Old Christ Church on Arch Street, where he had worshipped during his time in Philadelphia before and during the Revolution. Construction on a church for an unrecorded congregation was also pushed forward by means of a gift from him of $9.34. In May of 1792, he contributed $4 toward the construction of a Dutch Roman Catholic Church in Baltimore; $2 for building a new church of unknown denomination in Gloucester, New Jersey; and $3 for the same purpose for a church in Dauphin County, Pennsylvania.[56] Among the other contributions to congregations he assisted was one for a group trying to build a church in Martintown; one for an "African Church," presumably for an African American congregation; another for a "Universal Church" in Philadelphia; and still another for a Catholic church in the same city.[57]

9

CHURCH AND STATE

Washington's Vision for America

TWO THEMES RUN THROUGH George Washington's vision of the role
of religion in American life: the need to reduce the divisions caused
by religious differences and the need to encourage the unifying aspects of religion.[1] Especially in his last quarter century, as he struggled
to unite thirteen often provincial and fractious colonies into one united
whole, toleration of differing religious traditions, both privately by individuals and publicly by the government, was something he idealistically
saw, and heartily approved of, as a unique and basic quality of the new
United States. It can also be seen as an extension of the beliefs he was
likely to have been taught as a child and had seen his elder brother push
in the Virginia legislature.

Washington, however, went past support of mere toleration to take up
the cause of religious freedom, where the only being to whom a citizen
had to answer in terms of his religious beliefs, or lack thereof, was God.
Looking back on history, he could see what a divisive force religion had
often been in the past. Writing to a correspondent in Ireland about the
unhappy experiences of that country, he expressed the opinion that "Of
all the animosities which have existed among mankind those which are
caused by a difference of sentiment in Religion appear to be the most
inveterate and distressing and ought most to be deprecated." He went on
to say that he hoped "the enlightened & liberal policy which has marked
the present age" would be enough to have "at least reconciled Christians

of every denomination so far that we should never again see their religious disputes carried to such a pitch as to endanger the peace of Society."[2] Washington's idealism on this score extended well beyond fellow Christians. He also knew just how rare this American experiment in religious liberty was. As he stated to the Jewish communities in several large American cities early in his presidency, "The liberal sentiment towards each other which marks every political and religious denomination of men in this country stands unrivalled in the history of nations."[3]

Along with guarantees of liberty of conscience, which would protect the new country from the religious conflicts that had marked past centuries in Europe, Washington also felt that religion could be a unifying force. Without a citizenry that had internalized a strict moral code, democracy could easily descend into anarchy, and as Washington reminded his countrymen in his Farewell Address, not even an educated citizenry— and Washington was a man who placed a high value on education—could make up for a lack of religion in people's lives: "Let us with caution indulge the supposition, that morality can be maintained without religion. Whatever may be conceded to the influence of refined education on minds of peculiar structure, reason and experience both forbid us to expect that National morality can prevail in exclusion of religious principle."[4] Those who might have disagreed with Washington on this point had only to look at the experience of Revolutionary France, anticlerical and antireligious as it was, to see the dangers inherent in disregarding his advice. Throughout his public career, he encouraged his fellow citizens in the practice of their religious beliefs and assured them of their right to do so.[5]

Given the melding of religion and political life in eighteenth-century America, it is not surprising that, early in Washington's public career, his emphasis was on the unifying aspects of religion. During the French and Indian War, Washington tried unsuccessfully to get a chaplain assigned to his unit on the frontier, at the expense of the colony of Virginia. The day after Washington finished building Fort Necessity in the spring of 1754 was a Sunday. The twenty-two-year-old noted in his diary that two or three families of Shawnee Indians had arrived that day and that, although there was no chaplain, "We had Prayers in the Fort."[6] He apparently wrote a letter, which has since been lost, to his mentor, Col. William Fairfax of Belvoir Plantation, about his experiences that week, leading Fairfax to write in response to learning about the service:

I will not doubt your having public Prayers in the Camp especially when
the Indian Familys were your Guests, that They seeing our plain Manner
of Worship may excite their Curiosity to be inform'd Why we dont use the
idolatrous and Superstitious Ceremonys of the French which being wel ex-
plaind to their Understandings will more and more dispose Them to receive
our Baptism and unite in strictest Bonds of cordial Friendship.[7]

The officers continued leading services over the next several years. In the
summer of 1756, Lt. Col. Adam Stephen, the Scotsman who was Washington's second in command, wrote to him from Fort Cumberland in Maryland to say that his men "had Sermon these two last Sundays; The Genuine product of Fort Cumberland. Capt. Woodward Officiats." Stephen
went on to ask that if Washington happened to "come across a Cargo of
Second hand Sermons please to forward them by the first Waggons, for as
we have no Books the Art of making [sermons] will soon fail us."[8] It may
well have been the inadequacy felt by the officers in trying to fulfill the
role of chaplain that led Washington to convey to the governor of Virginia
their need for the presence of a professional clergyman: "The want of a
chaplain does, I humbly conceive, reflect dishonor upon the regiment, as
all other officers are allowed. The gentlemen of the corps are sensible of
this, and did propose to support one at their private expense. But I think it
would have been a more graceful appearance were he appointed as others
are."[9] Several weeks later he brought up this subject again, commenting
to the governor, "As touching a chaplain, if the government will grant a
subsistence, we can readily get a person of merit to accept of the place,
without giving the commissary any trouble on that point, as it is highly
necessary we should be reformed from those crimes and enormities we
[the soldiers] are so universally accused of."[10]

   The divisiveness and bitterness that could result from not putting more
of a barrier between religion and politics became sharply visible in the
years between the French and Indian War and the Revolutionary War. The
idea of separating the government of a nation from its religion was a relatively new concept in the eighteenth century. (One might argue that it still
is.) Like Virginia, many of the other colonies pre-Revolution had recognized the Church of England as their state church.[11] As the colonies moved
closer to a break with the mother country, ministers on both sides of the
conflict used their pulpits to promote highly partisan political opinions.

As demonstrated earlier, in the case of George Washington and the Loyalist Anglican clergy, such actions may well have damaged the image of the clergy—and consequently the church—in the eyes of many parishioners, and might partially account for the falling away of Americans from their local congregations in the last decades of the eighteenth century.

Loyalist Jonathan Boucher, who had taught Martha Washington's son for a number of years before the war, found himself in a difficult position at this period, because of a conflict between his political views and those of his congregation. In his autobiography, Boucher recalled those days:

> I happened one Sunday to recommend peaceableness; on which a Mr. Lee and sundry others . . . rose up and left the church. This was a signal to the people to consider every sermon of mine as hostile to the views and interests of America; and accordingly I never after went into a pulpit without something very disagreeable happening. I received sundry messages and letters threatening me with the most fatal consequences if I did not . . . preach what should be agreeable to the friends of America. All the answer I gave to these threats was . . . that I never could suffer any merely human authority to intimidate me from performing what in my conscience I believed and knew to be my duty to God and His Church. And for more than six months I preached . . . with a pair of loaded pistols lying on the cushion.[12]

The situation between Boucher and his congregation continued to deteriorate. Several times he was set upon by mobs in the church, and at one point the minister climbed the steps of the pulpit, "with my sermon in one hand and a loaded pistol in the other, like Nehemiah." After several such incidents, Boucher and his wife decided that, for his own safety, he should return to England; he sailed away with several friends in September of 1775.[13]

Ministers on the patriot side politically were just as likely to say something from the pulpit on the subject of the approaching war as the Loyalists. As one young American wrote in the spring of 1775:

> The clergymen of New England are, almost without exception, advocates of whig principles; there are a few instances only of the separation of a minister from his people, in consequence of a disagreement in political sentiment. The tories censure, in a very illiberal manner, the preacher who speaks boldly for the liberties of the people, while they lavish their praises

on him who dares to teach the absurd doctrine, that magistrates have a
divine right to do wrong, and are to be implicitly obeyed. It is recommended
by our Provincial Congress, that . . . ministers . . . adapt their discourses to
the times, and explain the nature of civil and religious liberty, and the duties
of magistrates and rulers. Accordingly, we have from our pulpits the most
fervent and pious effusions to the throne of Divine Grace in behalf of our
bleeding, afflicted country.[14]

A young Englishman traveling in America about this same time expressed
frustration about the anti-British, political tone of sermons in the churches
he attended. On Sunday, March 16, 1777, Nicholas Cresswell "Heard a Sermon preached by the Revd. David Griffith. A political discourse. Indeed,
there is nothing else to be expected now."[15]

Another Englishman seemed to blame the growing division between
Britain and the American colonies on the sermons of both Anglican and
dissenting ministers. Writing in October of 1776 from his post in New
York, this apparently thoughtful, committed Anglican commented:

> The Clergy of this Country; both those of the Establishment & of the Pres-
> byterian Interest . . . are Fire-brands to a man. . . . These have fomented half
> the present Divisions; nor is it likely that they will be quiet in future, but
> under a Power that may controul them both. One would think . . . that God
> had a great temporal Interest in this World, which wholly depended upon
> the management & Exaltation of their Party; and that, having so good an
> End, even Spite & malice might be employed as the means.[16]

Some of the dangers in not separating God and government—from
the perspective of the church—can be found in the experiences of Anglican clergyman Jacob Duché, the rector at Christ Church and St. Peter's in
Philadelphia. Extremely popular, Duché clearly supported the American
cause in the first years of the Revolution and gave prayers at the openings
of both the first and second Continental Congresses. On September 6,
1774, a motion was made to begin the first Continental Congress with a
prayer and, since many of the delegates were Anglican, Samuel Adams of
Massachusetts suggested that an Anglican minister officiate. When two
delegates objected on the grounds that the members held "a diversity of
religious sentiments," Adams responded with the ecumenical statement
that he himself "was no bigot, and could hear a prayer from any gentleman

of piety and virtue, who was at the same time a friend to his country; and nominated Duché." The following day, at 9 o'clock in the morning, wearing "full pontificals," the minister opened the session with several prayers from the liturgy, read Psalm 35, and proceeded to strike out "into an extemporary prayer." John Adams recorded in his diary that Reverend Duché's first prayer in Congress on September 7, 1774, was "as pertinent, as affectionate, as sublime, as devout, as I ever heard offered up to Heaven. He filled every Bosom present." Another delegate present that day called it "one of the most sublime, catholic, well-adapted prayers I ever heard."[17]

Duché would remain in the American fold for the next two years. He sent one of his sermons, published under the title *The Duty of Standing Fast in Our Spiritual and Temporal Liberties,* to George Washington, who had recently been named commander of the American forces, in the summer of 1775. In the accompanying letter, Duché assured Washington that he had "long been an Admirer of your amiable Character, and was glad of this Opportunity of paying you my little Tribute of Respect." He went on to say that he prayed for Washington and his soldiers "continually," but hoped that "a speedy and happy Reconciliation could be accomplished without the Effusion of one more Drop of valuable Blood. I know well, that your Humanity, and Christian Meekness, would ever prompt you to form the same benevolent Wish; and that the Love of Military Glory will in your Breast always give Way to the Love of Peace, when it can be virtuously and honourably obtained." He closed with the blessing, "May Heaven crown all your truly Patriotic Undertakings with Success, cover your Head in the Day of Danger, and restore you unhurt to the Arms of your friends and your Country."[18] When independence from England was declared on July 4, 1776, just days before he was named chaplain to the Continental Congress, Duché made a highly partisan prayer on behalf of the American cause:

> Look down in mercy . . . on these our American states, who have fled to thee from the rod of the oppressor, and thrown themselves on thy gracious protection, desiring to be henceforth dependent only on thee; to thee have they appealed for the righteousness of their cause . . . take them, therefore, heavenly Father, under thy nurturing care; give them wisdom in council, and valor in the field; defeat the malicious designs of our cruel adversaries; convince them of the unrighteousness of their cause, and if they still persist in their sanguinary purposes, O! let the voice of thine own unerring

justice, sounding in their hearts, constrain them to drop the weapons of war from their unnerved hands in the day of battle. Be thou present, O God of wisdom, and direct the councils of this honorable assembly; enable them to settle things on the best and surest foundation, that the scene of blood may be speedily closed . . . shower down on *them,* and the *millions* they here represent, such temporal blessings, as thou seest expedient for them in this world, and crown them with everlasting glory in the world to come.[19]

Reverend Duché's faith in the fight for independence wavered several years into the conflict, after the British took Philadelphia and he was thrown in jail. After winning release by switching his allegiance to the Crown, Duché wrote to George Washington in the fall of 1778, asking him to "abandon the American cause and resign his command of the army, or at the head of it, to force Congress immediately to desist from hostilities and to rescind their declaration of Independence." If this is not done, he says, "You have an infallible resource still left, *negotiate for America at the head of your army.*"[20] Washington, though trying to put the best face on Duché's actions, was concerned about the effect this letter might have on his own reputation and confided to a mutual friend that he was

> not more surprized than concerned, at receiving so extraordinary a letter from Mr. Duche, of whom, I had entertained the most favorable opinion, and I am still willing to suppose, that it was rather dictated by his fears, than by his real Sentiments; But, I very much doubt, whether the great numbers of respectable characters, in the State and Army, upon whom he has bestowed the most unprovoked and unmerited abuse, will ever attribute it to the same cause, or forgive the Man, who has artfully endeavoured to engage me to sacrifice them, to purchase my own safety.[21]

Washington sent the letter to Congress, feeling it was "a duty which I owed to myself, for had any accident have happened to the Army intrusted to my command . . . might it not have been said that I had in consequence of it [the letter], betrayed my Country? and would not such a Correspondence if kept a secret have given good Grounds for the suspicion."[22]

Duché left for England at the end of 1777, where he served as the secretary and chaplain to an orphanage. In 1783 he wrote Washington to ask about returning to the United States, which led Washington to respond that he felt no "personal Enmity" to anyone and that he, as a private citizen, would cheerfully give permission for the exile's return. He went on, however, to caution that, "removed as I am from the people and the policy of the State in which you formerly resided and to whose determination your case must be submitted," it was up to the judges in Pennsylvania to decide Duché's fate.[23] The minister would finally return to Philadelphia in May of 1792, but one has to wonder about the efficacy of his ministry, as well as his reception among former congregants, who very likely felt betrayed and abandoned by their former pastor's changing politics.[24]

As tensions grew between Britain and the American colonies, Washington was one of many in the Virginia legislature to encourage their fellow citizens to turn to God for guidance. The House of Burgesses, including Fairfax County representative George Washington, felt the need in May of 1774 to order a day of fasting, seemingly as a way of both proving their righteousness to God and to ensure that they were on the right path as far as relations with England were concerned. For precedent, they looked to resolutions dating back almost twenty years, to the days of the French and Indian War. Washington voted to support the resolution about the fast day and seemingly wrote to his minister, Lee Massey at Pohick Church, as other delegates wrote to theirs, to announce from their pulpits the upcoming fast and to encourage members of their congregations to undertake the fast, as well.[25] On Wednesday, June 1, 1774, George Washington recorded in his diary that he "Went to Church & fasted all day." He attended Bruton Parish Church in Williamsburg that day, where Thomas Price, a native Virginian, graduate of the College of William and Mary, and chaplain of the House of Burgesses, preached a sermon based on an event in the life of the patriarch Abraham.[26] Like Price, other ministers throughout Virginia gave prayers and sermons concerning the uneasy relationship between Britain and her North American colonies.[27]

Washington's balancing of the two themes, religious freedom and the need for religion in society, can readily be seen in his experiences during the Revolution. In marked contrast to the situation in Virginia before the war, where dissenters had to apply to the government for licenses to preach and have their "meeting houses" (not "churches," which were only Anglican), Washington came to believe that religious freedom was a natural right of all men, which the new United States would protect. In the fall of 1775, when sending Benedict Arnold to Canada, in the hopes of enlisting the Canadians in the fight against Britain, Washington directed that his subordinate "avoid all Disrespect to or Contempt of the Religion of the

Country [Catholicism] and its Ceremonies," because "Prudence, Policy, and a true Christian Spirit, will lead us to look with Compassion upon their Errors without insulting them." He reminded Arnold that, at a time when the Americans were "contending for our own Liberty, we should be very cautious of violating the Rights of Conscience in others, ever considering that God alone is the Judge of the Hearts of Men, and to him only in this Case, they are answerable."[28] As head of the Continental Army, Washington proved that he was not above using his rank and power to suppress religious intolerance. In the fall of 1775, for example, he learned that his troops were about to celebrate a traditional English holiday, Guy Fawkes Day, in the customary manner. The commander was outraged:

> As the Commander in Chief has been apprized of a design form'd for the observance of that ridiculous and childish custom of burning the Effigy of the pope—He cannot help expressing his surprise that there should be Officers and Soldiers in this army so void of common sense, as not to see the impropriety of such a step at this Juncture; at a Time when we are solliciting, and have really obtain'd the friendship and alliance of the people of Canada, whom we ought to consider as Brethren embarked in the same Cause. . . . to be insulting their Religion, is so montrous, as not to be suffered or excused; indeed instead of offering the most remote insult, it is our duty to address public thanks to these our Brethren, as to them we are so much indebted for every late happy Success over the common Enemy in Canada.[29]

While, in this instance, Washington might be seen as merely protecting a political alliance, the fact that toleration for other practices and beliefs was so much a part of his own value system and a positive aspect of what he wanted for the country as a whole suggests that he simply could not understand the mentality of some of his soldiers on the issue of religious prejudice and could not allow the outward expression of such prejudice to continue. Washington's stance on this issue certainly enhanced his reputation, both in America and throughout the world. In a sketch written in May 1779 and published in England the next year, Marylander John Bell noted that the American commander was "a total stranger to religious prejudices, which have so often excited Christians of one denomination to cut the throats of those of another."[30]

In setting up the Continental Army during the Revolution, Washington was saved from having to beg for a chaplain, as he had on the Virginia frontier, because the Continental Congress gave the authorization for clergymen to serve with military units in the summer of 1775. Although not specifically mentioned therein, the Articles of War, which were passed at the end of June, certainly implied the presence of chaplains. For example, Article 2 recommended that, "all officers and soldiers, diligently . . . attend Divine Service" and listed acceptable punishments for those who behaved "indecently or irreverently" during services. Article 64 forbade sutlers to conduct business at a number of times, including "upon Sundays, during divine service or sermon," and detailed the penalty for offenses against this rule. Chaplains were first specifically mentioned about a month later, on July 29, 1775, in a pay scale for soldiers in the army, granting them a salary of twenty dollars per month, the same as for a captain.[31] Information pieced together from a variety of sources indicates that, during the eight years of the war, at least 218 men served as chaplains to the American forces. Another sixteen clergymen have been identified as ministering to the soldiers, but their status as chaplains is unclear.[32]

In his role as commander of the Continental Army, Washington encouraged the religious life of his soldiers. He announced very early in the conflict that he "requires and expects, of all Officers, and Soldiers, not engaged on actual duty, a punctual attendance on divine Service, to implore the blessings of heaven upon the means used for our safety and defence."[33] The numerous references to Washington's attendance at services during the war indicate that he was not asking his soldiers to do something he himself was unwilling to do. For example, on Sunday, July 23, 1780, an army surgeon noted that he went to a service led by Chaplain Samuel Blair, a Presbyterian from Pennsylvania. That day, the "troops were paraded in the open field, the sermon was well calculated to inculcate religious principles and the moral virtues. His Excellency General Washington, Major-Generals Greene and Knox, with a number of other officers, were present."[34]

Surviving correspondence shows that, even toward the end of the war, Washington was willing to consider additional ways for the government to promote the practice of religion among his men. In the spring of 1783, he was approached by a prominent Presbyterian clergyman with a plan to have the government give an American translation of the Bible to each soldier in the army. The minister, John Rodgers, had been greatly influenced by the work of British evangelist George Whitefield and served as a pastor in New York City for several decades, except for the war years, when he chose to leave the British-occupied city. Washington quickly responded, thanking Rodgers for his congratulations "on the happy Event of Peace, with the Establishment of our Liberties and Independence." He expressed the wish, however, that "in the midst of our Joys, I hope we shall not forget that, to divine Providence is to be ascribed the Glory and the Praise." Washington liked Rodgers's plan and said that it "would have been particularly noticed by me, had it been suggested in Season," but by the time he had learned of it, two-thirds of the army had already disbanded and it was "now too late to make the Attempt." He went on to say that it "would have pleased me, if Congress should have made such an important present, to the brave fellows, who have done so much for the Security of their Country's Rights and Establishment."[35]

After the war began, the issue of declaring fast days was brought before the Continental Congress on a number of occasions, but they were by no means universally supported. As a member of the Virginia delegation, Thomas Jefferson stood in opposition to at least one of those proposals, doing so in a manner that seemed to "cast aspersions on Christianity." His colleague and friend from Massachusetts, John Adams, defended the motion, noting that he was "sorry to hear such sentiments from a gentleman [he] so highly respected" and that this was "the only instance" he had "ever known of a man of sound sense and real genius that was an enemy to Christianity."[36] One such fast was declared on July 20, 1775, and was mentioned in the journal of a Revolutionary War soldier:

This day is devoted to a Public Fast throughout the United Colonies, by the recommendation of Congress, to implore the Divine benediction on our country; that any further shedding of blood may be averted; and that the calamities with which we are afflicted may be removed. This is the first general or Continental Fast ever observed since the settlement of the colonies.[37]

Throughout the Revolution, Washington publicly endorsed efforts by various local and national legislative bodies to proclaim days of both fasting and thanksgiving and habitually ordered his army to comply with them:

The Honorable the Legislature of this Colony having thought fit to set apart Thursday the 23d of November Instant, as a day of public thanksgiving "to offer up our praises, and prayers to Almighty God, the Source and Benevolent Bestower of all good; That he would be pleased graciously to continue, to smile upon our Endeavours, to restore peace, preserve our Rights, and Privileges, to the latest posterity; prosper the American Arms, preserve and strengthen the Harmony of the United Colonies, and avert the Calamities of a civil war." The General therefore commands that day to be observed with all the Solemnity directed by the Legislative Proclamation, and all Officers, Soldiers and others, are hereby directed, with the most unfeigned Devotion, to obey the same.[38]

In a similar vein, he exhorted the Continental Army to observe a day of fasting, prayer, and humiliation, ordered by the Massachusetts legislature in 1776, directing that "All Officers, and Soldiers . . . pay due reverence, and attention on that day, to the sacred duties due to the Lord of hosts, for his mercies already received, and for those blessings, which our Holiness and Uprightness of life can alone encourage us to hope through his mercy to obtain."[39]

Washington himself, in his capacity as commander in chief, ordered days of thanksgiving, as in the spring of 1778, after word arrived at Valley Forge that the French had allied themselves with the Americans and would provide both military and financial support to the young country. In orders issued on May 5th of that year, Washington declared:

It having pleased the Almighty Ruler of the Universe propitiously to defend the cause of the United American States, and finally, by raising us up a powerful friend among the princes of the earth, to establish our liberty and independence on a lasting foundation; it becomes us to set apart a day for gratefully acknowledging the Divine goodness, and celebrating the important event which we owe to His benign interposition.[40]

Washington further spelled out details of the celebration, which was scheduled for the following day. After religious services in the morning, the soldiers were to be drawn up in formation, followed by a parade, artillery salutes, and cheers or huzzahs given in honor of the King of France, friendly European Powers, and the American States. The men would then be issued a gill of rum apiece. In addition, several death sentences were commuted and there was a general release of prisoners.[41] An officer who took part in the festivities recorded that George and Martha Washington and Lord Stirling and his wife, along with other generals and their spouses, "attended at nine o'clock at the Jersey brigade," when Washington's order was read aloud, "and after prayer a suitable discourse delivered to Lord Stirling's division by the Rev. Mr. Hunter."[42]

Hunter was Chaplain Andrew Hunter, a Presbyterian, who was serving with the 3rd New Jersey.[43] Following the service, at 11:30 a.m., the units "repaired to their alarm-posts," where they were inspected by Washington and the other generals and, "after the firing of the cannon and musketry, and the huzzas were given agreeably to the orders, the army returned to their respective brigade parades, and were dismissed." The day's celebrations were nowhere near their end, however:

> All the officers of the army then assembled, and partook of a collation provided by the general, at which several patriotic toasts were given, accompanied with three cheers. His excellency [Washington] took leave of the officers at five o'clock, on which there was universal huzzaing—Long live General Washington!—and clapping of hands till the general rode some distance. The non-commissioned officers and privates followed the example of their officers as the general passed their brigades. Approbation indeed was conspicuous in every countenance, and universal joy reigned throughout the camp.[44]

Washington's actions that day at Valley Forge won him praise from a prominent local minister. Henry Melchior Muhlenberg, often described as the father of the Lutheran Church in America, wrote in his journal on May 7th:

> I heard a fine example today, namely, that His Excellency General Washington rode around among his army yesterday and admonished each and every one to fear God, to put away the wickedness that has set in and become so general, and to practice the Christian virtues. From all appearances this gentleman does not belong to the so-called world of society, for he respects God's Word, believes in the atonement through Christ, and bears himself in humility and gentleness. Therefore the Lord God has also singularly, yea, marvelously, preserved him from harm in the midst of countless perils, ambuscades, fatigues, etc., and has hitherto graciously held him in his hand as a chosen vessel.[45]

The diary does not indicate how the pastor learned of Washington's actions or the more personal things about his private beliefs, but it might well have been from either a parishioner or his eldest son, John Peter Gabriel Muhlenberg, who was at Valley Forge that difficult winter.[46]

Washington not only ordered, but also attended religious services held out of gratitude for favorable events in the Revolution. For example, in the spring of 1776, after British forces left the city of Boston, following months of siege by the Americans, the citizens resumed the tradition of having a "Thursday lecture," which had existed from the time of the city's founding until the British occupation. George Washington and his staff were invited and they gathered at the council chamber, "from whence, preceded by the sheriff with his wand, attended by the members of the council, who have had the small-pox [there was an epidemic in the city at the time], the committee of the House of Representatives, the selectmen, the clergy, and many other gentlemen, they repaired to the old brick meeting-house [First Church]." The speaker that day was the Reverend Dr. Andrew Eliot, who took as his text Isaiah 33:20, comparing the experience of Boston with that of Jerusalem. Following "divine service," the gentlemen, including Washington, went to a nearby tavern for "an elegant dinner," at which "Joy and gratitude sat in every countenance, and smiled in every eye."[47] According to an army surgeon who was there at the time, it was Washington who specifically asked Dr. Eliot "to preach a thanksgiving sermon, adapted to the joyful occasion."[48]

It wasn't just among his own soldiers that Washington espoused the practice of religion, and more specifically, Christianity. He also showed that he had no qualms about using the government to promote this course of action. He had first come to know Native Americans on the Virginia frontier during a surveying expedition, when he was a teenager. Later, as a young officer in the French and Indian War, as well as during the Revolution, his interactions with native people became more frequent, as he both wooed some groups as allies and fought others in the forest. Several years into the War for Independence, when members of the Delaware nation brought three of the children of their principal chiefs to be educated by the colonists, Washington welcomed the children and assured the tribe that Congress would provide for their education. He went on to say that, "My ears hear with pleasure the other matters you mention. Congress will be glad to hear them too. You do well to wish to learn our arts and ways of life, and above all, the religion of Jesus Christ. These will make you a greater and happier people than you are. Congress will do every thing they can to assist you in this wise intention."[49]

By the end of the Revolution, it was clear that there was a definite religious cast to George Washington's picture of what life in the United States, not just his army, should be about and that it involved both freedom to practice one's faith, whatever it was, as well as the need for religion in the life of the people making up this new nation. He saw the war itself as having a much bigger purpose than simply winning independence from the mother country. When he announced the close of active hostilities in the last year of the war (it would be several months before the final peace treaty was signed), Washington tried to share with his soldiers his belief that what they had just accomplished meant more than just cutting ties with the mother country, or, as he phrased it, that they "might be impressed with a proper idea of the dignifyed part they have been called to act (under the smiles of providence) on the stage of human affairs." Anyone who had a part, however lowly, should be very happy "in erecting this steubendous *fabrick* of *Freedom* and *Empire* on the broad basis of Independency . . . in protecting the rights of humane nature and establishing an Asylum for the poor and oppressed of all nations and religions."[50] In one of his most frequently quoted statements, taken from a letter written just two months later, Washington painted a picture of a land blessed by God with a generous and cooperative citizenry:

> I now make it my earnest prayer, that God would have you, and the State over which you preside, in his holy protection, that he would incline the hearts of the Citizens to cultivate a spirit of subordination and obedience to Government, to entertain a brotherly affection and love for one another, for their fellow Citizens of the United States at large, and particularly for their brethren who have served in the Field, and finally, that he would most graciously be pleased to dispose us all, to do Justice, to love mercy, and to demean ourselves with that Charity, humility and pacific temper of mind, which were the Characteristicks of the Divine Author of our blessed Religion, and without an humble imitation of whose example in these things, we can never hope to be a happy Nation.[51]

The circular was widely published in newspapers throughout the country and served to further enhance Washington's reputation. When he read these last words of what he described as Washington's "very grave and important" address, Pastor Henry Melchior Muhlenberg responded in his journal, "How sublime and splendid is the character of a genuine Christian! . . . How rare are such true professions in the present generation of this so-called great world!"[52]

One "side effect" of the American Revolution had been the spread of ideas about liberty, including religious liberty, throughout Europe, as foreign officers who had served with the Continental Army returned to their homes and sought to effect change there. Knowing Washington's interest in the subject of religious freedom, his younger friend and protégé, the Marquis de Lafayette, kept the man he considered his adopted father informed about measures he was taking in France to improve conditions for the Protestant minority in that country in the years between the American and French Revolutions. Since 1685, the Huguenots had been "deprived of all religious and civil liberties," after the king, Louis XIV, revoked the 1598 Edict of Nantes, which had given them a great deal of religious freedom. These restrictions had been responsible for the emigration of over 400,000 Huguenots, who left France primarily for England, Prussia, Holland, and the New World.[53] Lafayette initially informed Washington about the problems he saw in the spring of 1785, in a letter written in code because of its sensitivity:

> [Protestants] in [France] are under intolerable [Despotism]—altho' oppen ersecution does not now Exist, yet it depends upon the whim of [king]; [queen], [Parliament], or any of [the ministers]—marriages are not legal among them—their wills Have no force By law—their children are to Be Bastards—their parsons to Be Hanged—I Have put it into My Head to Be a [Leader] in that affair, and to Have their Situation changed—with the view I am Going, under other pretences to Visit their chief places of abode . . . it is a Work of time, and of Some danger to me. . . . But I Run My chance. . . . Don't Answer me about it, only that You Had my Ciphered letter By M. [John Quincy] Adams—But when in the Course of the fall or winter You will Hear of Some thing that Way, I wanted You to know I Had an Hand in it.[54]

Washington responded with a note of caution on the need to move carefully on this matter, reminding the young man that "it is a part of the military art to reconnoiter & feel your way, before you engage too deeply." Ever the realist, he went on, "More is oftentimes effected by regular approaches, than by an open assault; from the first too, you may make a good retreat—from the latter (in case of repulse) it rarely happens."⁵⁵ About a year later, Lafayette reported that he had "Great Hopes to See the affairs of the Protestants in this Kingdom put on a Better footing—not Such by far as it ought to Be—But Much Mended from the Absurd, and Cruel laws of lewis the fourteenth."⁵⁶ Finally, in February of 1788, he proudly informed Washington that, "The Edi[c]t Giving to the Non Catholic Subjects of the king a Civil Estate Has Been Registered. . . . I was well pleased last Sunday in introducing to a Ministerial table the first protestant Clergyman Who Could Appear at Versailles Since the Revolution of 1685."⁵⁷

Washington was certainly aware of arguments against liberty of conscience. Shortly after the close of the Revolution, he was contacted by Jonathan Boucher, the Anglican minister who had schooled his stepson, Jack Custis, many years before. In a letter to Washington in the spring of 1784, this staunch Loyalist, who had moved back to England, argued for the maintenance of a state church. Boucher wanted Washington to "do something for the Religious Interests of your Countrymen" and specifically mentioned his concerns that "your Countrymen" "can neither be so good nor so happy as They have been, if They are not so religious." Comparing "Many of the Speculations which the late unsettled Times have given Birth to" to Washington's "Persimmons before the Frost," which were "Fair to the Eye & specious; but really disgusting & dangerous," he went on to specifically focus on notions of religious equality, something he found "romantic & mischievous in the Extreme . . . suffice it, for the present, to remind You, that the Practice of the whole World is against You. . . . I hardly know a Point more capable of Demonstration—from History & Experience—than this is, that, to secure permanent national Felicity, some permanent national Religion is absolutely necessary." Boucher went on to say that he hoped Virginia and Maryland would not be swayed by talk of equality among the various religious groups and denominations and to express his belief that they "certainly would not," if a state church was "espoused & patronized by a Person that is popular." He then pointedly noted that, "It is in this Light I view You." That Washington failed to answer this letter probably says a great deal about his reaction to the minister's suggestions.⁵⁸

Some of the conflicts between Washington's desire to promote religion in public life, while not infringing on the rights of each individual to make their own choice in religious matters, can be seen in his response to a proposal known as the General Assessment. In the years just after the Revolution, the Virginia legislature discussed the institution of a tax that would have allowed citizens of the state to see that a proportion of their local taxes was given to the church of their choice. Some very prominent statesmen supported this measure, including Patrick Henry, Edmund Randolph, and Washington's boyhood friend, Richard Henry Lee, who wrote of the proposal:

> I conceive that the Gen. Assessment, and a wise digest of our militia laws are very important concerns: the one to secure our peace, and the other our morals. . . . the experience of all times Shows Religion to be the guardian of morals—and he must be a very inattentive observer in our Country, who does not see that avarice is accomplishing the destruction of religion, for want of a legal obligation to contribute something to its support. The declaration of Rights, it seems to me, rather contends against forcing modes of faith and form of worship, than against compelling contribution for the support of religion in general. I fully agree with the Presbyterians, that true freedom embraces the Mahomitan and the Gentoo as well as the Christian religion. And upon this liberal ground I hope our Assembly will conduct themselves.[59]

Washington's longtime neighbor, George Mason, and his young friend, James Madison, vigorously opposed any attempts to make the citizens of Virginia pay taxes to provide teachers and ministers for the church. Washington could see their point, but disagreed to a certain extent. He assured Mason:

> Altho' no mans sentiments are more opposed to *any kind* of restraint upon religious principles than mine are; yet I must confess, that I am not amongst the number of those who are so much alarmed at the thoughts of making people pay towards the support of that which they profess, if of the denominations of Christians; or declare themselves Jews, Mahomitans or otherwise, & thereby obtain proper relief.[60]

In other words, believers in whatever faith should put their money where their hearts and souls were. Washington noted, however, that, for political reasons, he wished the bill to support the church had never been brought up and hoped it would die a quiet death. He feared that such a law would be "impolitic," because, even though it was supported by a majority of the people, it was viewed with "disgust" by "a respectable minority," including his two friends, Mason and Madison.[61]

Washington's efforts to get the government involved in support for missions among Native Americans continued during the years between the end of the Revolution and the beginning of his presidency. About a year after his return from the war, Washington was contacted by Britain's Countess of Huntingdon concerning her regret "that so little pains have been taken to bring [Native Americans] from darkness to light, to make them Christians, and good and useful Citizens." She asked his support for her scheme of settling pious Christians from Europe among the tribes on the frontier, noting that she was aware of his wish to retire from public life, but was "confident the Design will not want any assistance you can give it." The countess then hit him with both barrels, writing that she was "confident of this, because I am confident that the man who is the Christian & the Soldier cannot be insensible to the duty and to the glory of extending the knowledge of religion and Civil Life to heathen & savage Nations; and of making useful Arts and peaceable industry flourish where ignorance & barbarity now prevail."[62] In a long letter, Washington replied that the countess's plans "meet my highest approbation; & I should be very happy to find every possible encouragement given to them." He went on to say:

> It has ever been my opinion, since I have had opportunities to observe, & to reflect upon the ignorance, indolence & general pursuits of the Indians, that all attempts to reclaim, & introduce any system of religeon or morality among them, would prove fruitless, until they could be first brought into a state of greater civilization; at least that this attempt should accompany the other—& be enforced by example: & I am happy to find that it is made the groundwork of your Ladyships plan.[63]

When he forwarded the countess's letters and accompanying materials to the president of Congress, Washington wrote that he found the plan "not only unexceptionable in its design and tendency, but [it] has humanity & charity for its object—and may, as I conceive, be made subservient to valuable political purposes." In discussing the pros and cons of the plan, he admitted that he could see only one detrimental aspect—the fact that it involved bringing a large number of Europeans into the country, "who may bring with them strong prejudices against us, and our forms of Government; and equally strong attachments to the Country & constitution they leave; without the means, being detached & unmixed with Citizens of different sentiments, of having them eradicated." Washington also noted that he had written the countess that, although "it would by no means comport with the plan of retirement I had promised myself, to take an active or responsible part in this business," that he "would give every aid in my power consistent with that ease, & tranquillity I meant to devote the remainder of my life [to,] to facilitate her views."[64] Several months later, after Congress reacted negatively to the countess's plan, Washington wrote her to "express my concern that your Ladyships humane & benevolent views are not better seconded."[65]

After a brief respite of only three years, Washington was called back into public life, first as president of the Constitutional Convention, and then, two years later, as the first president of the United States. While he continued to encourage his fellow citizens in the practice of their religious beliefs, freedom of religion became an even more important issue. The Constitution produced under his leadership specified that "no religious Test shall ever be required as a Qualification to any Office or public Trust under the United States," opening public office to anyone, regardless of their beliefs, or lack thereof.[66] The ecumenicity that had been such a prominent part of Washington's private personality was quite visibly shown in the official procession at his first inauguration. At this point, the Jewish population in the United States was very small. Numbering perhaps 1,500 to 2,500 people at the time of the Revolution—or less than one-half of 1 percent of the total white population in the thirteen British colonies—the few Jews in the country still faced some of the same long-standing resentments they had experienced in Europe. The fact that most supported the American cause during the struggle for independence may have played a part in raising their community in the eyes of their fellow citizens.[67] Among the thirteen clergymen who took part in the ceremonies on that day was Gershom Mendes Seixas, the *hazzan,* or cantor, for Congregation Shearith Israel in New York City and a trustee of Columbia College.[68]

About a year later, Washington made one of his most important public statements on the subject of religious freedom to another Jewish community. During George Washington's official tour of Rhode Island in the summer of 1790, Moses Seixas, a merchant and fellow Freemason, who was the warden of Congregation Yeshuat Israel in Newport, initially addressed the president on behalf of his fellow congregants. After welcoming Washington to the city, Seixas, who had been a "quasi-Loyalist" during the Revolution, looked back on those difficult days, when God "shielded your head in the day of battle," and rejoiced in the thought that the deity was still looking out for the "Chief Magistrate in these States." He went on to remind Washington that the congregation had previously been "Deprived . . . of the invaluable rights of free Citizens" and now saw the new government, "whose basis is Philanthropy, Mutual Confidence and Publick Virtue" as the work of "the Great God, who ruleth in the Armies Of Heaven and among the Inhabitants of the Earth, doing whatever seemeth him good." Seixas concluded by thanking God for "all the Blessings of civil and religious liberty which we enjoy under an equal and benign administration" and added a plea for divine blessings on Washington himself, together with the hope that, "when like Joshua full of days and full of honour, you are gathered to your Fathers, may you be admitted into the Heavenly Paradise to partake of the water of life, and the tree of immortality."[69] In response, Washington noted his appreciation for these "expressions of affection and esteem" and assured the congregation that they could expect safety and continued freedom in the future:

> The Citizens of the United States of America have a right to applaud themselves for having given to mankind examples of an enlarged and liberal policy: a policy worthy of imitation. All possess alike liberty of conscience and immunities of citizenship. It is now no more that toleration is spoken of, as if it was by the indulgence of one class of people, that another enjoyed the exercise of their inherent natural rights. For happily the Government of the United States, which gives to bigotry no sanction, to persecution no assistance requires only that they who live under its protection should demean themselves as good citizens, in giving it on all occasions their effectual support.[70]

Washington closed his response with a benediction: "May the father of all mercies scatter light and not darkness in our paths, and make us all in our several vocations useful here, and in his own due time and way everlastingly happy."[71]

Washington elaborated on these ideas to other religious groups that had experienced varying degrees of persecution in both Europe and America.

Shortly after his inauguration, the General Assembly of the Presbyterian Church wrote a flattering letter, in which they commented on "the piety" of Washington's character. Having stated that "Public virtue is the most certain means of public felicity, and religion is the surest basis of virtue," sentiments with which Washington would have agreed, they assured him that they were especially happy to have a leader who was "steady, uniform, [an] avowed friend of the christian religion, who has commenced his administration in rational and exalted sentiments of Piety, and who in his private conduct adorns the doctrines of the Gospel of Christ, and on the most public and solemn occasions devoutly acknowledges the government of divine Providence."[72] In his response to this group, Washington enumerated all the elements necessary to promote the welfare and happiness of the country, as well as the duties of religious people as citizens:

> While I reiterate the possession of my dependence upon Heaven as the source of all public and private blessings; I will observe that the general prevalence of piety, philanthropy, honesty, industry and oeconomy seems, in the ordinary course of human affairs are particularly necessary for advancing and confirming the happiness of our country. While all men within our territories are protected in worshipping the Deity according to the dictates of their consciences; it is rationally to be expected from them in return, that they will be emulous of evincing the sincerity of their profession by the innocence of their lives, and the beneficence of their actions: For no man, who is profligate in his morals, or a bad member of the civil community, can possibly be a true Christian, or a credit to his own religious society.[73]

He wrapped up with his thanks to the group for their "laudible endeavors to render men sober, honest, and good Citizens, and the obedient subjects of a lawful government," an interesting and telling phrase given his own recent rebellion against a government he had felt was not legitimate. The closing was revealing, as well, about how Washington saw himself, as he thanked the Assembly "for your prayers to Almighty God for his blessing on our common country and the humble instrument [himself], which he has been pleased to make use of in the administration of it's government."[74]

Later that same year, a letter from the ministers and elders representing the Presbyterian churches in Massachusetts and New Hampshire began an exchange that allowed Washington to elaborate his views on the differing roles of religious groups and the government. The Presbyterians began by congratulating both him and the country on the blessing they had received through his election to the presidency and went on to state that any qualms they might have had about the form of the new government were now eased. They took care to mention, however, that they would like to have seen some sort of specifically Christian statement in the Constitution, which had been produced by a national convention headed by Washington: "Among these [possible objections to the Constitution] we never considered the want of *a religious test* [for public office], that grand engine of persecution in every tyrant's hand: But we should not have been alone in rejoicing to have seen some Explicit acknowledgement of the *only true God and Jesus Christ, whom he hath sent* inserted some where in the *Magna Charta* of our country." They wrote that Washington himself had "amply remedied" this omission, "in the face of all the world, by the piety and devotion, in which your first public act of office was performed—by the religious observance of the Sabbath, and of the public worship of God, of which you have set so eminent an example—and by the warm strains of christian and devout affections, which run through your late proclamation, for a general thanksgiving."[75] In his response, Washington very graciously thanked the group, but gently reminded them that the government was going to stay out of religion, not promoting any particular one but basically encouraging all, while it would leave to religious leaders the task of converting the citizens:

> The path of true piety is so plain as to require but little political direction.
> To this consideration we ought to ascribe the absence of any regulation,
> respecting religion, from the Magna-Charta of our country.
>
> To the guidance of the ministers of the gospel this important object
> is, perhaps, more properly committed—It will be your care to instruct the
> ignorant, and to reclaim the devious—and, in the progress of morality
> and science, to which our government will give every furtherance, we may
> confidently expect the advancement of true religion, and the completion of
> our happiness.[76]

Washington closed with a prayer to "the munificent Rewarder of virtue that your agency in this good work may receive its compensation here and hereafter."[77] Several years later, to a Swedenborgian congregation in Baltimore, Washington wrote that America had used the "light of truth and reason" to triumph over "the power of bigotry and superstition." Noting that "every person may here worship God according to the dictates of his own heart," Washington boasted that the United States was a place where "a man's religious tenets will not forfeit the protection of the laws, nor deprive him of the right of attaining and holding the highest offices that are known."[78]

As the country's new leader, Washington's views on religious freedom were an issue of great concern to a number of religious groups in the country. Shortly after his inauguration as president, for example, Washington received an address from the United Baptist Churches in Virginia, a group that had undergone considerable persecution in the decade before the American Revolution. Arguing that their authority to preach came from God, not the colonial government, Baptist ministers were jailed in Fredericksburg, Virginia, in June of 1768, and over the next few years in Culpeper, and in Caroline, Chesterfield, Essex, Fauquier, Middlesex, Orange, and Spotsylvania Counties, where they continued to preach through their prison bars. Some were dragged from their pulpits and threatened with death, others were beaten, scourged, slashed with knives, and ordered to leave the area.[79] This persecution drove home to a number of the Virginia Founding Fathers, including Patrick Henry, Thomas Jefferson, James Madison, and George Mason, the need for government to explicitly recognize freedom of religion.[80]

As Madison wrote to a friend in 1774:

> That diabolical, hell-conceived principle of persecution rages among some, and, to their eternal infamy the clergy can furnish their quota of imps for such purposes. This vexes me the worst of anything whatever. There are at this time in the adjacent country not less than five or six well-meaning men in close jail for publishing their religious sentiments, which, in the main, are very orthodox.... So I must beg you to ... pray for liberty of conscience to all.[81]

Two years later, Madison's lobbying was largely responsible for the inclusion of the Sixteenth Article in the Virginia Declaration of Rights, which states: "Religion, or the duty which we owe our Creator, and the manner of discharging it, can be directed by reason and conviction, not by force or violence; and, therefore, all men are equally entitled to the free exercise of religion according to the dictates of conscience, and that it is the mutual duty of all to practice Christian forbearance, love, and charity towards each other."[82]

When the Virginia Baptists wrote to Washington at the beginning of his presidency, they elaborated on their fears upon reading the Constitution of 1787. Although it did not guarantee their right to worship freely, they also acknowledged their trust that Washington would be the first person to hold the office of president and that he would protect them from intolerance in the future:

> When the constitution first made its appearance in Virginia, we, as a Society, had unusual strugglings of mind; fearing that *the liberty of conscience,* dearer to us than property or life, was not sufficiently secured. Perhaps our jealousies were heightened on account of the usage that we received under the royal government, when Mobs, Bonds, Fines, and Prisons were our frequent attendants. . . . But amidst all the inquietudes of mind, our consolation arose from this consideration "The plan must be good for it bears the signature of a tried, trusty friend"—and if religious liberty is rather insecure, "The administration will certainly prevent all oppression for a Washington will preside"—According to our wishes the unanimous voice of the Union has called you, Sir.[83]

In his response, Washington spoke of the "horrors of spiritual tyranny" and sought to reassure the Baptists that he understood their concerns and was willing to do more in the future to protect everyone's freedom of conscience in matters of religion:

> If I could have entertained the slightest apprehension, that the constitution framed in the convention, where I had the honor to preside, might possibly endanger the religious rights of any ecclesiastical society, certainly I would never have placed my signature to it. . . . For you doubtless remember, that I have often expressed my sentiments, that every man, conducting himself as a good citizen, and being accountable to God alone for his religious opinions, ought to be protected in worshipping the Deity according to the dictates of his own conscience.[84]

About this same time, Washington was contacted by the Quakers, a denomination whose beliefs and customs—especially pacifism—had put them at odds with their countrymen in the past.[85] The new president reassured them of his belief that, among its other purposes, government was intended "to protect the Persons and Consciences of men from oppression" and that leaders were "not only to abstain from it [oppression] themselves, but according to their Stations, to prevent it in others." As with the Baptists, he took care that the Quakers would understand his commitment to religious liberty:

> The liberty enjoyed by the People of these States, of worshipping Almighty God agreable to their Consciences, is not only among the choicest of their *Blessings,* but also of their *Rights*—While men perform their social Duties faithfully, they do all that Society or the State can with propriety demand or expect; and remain responsible only to their Maker for the Religion or modes of faith which they may prefer or profess.[86]

He closed with the assurance that "in my opinion the Consciencious scruples of all men should be treated with great delicacy & tenderness, and it is my wish and desire that the Laws may always be as extensively accomodated to them, as a due regard to the Protection and essential Interests of the Nation may Justify and permit."[87]

Roman Catholic leaders approached Washington on a similar mission in the late winter of 1790 to remind him that they had "a well founded title to claim . . . equal rights of citizenship, as the price of our blood spilled under your eyes, and of our common exertions for her [the country's] defence . . . rights rendered more dear to us by the remembrance of former hardships." They told the president that they prayed for the preservation of those rights they had achieved and "expect the full extension of them from the justice of those States, which still restrict them."[88] Washington responded that he fully expected those rights to be extended:

> As mankind become more liberal they will be more apt to allow, that those who conduct themselves as worthy members of the Community are equally entitled to the protection of civil Government. I hope ever to see America among the foremost nations in examples of justice and liberality. And I presume that your fellow-citizens will not forget the patriotic part which you took in the accomplishment of their Revolution, and the establishment of their Government: or the important assistance which they received from a nation in which the Roman Catholic faith is professed [France]. . . . May the members of your Society in America, animated alone by the pure spirit

of Christianity, and still conducting themselves as the faithful subjects of our free Government, enjoy every temporal and spiritual felicity.[89]

It was during Washington's first year as president that the Bill of Rights was proposed by Congress to enumerate the rights of American citizens and allay some of their fears under the new Constitution. In the preamble, Congress noted that this action was being taken in response to requests by a number of state ratifying conventions, which, at the time they approved the Constitution, had "expressed a desire, in order to prevent miscon-struction or abuse of its [the Constitution's] powers, that further declara-tory and restrictive clauses should be added" and to extend "the ground of public confidence in the government." Ratified by the states two years later, the first clause in the first of those ten original amendments specifi-cally guaranteed freedom of religion from any kind of federal government control: "Congress shall make no law respecting an establishment of reli-gion, or prohibiting the free exercise thereof; or abridging the freedom of speech, or of the press; or the right of the people peaceably to assemble, and to petition the Government for a redress of grievances."[90]

The passage of this important document took away the possibility that a future leader, who was not "a Washington," might revert to the idea of a state church, under which nonconformists could be victimized.

A treaty, negotiated with a Muslim power in North Africa during Washington's administration as president, can similarly be seen as an at-tempt to allay fears or concerns held by followers of another religion, in this case, Islam. Article 11 of the Treaty of Peace and Friendship with the Bey and Subjects of Tripoli states in its entirety:

> As the government of the United States of America is not in any sense
> founded on the Christian Religion,—as it has in itself no character of
> enmity against the laws, religion or tranquility of Musselmen,—and as the
> said States never have entered into any war or act of hostility against any
> Mehomitan nation, it is declared by the parties that no pretext arising from
> religious opinions shall ever produce an interruption of the harmony exist-
> ing between the two countries.[91]

The treaty was signed in Tripoli on November 4, 1796, and in Algiers on January 3, 1797. It was presented to the Senate on May 29, 1797, almost three months after Washington's retirement from the presidency and ratified by the United States on June 10th of the same year. The first clause of this section is often singled out for quotation, without the rest of the paragraph that puts it in context, and erroneously attributed to Washington by those who would like to see him as an unbeliever. Actually, it was quite likely the work of Joel Barlow, a poet and former Congregationalist chaplain in the Continental Army, who later served his country as a diplomat.[92] Washington knew Barlow slightly and had a good opinion of his abilities, writing shortly after learning of the younger man's arrival in Algiers as the U.S. consul, that "It has ever been my opinion from the little I have seen, and from what I have heard of Mr. Barlow, that his abilities are adequate to any employment; and, improved as they must have been by travel and the political career he has run, there can be little doubt of his fitness as a negotiator for some of the Countries above mentioned, with proper instructions."[93]

Writing several years later of Barlow's negotiations with the Barbary States, Washington offered his belief that the diplomat had discharged the functions "at that time with ability and propriety."[94] Although Washington was no longer president at the time of the treaty's submission for ratification, and it was signed by his successor, John Adams, it would appear, given his statement to the Presbyterians about the differing roles of the government and religious groups, that he would very much have agreed with the sentiment that the United States government was not based on the Christian religion.

As head of the civilian government, Washington continued, as he had during the Revolution, to encourage his countrymen to thank God for his many blessings to them. During his first year as president, Washington sent a confidential note to James Madison, seeking his advice on whether to ask the Senate for their opinions on a number of questions, including "a day of thanksgiving."[95] When the issue was presented to Congress, debate followed, in which critics faulted the proposal as smacking too much of European tradition and that it was "a business with which Congress have nothing to do; it is a religious matter, and, as such, is proscribed to us. If a day of thanksgiving must take place, let it be done by the authority of the several States." Supporters of the proclamation countered with precedents set both in the Bible and by the Continental Congress, and eventually prevailed.[96] On October 3, 1789, Washington issued the United States' first Thanksgiving Proclamation, ordering that Thursday, November 26th, "be devoted . . . to the service of that great and glorious Being, who is the beneficent Author of all the good that was, that is, or that will be."

Washington sent the proclamation to each state governor, with the request that they make it "known in your State in the way and manner that shall be most agreeable to yourself." The proclamation was widely published, both in newspapers and as a broadside, and many churches announced that they were using this occasion to take up special collections for the poor. After learning about one of these collections, the President sent $25 to the pastor of the two Presbyterian churches in New York "to be applied towards releiving the poor of the Presbyterian Churches."[97] Several years later, on January 1, 1795, Washington proclaimed that Thursday, February 19th, of that year was to be a "Day of Public Thanksgiving and Prayer." When the day arrived, he attended special services at Christ Church in Philadelphia, at which William White, the Episcopal bishop of Pennsylvania, preached a sermon on the "Connection between Religion and Civil Happiness."[98]

In his official capacity as president, Washington extended government support to missionary work among Native Americans, as part of an overall plan to encourage them to take up the settled, agricultural way of life shared by the majority of the citizens of the United States. He wrote to one Christian group shortly after his inauguration that "In proportion as the general Government of the United States shall acquire strength by duration, it is probable they may have it in their power to extend a salutary influence to the Aborigines in the extremities of their Territory. In the meantime, it will be a desirable thing for the protection of the Union to co-operate, as far as circumstances may conveniently admit, with the disinterested endeavours of your Society to civilize and Christianize the Savages of the Wilderness."[99]

In October of 1791, in an address to the Senate and House of Representatives, Washington noted that "considerable numbers of individuals" from tribes that had formerly been hostile to the United States had "lately renounced all further opposition, removed from their former situations, and placed themselves under the immediate protection of the United States." He then expressed a desire "that all need of coertion, in future, may cease; and that an intimate intercourse may succeed; calculated to advance the happiness of the Indians, and to attach them firmly to the United States." After outlining his plan for dealing justly with the native peoples, Washington reminded his listeners that, "A System corrisponding with the mild principles of religion and philanthropy towards an un-enlightened race of men, whose happiness materially depends on the conduct of the United States, would be as honorable to the national character as conformable to the dictates of sound policy."[100]

Largely in response to this address, Washington was contacted by Roman Catholic priest John Carroll in March of 1792 "on the subject of the instructing the Indians within, and contiguous to the United States, in the principles and duties of christianity." While noting that some tribes were then unreachable because of their active state of hostility with the new government, and that certain other individuals or entities seemed to have jurisdiction over particular groups of Indians, Washington praised Carroll's intentions:

> Impressed as I am with an opinion, that the most effectual means of securing the permanent attachment of our savage neighbors, is to convince them that we are just, and to shew them that a proper and friendly intercourse with us would be for our mutual advantage: I cannot conclude without giving you my thanks for your pious and benevolent wishes to effect this desirable end, upon the mild principles of Religion and Philanthropy. And when a proper occasion shall offer, I have no doubt but such measures will be pursued as may seem best calculated to communicate liberal instruction, and the blessings of society, to their untutored minds.[101]

Ironically, in the decades ahead, many native peoples, especially in the southeastern United States, took up Washington's challenge to learn a new way of life and adopt the culture of their Anglo-American neighbors. While Washington seems to have encouraged this major change, in order to include and possibly assimilate Native Americans into the population of the new country—again using religion as a means of unifying—later presidents would feel that the only way to protect them from annihilation was to remove them from contact with white settlers, across the Mississippi River. But that is a story for another book.

10

CONCLUSIONS

Washington's and Others'

EORGE AND MARTHA Washington died within two and a half years of one another, he on the evening of December 14, 1799, after suffering a short, but virulent illness, and she on the afternoon of May 22, 1802, following a more than two-week-long ordeal. The main description of George Washington's last hours comes from the pen of his longtime secretary and friend, Tobias Lear, who recorded not one mention of any conversations or acts relating to religion in his seemingly blow-by-blow account.[1] The problem is that Lear's account, while very full, may well not tell everything that went on that day. Other than a brief exchange, during which Washington sent his wife to his office to bring the two versions of his will stored there and then directed which one should be burned, Lear neglected to record any other conversation between these two people, who had been devoted to one another for forty years. Neither is there a recorded conversation of a personal nature between Washington and the senior doctor on his case, James Craik, who had been his close friend since the French and Indian War.

In his discussion of the events of the evening before Washington's death, when the symptoms of his fatal illness were just beginning to appear, Lear noted that at about nine o'clock, Mrs. Washington went upstairs to spend a little time with her youngest granddaughter, Nelly Custis Lewis, who was recovering from the birth of her first child.[2] George Washington continued reading with and talking to Lear, before going up himself.

Lear never mentioned that Washington, too, seems to have gone to Nelly's room to see the baby, a fact attested to many years later by Frances Parke Lewis Butler, who wrote, "I was born at Mt. Vernon, on the 27th of Nov. 1799—seventeen days before Gen. Washington's death, and the night before he died he gave me the last blessing he ever gave to any one."[3]

Those who doubt George Washington's Christianity often cite Lear's account and the fact that it recorded no prayers being said, no death-bed confession of faith, and no minister being called to the bedside. They do not take into account that Lear's record, as wonderful as it is, is very likely not complete.[4] They also overlook the virulence of the infection that killed Washington in less than twenty-four hours, and what quite possibly no one in that room—except Washington—was ready to believe, until almost the very end, when it would be too late to get a minister there: that the illness was going to be fatal. Regarding the last point, they forget that Washington did not belong to a church that required the presence of a priest to give last rites at a deathbed. At this point, Washington was surrounded with people who, for the most part, had known him for years and would have been familiar with his beliefs. There was no need for a confession of faith, especially given the fact that Washington could barely talk.

As far as prayers are concerned, Martha Washington's grandson later indicated that his grandmother was in the room, praying silently, throughout her husband's final illness.[5] Granted, the young man was away from Mount Vernon at the time of the death, did not write his account until many years later, and had a tendency to romanticize. He also, however, had had plenty of time to talk to those who actually were in the room to learn what had happened. It is also possible that George Washington, who could barely speak throughout his last hours, might have been praying silently. He and Mrs. Washington may well have prayed and talked about end-of-life issues in the three or more hours between when he woke his wife to tell her that he was very ill and the time the maid came into the room to light the fire and was sent for help. There is simply no way to know what Lear might have left out.

At least one historian, who has looked into the matter of George Washington's death and what it can tell us about his religious beliefs, has suggested that, rather than Christian, Washington's final hours show a strong influence of Stoic philosophy. It has even been suggested that, in this matter, Washington was following the example of his patrons, the Fair-

fax family at nearby Belvoir Plantation.⁶ These assertions are interesting
in light of the fact that the surviving books from Washington's library at
the Boston Athenaeum include about fifty volumes on various aspects of
religion and only one on philosophy, *Seneca's Morals* by Roger L'Estrange,
which was published in London in 1746 and acquired by Washington
about 1749. The overwhelming preponderance of books dealing with religion perhaps points to a much greater interest on Washington's part in
that subject than he had in philosophy—and certainly to much greater
exposure and influence.⁷ Stoicism was also not incompatible with Christianity, as evidenced by the work of late sixteenth- and early seventeenth-
century scholars known as the Christian Stoics, "who sought to reconcile
the teachings of ancient Stoicism with their own Christianity to produce
a credible religion."⁸

Contrary to the assertions of recent scholars, the Fairfaxes were a devout
Anglican/Episcopal family. As noted earlier in this work, it was the patriarch, Col. William Fairfax, who congratulated George Washington enthusiastically upon learning that the younger man had led a Sunday service
at which there were several Native Americans present. Many years before,
Colonel Fairfax had confided to his mother that he "often wished that I had
been a Parson." He noted in other letters to her that he "intend[ed] with
God's leave to make another trial of interest in England" and expressed his
"trust in God [that] I shall never procure the disesteem of any relation."
On another occasion, upon being separated from his wife for a brief time,
Fairfax wrote that "Yet I trust in God, she will not want any thing to comfort her sorrows."⁹ Colonel Fairfax not only expressed his religious beliefs
privately, but also served publicly as a vestryman for his local parish.¹⁰

There is also evidence to suggest that several of the Fairfax children
were orthodox Christians. Oldest son George William Fairfax, like his
friend of many years, George Washington, served as a vestryman and
churchwarden at Pohick Church from 1757 until 1773.¹¹ He also imported
two prayer books and a Bible for the use of the parish and purchased a
pew in the new church.¹² After moving to England a few years before
the start of the Revolution, George William maintained his friendship
with George Washington until his death in 1787. Washington learned of
his friend's passing in a letter from a British merchant, who had visited
Fairfax during his final illness. The Englishman wanted Washington to
know that he had witnessed Fairfax's "Firmness of Mind & christian patience with which he sustained his Malady; they continued with him to

the last, & the Remembrance of them to those of his Friends who were admitted to the Scene will serve as an Example & Admonition, & to those who were not the Reflection upon them may alleviate their Sorrow for his Departure."[13]

George William's younger sister, Sarah Fairfax, was married to Alexandria merchant John Carlyle. Shortly after their engagement, Carlyle wrote to his brother back in Scotland about the virtues of his betrothed, confiding that, "A Woman of A Virginia Education [upbringing] I Always Was Afraid of [but] The young Lady that I Am under Ingagmts with [engaged to] has had A Good, Relegious one."[14] Carlyle's assessment of his fiancée is backed up by a letter she wrote seven years later to George Washington, who was then serving on the frontier. She expressed that, upon receiving his last letter, she felt pleasure at learning that he was in good health, but pain about the "many Risques" he faced on the battlefield. She then acknowledged her belief that "your good Constitution and a kind protecter will bring you out of them all as it has In the last Ingagement preserved you from harm." After admonishing the young man to quit moping out of homesickness, she suggested that he turn his thoughts instead to the prospect "of preserveing your Country from the Insults of an Enimy." Just before closing, she expressed the hope that "as god has blessed your first Attempt . . . he may Continew his blessings."[15]

Bryan Fairfax, the youngest son in the Belvoir family, was the one who showed the greatest evangelical leanings. As a young man, he went through a conversion experience during the French and Indian War, while serving on the Virginia frontier. Of that event, he wrote that "From twelve at night till two it was my turn to stand sentinel at a dangerous post. I had a fellow sentinel, but I desired him to go away which he willingly did. As soon as I was alone, I kneeled down, and determined not to rise, but to continue crying and wrestling with God, till he had mercy on me." A Loyalist during the American Revolution, Bryan Fairfax remained a friend to George Washington and became a minister of the new Protestant Episcopal Church in 1789. He was later described as someone who, although he preferred his own church, "was free from bigotry, and accepted the moderate Calvinistic interpretation of the thirty-nine articles." It was also said of him that, "As a preacher while not eloquent, he was logical and practical."[16] Between 1798 and 1799, Fairfax traveled to England, where he was next in line to inherit the title Baron of Cameron. As he was setting off from home, he wrote a letter to his old friend, George Washington, assuring him that "I have not ceased almost daily to pray for you for more than twenty years."[17] While in England, he came to know Lady Anne Agnes Erskine, the longtime friend and companion of the Countess of Huntingdon, and her successor as one of four trustees carrying on her evangelistic work. Noting that he considered Lady Erskine "another Sister," Bryan Fairfax enthusiastically described their time together in letters to Washington.[18] Not long after his return to America, Bryan Fairfax walked with the principal mourners at the funeral of George Washington, who bequeathed to him "a Bible in three large folio volumes, with notes, presented to me, by the Right Reverend Thomas Wilson, Bishop of Sodor and Man."[19] None of these Fairfaxes sound like people who had given up Christianity for Stoicism alone.

Given the controversy about the absence of any religious statements by the dying Washington, it might be instructive to compare his death to that of someone whose religious beliefs are not in question. Episcopal bishop William White, who had been the Washingtons' pastor during their years in Philadelphia, fell ill at the end of June 1836, but seemed to be recovering, when he had a bad fall on the night of July 2. His condition deteriorated after that mishap, and he died fifteen days later at the age of eighty-eight. The bishop was in full possession of his faculties during this period and was well aware that he was dying. According to his biographer, Bishop White

> evidently viewed it [the fact of his dying] with the composure which might be expected from the whole tenor of his life; from his having long and habitually fixed his thoughts on his approaching departure; and from the evenness and moderation of his disposition and feelings. His end was therefore marked by the serenity, and by the deep-seated and sweetly calm religious consolation and trust in the mercy of God through the Redeemer, which were in perfect consistency with his own declared principles of religion, and with the uniform character of his feelings, conversation and life.[20]

While it might seem that the only thing the bishop and Washington had in common in their deaths was their composure, there was something else as well. Particularly interesting is his biographer's description of the bishop's customary reserve on personal matters, very much like Washington's, which led him to refrain from speaking about his religious beliefs, as opposed to preaching and writing about them as part of his profession:

At no period of his life had he been disposed to speak of the influences of religion upon himself. That his heart and conduct were controlled and regulated by its principles was undoubted. But the inclinations and feelings which were the result were always of that retired and unobtrusive kind which fill and satisfy the soul, while (in the language of Scripture) "with them a stranger intermeddleth not." They were manifested only by their fruits.[21]

White's biographer suggests that this "reluctance" to talk about his beliefs should not lead one to "doubt of their existence or their power," because the "deepest and strongest feelings are less apt than others to vent themselves in words, or to excite the desire of making them subjects of discourse." He went on to remind his readers that the bishop's "aversion to every thing approaching to self display led him, from principle, to avoid this course" and that "[s]uch being his previous views and dispositions, they still continued, as might naturally be expected, to influence him during his last illness. He was not disposed, of his own accord, to speak concerning the state of his mind, his expectations or consolations." It was only when two other bishops came to visit him on his deathbed that White "spoke at all upon the subject." Prompted by his visitors, he then "fully expressed, with greater warmth and animation than it was believed his weakness would have allowed, and than was usual with him, his reliance upon the merits of the Redeemer alone for acceptance; and the comfort, the 'charming' gratification, of being enabled to trust in the divine goodness, and to realize the protecting care of God in life and in death."[22] In comparing the deathbed scenes of George Washington and Bishop White, I would submit that the two men exhibited the same "stoic" traits and the same reticence to talk about their faith, which were simply a continuation of the way they had lived their lives. Unlike the bishop, Washington had no need to make a statement of faith, because he was surrounded by people who knew him, and those beliefs, very well.

In the two years following her husband's death, Martha Washington received many letters of condolence, both from dear friends and from people she had never met. One of the first to arrive, probably among the most precious to her, came from their close friend from Philadelphia, Elizabeth Willing Powel, reminding the new widow that, "the healing Hand of Time, and pious resignation to the inscrutable decrees of God can alone tranquilize your Soul." While Mrs. Washington had "lost the man of your choice the protector and support of your declining years," she could take comfort in the belief that her late husband was "removed to regions of bliss." Mrs. Powel mentioned that she had been told that Washington "ended his glorious well spent Life," retaining to the end "the faculties of his mind," and that he had "died as he had lived like a man and christian."[23]

Some of the differences in expression between the Washingtons' Anglican/Episcopal faith and those of the more evangelical believers of the period can be found in the correspondence between Martha Washington and the daughter of a longtime friend who had married a Methodist minister several years before George Washington died. The younger woman began by reminding the new widow that "God is Wise—and He does all things Well—Submission to his Will, and a Gracious improvement of his dispensations is all he will require." She then went on to offer some advice, recommending that religion offered a promise of "happiness far beyond anything this vain World can either give or refuse." She related a little of her conversion experience, twelve years before, when she was at a stage in life "when the Whole Creation was to me a dreary void, from which I turned with disgust." Throwing herself "helpless at the Feet of Jesus The Friend of the distresed," she found that "A new Creation of Love, Peace, and Joy were opened in my Soul.—I found myself united to God" and confessed that an "earnest fever and desire for the universal Salvation of Mankind assured me [that the] law of love was written by the finger of God, in this new heart he had given me." She also wanted to reassure Martha Washington that her relation of this change in her life was not done out of "any desire to exalt myself in your estimation," but "that you may be induced to make the same surrender, and be as blessed in the event." The younger woman closed by asserting her

earnest Wish to meet you at the Right Hand of the Judge of all the Earth. With a Palm of Victory in your Hand, and your Robes Washed in the Blood of the Lamb. God bless, Comfort, sustain, and enrich you with every Grace of his Holy Spirit, bring you safely through the pangs of the New birth hereafter, crown you with Glory everlasting, in the bright region of eternal day.[24]

Martha Washington, a quintessential Virginia Anglican of the eighteenth century, seems to have had trouble relating to the emotionalism of this letter. Through a secretary, she responded by thanking the young woman for the sympathy expressed in her letter, as well as for her prayers "for my present comfort and future happiness." She noted that the "precepts of our holy Religion have long since taught me, that in the severe and trying scenes of life, our only sure Rock of comfort and consolation is the Divine Being who orders and directs all things for our good." Where the younger woman had poured out the details of her conversion, Mrs. Washington made no comment on that pivotal event in her life, but assured her of the "great pleasure" she felt "that you experience those comforts which the Scriptures promise to those who obey the Laws of God." In closing, she wrote simply, "That you may continue to enjoy the blessings of this life—and receive hereafter the portion of the Just is the prayer of your sincere friend & ob[edien]t Serv[an]t."[25]

Martha Washington's own death was quite different from that of her second husband. The illness to which she succumbed did not take away her ability to speak, so that she could converse easily with those around her. In addition, there was no doubt that she was dying, and there was ample time to call a minister. When her husband of almost forty-one years died in December of 1799, Martha Washington was sitting at the foot of his bed. According to Tobias Lear, Mrs. Washington asked "with a firm & collected voice, *Is he gone?*" Upon learning that the answer was yes, she responded, *"'Tis well . . . All is now over. I shall soon follow him! I have no more trials to pass through!"*[26] In the two years between the loss of her beloved husband and her own demise, Mrs. Washington stayed busy and continued to charm visitors to Mount Vernon, as she had for years, but she never wavered from her belief, expressed so profoundly in the first minutes after George Washington's death, that she would soon be leaving this world, as well.

By the spring of 1802, it was becoming obvious to those who knew her that Martha Washington was failing. Cornelia Lee, who was probably a friend of Mrs. Washington's grandchildren, was one of the daughters of the late William Lee of Greenspring. The young woman came to stay with the elderly widow for several days in March and recorded that they "had an agreable visit indeed." She found Mrs. Washington suffering from "a wretched cold" and thought the "poor old Lady looks badly," commenting prophetically that, "I fear she will not be long here." Apparently she told a mutual acquaintance "that Life was no longer desirable. The loss she had was such that every thing was indifferent to her."[27] By May 20th, when Philadelphian Thomas Cope came to Mount Vernon, Mrs. Washington had been seriously ill for two weeks and was confined to her bed. Dr. James Craik, who was caring for her, felt that she "has not many days to survive." Craik had finally convinced her to move from her little room on the third floor and "lodge in some other part of the house more airy & commodious," if she survived, but "of this there is little probability as her health has been wasting for the last twelve months & yesterday a chilly fit deprived her, during the paroxysm, of the power of speech." Dr. Craik feared that another seizure of that sort "must deprive her of life."[28]

More details about Martha Washington's final illness can be found in a letter written by Thomas Law, the husband of her eldest granddaughter, Eliza, to one of his sons. According to Law, Mrs. Washington had been suffering from a fever for about three weeks. Unlike her late husband, for whom the end came quickly, she had time to make preparations for her death, gathering her grandchildren around her and giving them advice, sending for the minister and taking communion, and, finally, directing "a white gown to be brought which she has previously laid by for the last dress." Law commented that "Fortitude & resignation were display'd throughout, she met death as a relief from the infirmities & melancholy of old age—all she valued in life had been take[n] from her." Her "well spent life" ended at noon on Saturday, May 22, 1802, and Law noted that, "On Tuesday I join a real mourner the solemn procession & then bid adieu to this mansion under whose hospitable roof I beheld examples of rectitude & beneficence."[29]

Grandson George Washington Parke Custis filled in further details of his grandmother's last days in a biographical sketch done many years after the fact:

Mrs. Washington became alarmingly ill from an attack of bilious fever. From her advanced age, the sorrow that had preyed upon her spirits, and the severity of the attack, the family physicians gave but little hope of a favorable issue. The lady herself was perfectly aware that her hour was nigh; she assembled her grandchildren at her bedside, discoursed to them on their respective duties through life, spoke of the happy influences of religion upon the affairs of this world, of the consolations they had afforded her in many and trying afflictions, and of the hopes they held out of a blessed immortality; and then surrounded by her weeping relatives, friends, and domestics, the venerable relict of Washington resigned her life into the hands of her Creator, in the seventy-first year of her age.[30]

Both George and Martha Washington began their wills with the words, "In the name of God amen." The couple also took care to provide for certain charitable concerns after their lifetimes. In addition to leaving his entire estate to his widow and freeing those slaves who belonged to him, George Washington left money for several educational institutions, including a gift of twenty shares of his stock in the Bank of Alexandria, valued at about $4,000, to support "a Free school" in that city for the education of "Orphan children, or the children of such other poor and indigent persons as are unable to accomplish it with their own means; and who, in the judgment of the Trustees of the said Seminary, are best entitled to the benefit of this donation." In her will, Martha Washington made a bequest of £100 to the vestry of Truro Parish for the purchase of a glebe, or parsonage.[31]

News of George and Martha Washington's deaths went around the country by letter and newspaper. One of the earliest is particularly interesting for the light it sheds on Washington's last hours. On Monday, December 16, 1799, less than two days after his death, the *Alexandria Times and District of Columbia Daily Advertiser* informed its readers, who were also Washington's neighbors, that, "It is our painful duty first to announce to our Country, and to the world, the death of their illustrious benefactor—GEORGE WASHINGTON." Basing their account on information received from two of Washington's physicians, James Craik and Elisha Cullen Dick, the editors went on to briefly describe the illness that "put a period to his mortal existence," and then mentioned that, "conscious of his approaching dissolution, he bore the excruciating agonies of a violent and painful disease with that heroic and Christian fortitude for which he was ever distinguished, and expired in the possession of that serenity of mind resulting from a consciousness of integrity, and a well-spent life." Another article in the same newspaper, written a few days later following the funeral, mentioned the "short, but painful" nature of Washington's final illness and his "heroic magnanimity and Christian fortitude."[32] Here again, as in Eliza Powel's note to Martha Washington, which was mentioned earlier, is evidence that, at the time, Washington's serenity as he came face to face with death, was attributed, not to the influence of Stoicism, but rather to his Christian beliefs.

One of those doctors hinted again at the source of Washington's calm in those last hours in a funeral oration given about two months after the death. Elisha Cullen Dick, a friend and fellow member of Washington's Masonic lodge in Alexandria, gave a public lecture at the Presbyterian Meeting House on the occasion of what would have been the late president's sixty-eighth birthday. Outlining for his audience the story of Washington's life, Dr. Dick touched only briefly on his subject's relationship to God, but took care to note that at the time of the American Revolution, Washington made a pledge "to himself, his fellow citizens and to his God," accepting the "sacred trust" of leading the Continental Army, determined "to give liberty to his country, or perish in the enterprise." While he did not remind the congregation of his presence at the event, he noted that at the close of Washington's exemplary life, "the soul of this great and good man took its final departure to the mansions of eternal rest." Among his closing words, the doctor gave the opinion that "heaven has reclaimed its treasure."[33]

Hundreds of eulogies for George Washington were given, and often published, in the aftermath of his death. While many of the eulogies, like that of Dr. Dick, dealt with aspects of the religious faith attributed to him, according to one scholar, only one openly questioned "whether Washington was a Christian and died in a state of grace." The author of that funeral sermon was Seth Williston, a missionary from Connecticut, who wrote in the preface to the published version of his work:

> It is true that the preacher nowhere in the sermon did pretend to decide absolutely whether Washington had a principle of GRACE. It is thought that this is going too far for him, or any other mortal. . . . The preacher's acquaintance with this great man's religious character was not such as to make it appear to him expedient, even to give his opinion of his piety. It is conceived that a man may have shining talents and may maintain what is called a good moral character and yet be destitute of the grace of God, or a new heart. . . . As a general and as a statesman, we place our Washington above the most, if not all of them; yet we dare not positively affirm that, when weighted in the balance of the sanctuary, he will not be found wanting. If our patriot was pious, as well as brave—if he was a man of prayer as well as a man of war, we rejoice. All the pious will be happy to sit with him at the feet of our exalted Prince, who is himself a man of war and a mighty conqueror. But the sending of great men all to heaven in funeral sermons, orations, and elegies, it is thought has a bad tendency. It is calculated to establish the self-righteous system, and to keep out of sight, the NECESSITY OF FAITH IN CHRIST.[34]

Rather than questioning Washington's beliefs, however, Williston actually was making a point about the majority of funeral sermons at this period and the sloppy theology of some of his contemporaries. He was merely stating that no human being should cast judgment on another person's soul, admitting that he had no personal knowledge of the late president's faith, and criticizing the habit of others, who assumed that, simply because someone was a good person, they were also Christian.

A similar point was made by Bishop James Madison of Virginia, who was also the president of the College of William and Mary. A relative of future president James Madison, a friend to Thomas Jefferson, and teacher of future president James Monroe, Bishop Madison gave a very popular oration on Washington's death at Williamsburg's Bruton Parish Church on February 22, 1800. He reminded the congregation:

> If, indeed, the illustrious WASHINGTON, whom all America deplores, and whom the whole civilized world will honour with their eulogies, had obtained only that celebrity, which extraordinary talents in war, in arts and sciences, or in politics, confer; if he had not been distinguished for his firm adherence to the truths of religion; if he had not served his God with a zeal worthy of his superior understanding, however full of glory he might have been in the eyes of man, Religion could not have added her voice to the general plaudit. But Religion joins in the universal wo[e]: she weeps over the tomb of WASHINGTON! great in arms, great in peace, great in piety! and, amidst her sorrows, feels a gleam of consolation in pronouncing his eulogium.[35]

From his own observations of Washington, during the time he served as chaplain to Gen. Henry Knox's brigade during the American Revolution, Presbyterian minister Alexander Macwhorter of Newark, New Jersey, brought his take on Washington's faith:

> General Washington was a uniform professor of the Christian religion. He steadily discountenanced vice; abhorred the principles of infidelity; and the practice of immorality. He was a constant and devout attendant upon divine worship. In the army he kept no chaplain of his own, but attended divine service with his brigades, in rotation, as far as conveniency would allow; probably to be an example to his officers, and encourage his soldiers to respect religion. He steadily attended the worship of God when president.

He was not in this respect like too many, who practically declare themselves superior to honoring their Maker in the offices of religion. He firmly
believed in the existence of God and his superintending providence. This
appears in almost all his speeches. He was educated in the Episcopal Church,
and always continued a member thereof, and was an ornament to the same.
He was truly of a catholic faith, and considered the distinction of the great
denominations of Christians rather as shades of difference, than anything
substantial or essential to salvation.[36]

Another former chaplain, Timothy Dwight, who was the grandson of
Congregational theologian Jonathan Edwards and who went on after the
war to become the president of Yale University and write a book-length
poem about the founding of the United States, expressed more caution
in his funeral sermon for George Washington, but came down on the
same side as Macwhorter. Dwight noted that doubts had been expressed
about Washington's Christianity, and commented that, "No one will be
surprised at this, who reflects, that this is a subject, about which in all
circumstances not involving inspired testimony, doubts may and will exist." In other words, it could not be otherwise, given the lack of any direct
statements by Washington on the subject:

The evidence concerning it must of course arise from an induction of
particulars. Some will induce more of these particulars, and others fewer;
some will rest on one class, or collection, others on another; and some will
give more, and others less, weight to those which are induced; according to
their several modes and standards of judging. The question in this, and all
other cases, must be finally determined before another tribunal, than that of
human judgment; and to that tribunal it must ultimately be left. For my own
part, I have considered his numerous and uniform public and most solemn
declarations of his high veneration for religion, his exemplary and edifying
attention to public worship, and his constancy in secret devotion, as proofs
sufficient to satisfy every person, willing to be satisfied. I shall only add,
that if he was not a Christian, he was more like one than any man of same
description, whose life has been hitherto recorded.[37]

Many readers will already be familiar with the famous funeral oration
by "Light-Horse Harry" Lee, the father of Confederate general Robert E.
Lee, which describes George Washington as "first in war, first in peace,

and first in the hearts of his countrymen." Fewer will know that William White, the Episcopal bishop of Pennsylvania and Washington's former pastor, gave a prayer and short address just prior to Lee's eulogy on January 26, 1800. Bishop White began with the words, "'Forasmuch as it hath pleased Almighty God, in his wise providence, to take out of this world,' our beloved brother in Christ, and our ever honoured fellow-citizen, George Washington, formerly president of these United States; and, at the time of his decease, commander-in-chief of the armies of the same; let us bow down our souls in lowly submission, under this afflictive dispensation."[38] The first part of the quote relates to the burial service from the Anglican prayer book, which begins "Forasmuch as it hath pleased Almighty God of his great mercy to take unto himself the soul of our dear *brother* here departed, we therefore commit *his* body to the ground."[39] That the bishop, who personally knew Washington, would describe him as "our beloved brother in Christ" suggests that White had no questions about the sincerity of Washington's beliefs. He could easily have left out the words "in Christ," without causing offense or even the odd raised eyebrow. Given the fact, discussed earlier, that the two shared a similar reticence in talking about their personal faith, the bishop had no qualms, given what he knew of Washington, in seeing the late president as a fellow Christian.

Newspapers throughout the country also told the news of Mrs. Washington's death and made mention of her religious faith. The news traveled rather slowly, finally reaching Newport, Rhode Island, on Saturday, June 5, 1802.[40] Inhabitants of Augusta, Georgia, learned of her demise on Wednesday, June 9, through a small article, outlined in black, on one of the inner pages, which was an almost verbatim copy of an article from the *Daily National Intelligencer* of May 26:

> DIED—At Mount Vernon, on the 22d ultimo, Mrs. MARTHA WASHINGTON, widow of the late illustrious General GEORGE WASHINGTON—To those amiable and christian virtues, which adorn the female character, she added dignity of manners, superiority of understanding, a mind intelligent and elevated. The silence of respectful grief is her best eulogy.[41]

The *New England Palladium* provided greater coverage, based on an article in an Alexandria newspaper, dated May 25, 1802. The wording suggests that the source for the information was probably Thomas Law. After noting the date of her death, the article went on:

Composure and resignation were uniformly displayed during seventeen days depredations of a severe fever. From the commencement she declared she was undergoing the last trial, and had long been prepared for her disso-lution. She took the sacrament from Mr. DAVIS, imparted her last advice and benedictions to her weeping relations, and sent for a white gown, which she had previously laid by for her last dress—thus in the closing scene, as in all preceding ones, nothing was omitted. The conjugal, maternal and domestic duties had all been fulfilled in an exemplary manner. She was the worthy partner of the worthiest of men, and those who witnessed their conduct could not determine which excelled in their different characters, both were so well sustained on every occasion. They lived an honor and a pattern to their country, and are taken from us to receive the rewards—promised to the faithful and just.[42]

The problem for anyone trying to sum up the religious beliefs of George Washington was formulated by historian Paul Boller over forty years ago:

> If to be a member of a Christian church, to attend church with a fair degree of regularity, to insist on the importance of organized religion for society, and to believe in an over-ruling Providence in human affairs is to be Chris-tian, then Washington can be regarded as Christian. . . . On the other hand, if to believe in the divinity and resurrection of Christ and his atonement for the sins of man and to participate in the sacrament of the Lord's Supper are requisites for the Christian faith, then Washington can hardly be considered a Christian except in the most nominal sense.[43]

This summation of the problem has been quite persuasive to the last gen-eration or two of historians. However, in my opinion, Boller and others have made several errors when they set about to define what makes a per-son a Christian. First, they hold Washington to a standard (an emotional conversion experience) that most people in his own denomination would not have said was necessary and wouldn't have held him to for at least an-other five to ten years. Second, they place too much emphasis on partici-pation in a ritual (communion), when the basis of salvation is, according to St. Paul in the New Testament, simply a matter of faith in Jesus.[44] Jesus taught that that faith would be manifested in a believer's life by the "fruits" he or she produced.[45] Washington himself wrote that, "With me, it has always been a maxim, rather to let my designs appear from my works than by my expressions."[46] Here was a man who was recognized by his peers for his goodness and integrity. He continually gave credit to God/Providence for the good things that happened in his life, while acknowledging that the bad things, too, were part of God's will and should be submitted to without a lot of griping. He supported the Church both financially and by his attendance at services throughout his life, and as a member of the religion committee in the House of Burgesses ensured that the Church, as an institution, would remain in place to meet the needs of his fellow Virginians. The children entrusted to his care received religious instruction while they were being raised in a home that was filled with religious books and sermons to read and decorated with at least some religious artwork, to reinforce what they were being taught. Washington supported efforts to distribute Bibles to his soldiers and to send missionaries among Native American peoples. These might all be seen as "good fruits."

Boller made a second error in making a judgment about someone else's faith, because no matter what a person says or does, the only one who can truly know the state of an individual's soul is God.[47] It is quite true that Washington might have been doing all the things mentioned in the preceding paragraph because, knowing his constituency as well as he did, they made him look good to the electorate and led them to trust—and elect—him. This cynical use of religion would not have been anything new in the world. Jesus himself warned his disciples about behaving like some of the religious leaders of that time, who prayed loudly in public, made generous donations in such a way that everyone knew about it, and overacted their weakness because of fasting, as a means of getting attention—all while missing the true point of what God wanted and expected of them.[48] More recently, have there not been numerous examples of religious leaders who sanctimoniously said all the right things, but later proved themselves, at best, to be no better than the sinners we all are, or, at worst, nothing more than hypocrites and charlatans, out to win nothing but political influence and money? As St. Paul reminded his fellow believers in the early years of the Christian Church, it was quite possible for a person to look really good, to even go so far as to be burned as a martyr for Christ's sake, but if they were doing it for false motives, they were lost.[49] Judging the sincerity of another person's beliefs is not something any of us can—or should—ever do.

Still others looking at Washington's life have erred in not trying to put Washington's religious beliefs and practices into the context of what was happening to the Anglican Church in America. Had they tried to do this—and paid more attention to traditions within his own family about changes in Washington's religious practice over his lifetime—they might have understood that the two things were related. Washington remained a lifelong Anglican, but may have felt that he couldn't leave the Church outright, perhaps because of the deep attachment of his wife or other family members to that denomination. It should also be noted that the fact that Washington's own connection to the Anglican/Episcopal Church seems to have weakened after the Revolution, for any of the myriad reasons discussed earlier or perhaps because of something else, does not necessarily mean that there was any lessening in his attachment to God.

Knowing all the words that have been written over the years about George Washington's life, including his religious life, I still think there is room for additional research on this subject. One issue crying out for serious scholarship concerns the many sermons and books on religion and philosophy in his library and what they might have to tell us about the interests and beliefs of the man who owned them. Another area with promise involves the place of Freemasonry in Washington's life. A dear friend, Dr. Thomas McDaniel, who is a retired professor of Old Testament Languages from Eastern Baptist Theological Seminary, for example, recently suggested that perhaps it was some teaching in Freemasonry, which gave Washington, and his fellow Masons among the other Founding Fathers, the theoretical underpinnings to disregard the teachings of both Jesus and St. Paul that good Christians should submit to the authorities that God had put over them.[50] This was an intriguing question, which I was unable to answer due to a lack of knowledge on the topic of Freemasonry. Finally, while in this work I have tried to look at the place of the Church in the lives of later members of the Washington and Custis families, they really deserve close attention from someone with more expertise in nineteenth century history than I can bring to the effort. So there is considerably more work in this field to undertake and I would like to challenge some young historians to think about taking up these topics.

In conclusion, while it is not possible to make definitive statements about the state of George Washington's soul, one can certainly learn something about the role religion played in his life. He was raised within the tolerant, liberal wing of the Anglican Church, as it developed in Virginia in the late seventeenth and early eighteenth centuries. Changes within the Anglican Church shortly before and after the American Revolution may have troubled him greatly, although he remained a member of the Church until his death. Changes either in the Anglican/Episcopal Church or within himself may have led him to stop observing the Christian ordinance of communion. He took part in the religious life of his social circle and local congregations throughout his life, wherever he happened to be. He supported both the Church and those less fortunate than himself financially. Finally, George Washington promoted a national atmosphere in which all were free to express their faith. In looking at George Washington's faith, we, like Timothy Dwight, might well say that "if he was not a Christian, he was more like one than any man of [the] same description, whose life has been hitherto recorded."[51]

NOTES

ABBREVIATIONS

DAB   *Dictionary of American Biography*
GW   George Washington
GW Diaries   *Diaries of George Washington*
GW Papers   *Papers of George Washington*
GW Writings *Writings of George Washington*
MVLA   Mount Vernon Ladies' Association Research Library, Mount
            Vernon Estates and Gardens, Mount Vernon, VA
MW   Martha Washington
OED   *Oxford English Dictionary*

PREFACE

1. Holmes, *Faiths of the Founding Fathers,* 134–40.

1. CONTROVERSY

1. For an example of some recent articles and an interchange on this subject, see David D. Kirkpatrick, "Putting God Back into American History," *New York Times,* February 27, 2005; Sally Quinn, "The G-Word and the A-List; In a Social Setting, There's One Subject Washington Avoids Religiously: God," *Washington Post,* July 12, 1999; J. S. White, "The God of Our Founding Fathers," *Washington Post,* July 25, 1999; John Lofton, "Of God and Revolution," *Washington Post,* August 8, 1999; C. W. Jones, "God and Revolution (Cont'd)," *Washington Post,* August 29, 1999. For an earlier twentieth century debate on the subject of George Washington's religious beliefs, see Briggs, "To Be Alone with God," *William and Mary Quarterly,* 3rd ser., 12, no. 3 (July 1955): 476–78; and Wall, Letter to the Editor, *William and Mary Quarterly,* 3rd ser., 12, no. 4 (October 1955): 678–79. For an organization promoting Spiritual Heritage Tours of Washington, D.C., during the year 2004, see http://www.spiritualheritagetours.com.

2. Brooks, "A Dinner at Mount Vernon," *New-York Historical Society Quarterly* 31, no. 2 (April 1947), 82; Remsburg, "George Washington." For some interesting examples of what a number of Jefferson's contemporaries were saying about him, see Edward Thornton to James Bland Burges, February 2, 1792, in Thornton, "A Young Englishman

Reports on the New Nation," *William and Mary Quarterly,* 3rd ser., 18, no. 1 (January 1961), 98; Abigail Adams to her sister, February 7, 1801, in *New Letters of Abigail Adams,* 265–66; Manasseh Cutler to Dr. Torrey, January 4, 1802, in Cutler and Cutler, *Life Journals and Correspondence of Rev. Manasseh Cutler,* 66–67.

3. Rev. J. T. Kirkland, December 29, 1799, quoted in Schroeder, *Maxims of George Washington,* 197; Kennedy, *The Faith of Washington.*

4. For Washington as a Deist, see "Deism," *New Encyclopaedia Britannica,* 15th ed., 26:608; Flexner, *George Washington: Anguish and Farewell,* 490 (also 300 and 442). For deism itself, see "Deism," *New Encyclopaedia Britannica,* 15th ed., 3:965, 26:606–8; Waring, *Deism and Natural Religion,* v–x. These Deist beliefs violated several thousand years of Judeo-Christian teaching in a number of ways. The emphasis on man's rationality led to a tendency to play down or deny the basic sinfulness of man's nature; the rejection of revealed religion meant that the scriptures lost their authority; and the idea of God as the watchmaker denied the Deity any continued role in the world or care about the affairs of the world after the point of the creation, when, for example, both the Old and New Testaments are the story of God's continual involvement with man and the rest of creation.

5. Waring, *Deism and Natural Religion,* x. Except for the final point, these arguments would not have been at odds with Christian theology, or, more specifically, with the writings of St. Paul to the Romans (see Romans 1:19–20 for his handling of the first, second, and fourth Deist propositions, and Romans 2:13–15 for the second and third).

6. Gay, *Deism,* 11.

7. Ibid., 10–11, 13.

8. Marshall, *Life of George Washington,* 5:375. Both the chief justice and his father had known Washington and members of his family for years (see Washington, *Diaries,* 2:133, 134n; 6:314–15, 314n, 315n). At least one reader, who had known the first president well, found John Marshall's character sketch of Washington exactly right (see Gouverneur Morris to John Marshall, June 26, 1807, in Marshall, *Papers,* 7:54, 56n).

9. Hutson, *Religion and the Founding of the American Republic,* 30, 32.

10. Sanford, *Religious Life of Thomas Jefferson,* 91–101, 174.

11. Henriques, "A Few Simple Beliefs," 185.

12. Holmes, *Faiths of the Founding Fathers,* 68, 133–60. Elsewhere in the book (pages 50–51), Holmes indicates another way to organize the religious beliefs of the founding generation: "If census takers trained in Christian theology had set up broad categories in 1790 labeled 'Atheism,' 'Deism and Unitarianism,' 'Orthodox Protestantism,' 'Orthodox Roman Catholicism,' and 'Other,' and if they had interviewed Franklin, Washington, Adams, Jefferson, Madison, and Monroe, they would undoubtedly have placed every one of these six Founding Fathers in some way under the category of 'Deism and Unitarianism.'"

13. Gier, "Religious Liberalism and the Founding Fathers," http://users.adelphia.net/~nickgier/foundfathers.htm.

14. Conversation between Dr. Robert Prichard, Professor of Church History and Liturgy at the Episcopal Seminary in Alexandria, Virginia, and Mount Vernon cura-

tor emerita Christine Meadows, November 6, 1997, related to me by the latter on that same day; the comment of Dr. Taylor Sanders of Lexington, Virginia, that Washington expressed the beliefs of the Latitudinarians was made during the discussion period at a seminar entitled "George Washington: Mourning and Memory," at Mount Vernon, on November 7, 1998; Lillback, *George Washington's Sacred Fire*, 907–18.

15. For the beliefs of the Latitudinarians, see Sheridan, *Jefferson and Religion*, 15; and John W. Turner, Department of Religious Studies and Programs at the Colonial Williamsburg Foundation, Williamsburg, Virginia, faxed communication to the author, August 10, 1999. For a scholarly treatment of the Latitudinarian movement within the Anglican Church, see Spellman, *Latitudinarians and the Church of England*, especially pages 16–23, on its development.

16. Spellman, *Latitudinarians and the Church of England*, 18, 24; Haller, *Rise of Puritanism*, 239, 247.

17. GW to Dr. James Anderson, December 24, 1795, *GW Writings*, 34:407.

18. "Funeral Sermon on the Death of General Washington, Delivered the 29th December, 1799, By the Reverend Doctor Muir" (broadside), MVLA (photostat). Many people today question whether Washington's association with the Freemasons is an indication that his religious beliefs were not only less than orthodox, but veered into the Deist camp (see, for example, Holmes, *Faiths of the Founding Fathers*, 48, 68, 105–6, 110, 146). Whereas Roman Catholics are forbidden to become Masons, Protestant Christians are (and were) not, and, especially in the eighteenth century, the ranks of the Masons included both clergymen and bishops, who found nothing incompatible with their dual affiliations (see Novak and Novak, *Washington's God*, 97).

19. James Muir to [?], January 27, 1800, MVLA (photostat).

20. Lear, *Letters and Recollections*, 133.

21. Thomas Jefferson, February 1, 1800, "The Anas," in Jefferson, *Writings*, 1:433–34.

22. See Steiner, *Religious Beliefs of Our Presidents*, 39.

23. Bishop William White to the Rev. B. C. C. Parker, November 28, 1832, in Wilson, *Memoir of the Life of the Right Reverend William White*, 190–91.

24. Hadfield, *An Englishman in America*, 14.

25. Abigail Adams to her sister, July 12, 1789, in *New Letters of Abigail Adams*, 15; Niemcewicz, *Under Their Vine and Fig Tree*, 102.

26. Bishop William White to the Rev. B. C. C. Parker, November 28, 1832, in Wilson, *Memoir of the Life of the Right Reverend William White*, 189–90.

27. Bishop William White to the Rev. B. C .C. Parker, December 21, 1832, ibid., 193.

28. Nelly Custis Lewis to Jared Sparks, February 26, 1833, quoted in Sparks, *Life of George Washington*, 522.

29. Ibid. According to one Mount Vernon visitor, Mrs. Washington was successful in her efforts to raise Nelly in her own image (see Brooks, "A Dinner at Mount Vernon," 75). It is interesting, in the light of allegations that George Washington was a Deist, and of Nelly's own strenuous protestations concerning the depth of his faith, that Nelly herself once vilified two Virginians involved in a family scandal with the words "They are both *Deists*" (Nelly Custis Lewis to Elizabeth Bordley Gibson, March 22, 1821, in Lewis, *George Washington's Beautiful Nelly*, 107).

30. Eliza Parke Custis [Law] to E[dmund] L[aw] Rogers, January 22, 1831, MVLA, RM-626/PS-4544 (photostat).

31. Joseph E. Fields, "The Correspondence and Papers of Martha Washington," in Fields, *Worthy Partner*, xxxi, 464–65; Meadows, "The Furniture," 485.

2. FOUNDATIONS

1. Quitt, "The English Cleric and the Virginia Adventurer," 164–68. In addition to Quitt's article, for a good overview of the life of the Reverend Lawrence Washington, see Hoppin, *Washington Ancestry*, 1:110–26. The Arminians would be a strong influence on John Wesley in the eighteenth century. Wesley edited a publication entitled *The Arminian Magazine*, in which he wrote that, "God willeth all men to be saved, by speaking the truth in love." In an even more liberal manifestation, Arminianism also influenced the development of Unitarianism in America at the end of the eighteenth and into the early nineteenth centuries (see "Arminianism," *New Encyclopaedia Britannica*, 15th ed., 1:569).

2. Quitt, "The English Cleric and the Virginia Adventurer," 168, 169.

3. Ibid., 171.

4. White, "The Epistle to the Reader," in *First Century of Scandalous, Malignant Priests*, A2.

5. Ibid., A5.

6. Ibid., 4.

7. Hoppin, *Washington Ancestry*, 1:125.

8. Quitt, "The English Cleric and the Virginia Adventurer," 173.

9. Hoppin, *Washington Ancestry*, 1:166–67; Freeman, *George Washington*, 1:17, 17n.

10. Nelson, *A Blessed Company*, 225.

11. Toner, *Wills of the American Ancestors of Washington*, 4.

12. Ibid., 3–4, 5. For the fact that Washington Parish was in Westmoreland County, see Nelson, *A Blessed Company*, 18, 68.

13. Toner, *Wills of the American Ancestors of Washington*, 7.

14. Ibid., 9.

15. For Martha Washington's family background, see Tyler, "Bruton Church," 171; and Cary, "Descendants of Rev. Rowland Jones," 192. For the Reverend Rowland Jones Jr.'s experiences in Williamsburg and elsewhere in Virginia, see Meade, *Old Churches, Ministers, and Families*, 1:146; and Goodwin, *Colonial Church*, 283. For his burial, see Massey, *Colonial Churches* 41.

16. Bond, *Damned Souls*, 175–76, 180.

17. Bond, "Anglican Theology and Devotion in James Blair's Virginia," 313–19, 322, 328–30, 333–35, 338.

18. Ibid., 331–33.

19. Bond, *Spreading the Gospel*, 31.

20. For more on John Wesley's influence on the church, see Marshall, *Eighteenth Century England*, 487–93.

21. Nelson, *A Blessed Company*, 284–85. For more on the lack of evangelical inroads in both the mother country and in colonies with a strong Anglican presence, see ibid., 453n24.

22. Freeman, *George Washington*, 1:47, 47n. For more on Reverend McCullough, see Nelson, *A Blessed Company*, 314. Among the surviving artifacts relating to Washington's christening are a wine glass and the Washington family Bible, which records both his birth and christening (MVLA, H-3408/A-1543 [for wine glass]; W-408 [for Bible]). Another relic of the christening is a child's robe of white brocaded silk lined with rose-colored silk, now at the National Museum of American History (see Klapthor and Morrison, *A Figure upon the Stage*, 102; and for the fabric, MVLA, W-469 [fragment]).

23. Warren, "The Childhood of George Washington," 5786–87.

24. Freeman, *George Washington*, 1:42–72. For background on the Washington family, see ibid., 1:15–42, and Hoppin, *Washington Ancestry*, 1:54–247.

25. For Augustine Washington's will, see Toner, *Wills of the American Ancestors of Washington*, 13–16. For Augustine Washington as a vestryman at Pohick Church, see *Minutes of the Vestry*, 11, 13, 18, 19, [158]; Freeman, *George Washington*, 1:53, 53n, 54.

26. Bond, *Spreading the Gospel*, 38; see also Isaac, *Transformation of Virginia*, 65.

27. Christine Heyrman, as quoted in Nelson, *A Blessed Company*, 218. For more on using the Bible as a primer to teach reading, see page 221 of this same source, as well as Isaac, *Transformation of Virginia*, 65.

28. The description of Weems by a fellow clergyman is taken from Meade, *Old Churches, Ministers, and Families*, 2:234–36. Throughout this paper, descriptions of ministers associated with the Washingtons will be quoted from Bishop Meade's work, because he relates more than just the bare facts about the lives of these gentlemen, giving some sense of their personalities. Invariably, however, the descriptions include something negative about the way the minister conducted himself or his church services. This is primarily the result of the growth of the evangelical movement within the Anglican/Episcopal Church itself. This difference in emphasis led to changes in social mores on subjects like drinking and card playing and caused nineteenth-century Episcopalians to look down on the personalities, methods, and messages of their eighteenth-century predecessors. For more on how and why Meade, specifically, was critical of the eighteenth-century Church in Virginia, see Nelson, *A Blessed Company*, 299–301.

29. Weems, *Life of Washington*, ix–xiii; Washington's birth and education are covered on pages 6–16. For the cherry tree story, see page 12; the lesson on sharing is found on pages 9–10.

30. Ibid., 12–16.

31. Warren, "The Childhood of George Washington," 5787, 5792, 5799–5803.

32. Custis, *Recollections and Private Memoirs*, 141.

33. Lawrence Lewis to George W. Bassett, May 15, 1831, quoted in Freeman, *George Washington*, 6:230–31. The spot mentioned by Lawrence is probably the so-called "Meditation Rocks," which are discussed and illustrated in Wayland, *Washingtons and Their Homes*, 73, 84.

34. Bassett, "Reminiscences of Washington," 78, MVLA, catalogue record for Washington Family Bible, W-408 (typescript).

35. Mary Ball Washington, "Mary Washington's Last Will," May 20, 1788, MVLA, PS-120 (photostat).

36. "FREDERICKSBURG [VA], August 27, 1789," *Gazette of the United States,* September 9, 1789, in Baker, *Washington after the Revolution,* 145–46.

37. "An Inventory of the Estate of Capn. Augustine Washington in King George, Stafford, and Westmoreland Counties," July 1, 1743, MVLA, PS-237 (photostat).

38. *Library of Dr. S. Weir Mitchell,* 56. Further evidence that Mary Ball Washington's interest in Anglican theology continued into her children's teenage years can be surmised from her ownership of a two-volume set of *Meditations and Contemplations* by James Hervey, which had been published in London in 1750. Hervey was a former student of John Wesley's and one of the early proponents of the evangelical movement in the Anglican Church in England, which might be seen as a reaction to the rationalism of the Latitudinarians. (For more on Hervey and the evangelicals in the Anglican/Episcopal Church, see Zabriskie, "The Rise and Main Characteristics of the Anglican Evangelical Movement in England and America.") While GW would have been out on his own by the time his mother acquired Hervey's book, its influence may have been particularly strong on her younger children and grandchildren. The two volumes are now in the collections at Mount Vernon, and bear the signatures of both Mary Ball Washington and her grandson, Lawrence Lewis. The evangelical movement predominated in the Virginia Church in the first half of the nineteenth century, when that grandson and his wife, Martha Washington's granddaughter Nelly, were active in the Episcopal Church (see Meade, *Old Churches, Ministers, and Families,* 2:231–32).

39. For Mary Ball Washington's ownership of this particular title, and for the tradition that she used it for the instruction of her children, see M'Guire, *Religious Opinions and Character of Washington,* 47–48. This author, Rev. Dr. Edward Charles McGuire, was the son-in-law of George Washington's nephew, Robert Lewis, and the pastor for forty-five years of St. George's Church in Fredericksburg, Virginia (see Sorley, *Lewis of Warner Hall,* 233). For the presence of Matthew Hale's book in the Mount Vernon library, see Prussing, *The Estate of George Washington,* 424.

40. "Hale, Sir Matthew," in *New Encyclopaedia Britannica,* 15th ed., 5:630–31.

41. Cushing, *George Washington Library Collection,* 56–58.

42. Pyle, "The Boyle Lectures (1692–1732)," 1–3.

43. Washington, *Rules of Civility,* 11–12, 14, 28, 61; Freeman, *George Washington,* 1:195–96, 196n. For the continued influence of these rules on Washington's life as an adult, see Sayen, "George Washington's 'Unmannerly' Behavior," 5–36, and Brookhiser, *Founding Father,* 127–31.

44. *Writings of George Washington,* by Jared Sparks, 2:481 [hereafter cited as Sparks, *Writings of George Washington*].

45. Freeman, *George Washington,* 1:244–45; Sparks, *Writings of George Washington,* 2:481–82. A caveat is necessary at this point about Sparks, who in editing the Washington papers was known to change things to suit himself. This propensity led Douglas

Southall Freeman to say that, "Unless papers appearing in *Sparks* are printed correctly elsewhere, or are verifiable from the manuscript, their literal accuracy never can be taken for granted. The meaning seldom is changed perceptibly" (Freeman, *George Washington,* 1:245n).

46. Washington, *GW Papers, Colonial Series,* 1:37n, 38n.

47. GW to Burwell Bassett, August 28, 1762, in *GW Writings,* 37:484–85.

48. GW to President Joseph Reed, December 12, 1778, ibid., 13:383; for the story of Haman, see Esther 3:7.

49. GW to Jonathan Trumbull, August 7, 1776, *GW Writings,* 5:390; for the Biblical quote, see Matthew 4:7 and Luke 4:12, both of which refer back to Deuteronomy 6:16.

50. GW to James Warren, March 31, 1779, in Washington, *GW Writings,* 13:312; see also Genesis 15:16.

51. GW, Circular to the States, June 9, 1783, *GW Writings,* 26:496. For the Biblical reference, see Micah 6:8.

52. GW to the Chevalier de Chastellux, August 20, 1784, *GW Writings,* 27:459–60.

53. From Matthew 6:19–21; see also Luke 12:33.

54. GW to the Mr. Chichesters, April 25, 1799, *GW Writings,* 37:194. The Golden Rule can be found in Matthew 7:12 and Luke 6:31.

55. GW to Rev. William White, December 31, 1793; GW to Charles Cotesworth Pinckney, July 8, 1796, and GW to George Washington Parke Custis, November 15, 1796, *GW Writings,* 33:220–21, 35:131 and 283. For the Biblical story, see Mark 12:42 and Luke 21:2.

56. GW to George Washington Parke Custis, June 13, 1798, *GW Writings,* 36:288.

57. GW to Howell Lewis, November 3, 1793, ibid., 33:148.

58. GW to John Augustine Washington, November 26, 1778, ibid., 13:335; for St. Paul's remarks, see 1 Corinthians 13:2.

59. GW to John Augustine Washington, March 31, 1776, *GW Writings,* 4:449. For the Biblical reference, see 1 Corinthians 15:51–52.

60. GW to Benjamin Lincoln, August 28, 1788, *GW Writings,* 30:63; for the Biblical quotes, see Proverbs 6:16; for similar use of language, see Proverbs 30:18, 29.

61. GW to Rev. William Gordon, October 15, 1797, *GW Writings,* 36:49; for the Biblical reference, see Proverbs 16:9.

62. GW to the Marquis de Lafayette, July 25, 1785, *GW Writings,* 28:206–7.

63. Genesis 1:28.

64. For Jesus's statement, see Matthew 11:28; for milk and honey, see Exodus 3:17 and 13:5, Numbers 13:27 and 14:8. For Abraham's going to the "land of promise," see Hebrews 11:9.

65. See Luke 3:4–6. For similar references to "preparing the way" from throughout the Bible, see also Deuteronomy 19:3; Isaiah 40:3, 57:14, 62:10; Malachi 3:1; Matthew 3:3, 11:10; Mark 1:2–3; and Luke 1:76, 7:27.

66. GW to the Marquis de Chastellux, April 25–May 1, 1788, *GW Writings,* 29:485.

67. Ibid. For similar uses of these words from Isaiah, see GW to the president of Congress, December 20, 1776; GW to the Marquis de Lafayette, September 30, 1779; and GW to Dr. James Anderson, December 24, 1795, ibid., 6:402, 16:369–70, 34:407.

68. GW to the Hebrew Congregation of Newport, Rhode Island (August 18, 1790), ibid., 31:93n. The Biblical references were taken from 1 Kings 4:25 and Micah 4:4. For other examples of Washington's use of the vine-and-fig-tree motif, see GW to Edmund Randolph, November 17, 1780; GW to William Fitzhugh, November 8, 1780; GW to John Sullivan, November 20, 1780; GW to Bartholomew Dandridge, December 18, 1782; GW to Chevalier de Chastellux, October 12, 1783; GW to Charles Thomson, January-ary 22, 1784; GW to Chevalier de Chastellux, February 1, 1784; GW to the Marquis de Lafayette, February 1, 1784; GW to the Marchioness de Lafayette, April 4, 1784; GW to the Comte de Rochambeau, September 7, 1785; GW to Charles Vaughan, November 18, 1785; GW to George Clinton, February 28, 1797; GW to Doctor James Anderson, April 7, 1797; GW to the secretary of the treasury, May 15, 1797; GW to John Quincy Adams, June 25, 1797; GW to the Earl of Radnor, July 8, 1797; GW to William Strick-land, July 15, 1797; GW to Sir Edward Newenham, August 6, 1797; GW to Governor John Henry, April 3, 1798; GW to the president of the United States, June 17, 1798; GW to Julian Ursyn Niemcewicz, June 18, 1798, ibid., 20:317, 328, 371; 25:445–46; 27:189, 312, 314, 317, 385; 28:255–56, 316; 35:407, 432, 446, 476, 493, 499; 36:4, 238, 291, 297.

69. "Address of the *General Committee* representing the United Baptist Churches in Virginia, assembled in the City of Richmond," May 8–10, 1789, in *GW Papers, Presidential Series,* 2:425n.

70. Lossing, *Mount Vernon and Its Associations,* 202; Bowen, *History of the Centennial Celebration,* 51–53.

71. For Washington kissing the Bible after taking the oath of office, see "William A. Duer, Description of the Inauguration," in First Federal Congress, *Documentary History,* 15:396. The secretary of the Senate, Samuel Otis, the man holding the Bible during the oath and while Washington kissed it, also left an eyewitness account of this event (see "Journal of the Secretary of the Senate, 1789–1813," in RG46, Records of the United States Senate [8E2/22/15/1], 187). Many thanks to my colleague, Christina Hills, for sharing the Otis description with me. The story of Washington adding the words "So help me God" after taking the oath of office has been told for years (see Freeman, *George Washington,* 6:192; Bowen, *History of the Centennial Celebration,* 52; Lossing, *Mount Vernon and Its Associations,* 202; Griswold, *Republican Court,* 141). Modern scholars, however, have indicated that there is no eighteenth-century documenta-tion for Washington making that statement, although those words appear to have been used at the period in judicial and military oaths (personal communication from Philander D. Chase, one of the senior editors at the Papers of George Washington project at the University of Virginia, ca. 2003; e-mail communication from Richard Holway, social science and history editor at the University Press of Virginia, August 15, 2005; personal communications with Christina Hills of the Mount Vernon staff, after she talked with Charlene Bickford at the Papers of the First Federal Congress project at George Washington University, August 16, 17, 18, 2005). For examples of oaths from this period using the words "so help me God, see *Virginia Statutes at Large,* 11:141, 220, 259, 274–75, 284, 464, 477.

72. Stokes, *Iconography of Manhattan Island,* 5:1244, MVLA (typescript).

3. CHURCH AFFILIATION

1. For information on the Washingtons' wedding, see Freeman, *George Washington,* 3:1–2. For the clergymen at George Washington's funeral, see Carroll and Ashworth, *George Washington,* 629, 629n.

2. For Reverend Mossom, see Goodwin, *Colonial Church,* 295, and Nelson, *A Blessed Company,* 316. For Daniel Parke Custis and John Custis as active members of St. Peter's Church (Daniel was a vestryman between 1740 and 1757 and churchwarden 1740–42; his father was a vestryman in 1735, 1739–44, and 1746, and churchwarden 1735–38 and again 1744–45), see Chamberlayne, *Vestry Book and Register of St. Peter's Parish,* 241, 242, 244, 245, 246, 250, 251, 254, 258, 261, 262, 263, 265, 266, 267, 270, 271, 274, 275, 278, 279, 280, 283, 284, 285, 288, 291, 292, 294, 299, 302, 305, 309, 313, 317, 320, 323, 325, 327, 328, 329, 331, 333–34, 502, 503, 505, 506. For the christening of Martha's siblings, see ibid., 520, 536, 552. For the fact that Reverend Mossom preached Daniel Parke Custis's funeral sermon, see "Schedule B: General Account of the Estate," [ca. October 1759], *GW Papers, Colonial Series,* 6:252.

3. Nelson, *A Blessed Company,* 195.

4. The information about Reverend Mossom was taken from Meade, *Old Churches, Ministers, and Families,* 1:386, 470. The claim that Reverend Jarratt introduced the Methodist movement to Virginia in the 1770s is from Bond, *Spreading the Gospel,* 38.

5. *GW Diaries,* 6:335n; Nelson, *A Blessed Company,* 308; Thompson, *United States Army Chaplaincy,* 216, 250; Brydon, "The Clergy of the Established Church in Virginia and the Revolution," 134.

6. Meade, *Old Churches, Ministers, and Families,* 2:260.

7. *GW Diaries,* 3:240n; 6:298, 298n.

8. For more on Muir's life and his dealings with George Washington, see Miller, *Artisans and Merchants,* 1:7; GW to William Pearce, February 24, 1794; GW to Rev. James Muir, February 24, 1794; and GW to William Pearce, June 14, 1795, in *GW Writings,* 33:279, 279n, 281–82, 282n, 34:214, and see also 36:137n; Powell, *History of Old Alexandria,* 106–10, 156, 161, 200–201, 208, 216, 240, 242.

9. Powell, *History of Old Alexandria, Virginia,* 155; GW to David Stuart, February 26, 1798, *GW Writings,* 36:170.

10. Bogard, *President Washington a Baptist;* "George Washington's Chaplain," *Pentecostal Evangel,* February 2, 1970; Honeywell, *Chaplains of the United States Army,* 55–56; "The John Gano Sword," *SAR Magazine,* 12–13; Thompson and Cummins, *This Day in Baptist History,* 165, 220, 300–301, 323, 327–28. It was Chaplain Gano who was asked to offer prayers when word that the United States and Britain had ceased hostilities reached Washington's headquarters at New Windsor on April 19, 1783 (see Thompson, *The United States Army Chaplaincy,* 252).

11. Griffin, *American Catholic Historical Researches,* 126–29. For a more recent recounting of this story, see Connell, *Faith of Our Founding Father,* 166–67.

12. For the fact that Washington served as godfather to his nephews, see Felder, *Fielding Lewis and The Washington Family,* 72 and 73, which is based on material in the

Lewis family Bible at Kenmore in Fredericksburg, Virginia. From the same source, we learn that in the case of nephew Charles Lewis, Martha Washington took her place as one of the child's two godmothers. For George Washington as godfather to Ferdinando Fairfax, see Freeman, *George Washington*, 3:227; *GW Diaries*, 2:154. For godson Daniel McCarty Chichester, see ibid., 2:158. For George Washington Lafayette as a godson, see GW to the Marquis de Lafayette, October 20, 1782, in *GW Writings*, 25:281. For Washington as godfather to the Schuyler daughter, see GW to Philip Schuyler, March 23, 1781, ibid., 21:360. For godson Walter W. Buchanan, see Decatur, *Private Affairs*, 67. For godson Benjamin Lincoln Lear, see ibid., 205; and Ashbel Green to Bernard Whitman, March 8, 1834, in MVLA, *Annual Report 1956*, 41–42.

13. "The Ministration of Public Baptism of Infants, to Be Used in the Church," *Book of Common Prayer*, 80. This prayer book belonged to Martha Washington and is inscribed with her name (MVLA, W-2139). Missing its title page, it was published by the Protestant Episcopal Church in America about 1790. I chose to quote the ceremony from this edition of the prayer book because it is probably the version from which the later godchildrens' services would have been taken.

14. Ibid., 80, 83. The Apostles' Creed is an ancient Christian statement of faith (see "The Apostles' Creed" at http://www.creeds.net/ancient/apostles.htm).

15. Ibid., 81, 83.

16. Sanford, *Religious Life of Thomas Jefferson*, 88; Holmes, *Religion of the Founding Fathers*, 104.

17. Thomas Jefferson to J. P. P. Derieux, July 25, 1788, in Jefferson, *Papers*, 13:418; see also Sheridan, *Jefferson and Religion*, 15, 72.

18. GW, Farewell Address, September 19, 1796, *GW Writings*, 35:229.

19. For more on the rite of baptism as practiced by Anglicans in Virginia in the eighteenth century, and the christening of Samuel Washington's child, see Nelson, *A Blessed Company*, 211–17, and *GW Diaries*, 2:87. In the Mount Vernon collection are two small bowls (roughly eight inches in diameter) of eighteenth-century Chinese porcelain, which descended in Martha Washington's family with the tradition that they had been used by the Dandridge family as "christening bowls" (MVLA, W-531/AA-3 and W-2405/A-1096).

20. GW, April 10, 24, and 25, 1787, *GW Diaries*, 5:131, 142, 143.

21. For Walter Magowan's career, see ibid., 2:37n; GW to Robert Cary & Company, October 12, 1761, and GW to Robert Cary & Company, March 10, 1768, *GW Papers, Colonial Series*, 7:77 and 77n, 8:72 and 73n. For the fact that Jacky was introduced to Latin and Greek by Mr. Magowan, see GW to Jonathan Boucher, May 30, 1768, ibid., 8:89–90. For Magowan's postemployment visits to Mount Vernon, see *GW Diaries*, 2:37, 39, 108, 109n, 116, 119, 136, 140, 153, 154, 157, 167, 168, 188, 189, 190, 218, 219, 229, 263, 264; 3:19, 20, 33, 34, 70, 82, 83, 114, 150, 153, 154, 155, 203, 245, 261, 263, 319, 320; 4:145, 146, 235.

22. Jonathan Boucher to John James, July 25, 1769, *GW Papers, Colonial Series*, 8:167n.

23. Meade, *Old Churches, Ministers, and Families*, 1:410–12, 2:184–85; see also *GW Papers, Colonial Series*, 8:90n, 387n; 9:211–13, 213n; and Nelson, *A Blessed Company*,

305. For the quote from Boucher concerning his enthusiasm for teaching young Custis, see Jonathan Boucher to GW, June 16, 1768, *GW Papers, Colonial Series*, 8:97.

24. GW to George William Fairfax, November 10, 1785, *GW Papers, Confederation Series*, 3:348–49.

25. MW to Mary Stillson Lear, November 4, 1796, in Fields, *Worthy Partner*, 293.

26. "Moravian Church," *New Encyclopaedia Britannica*, 15th ed., 8:310–11. For the influence of the Moravians on the Wesley brothers, see Cook, *Selina, Countess of Huntingdon*, 26–29.

27. GW to Tobias Lear, November 16, 1796, and December 14, 1796; GW to Rev. Jacob Van Vleck, December 7, 1796, *GW Writings*, 35:284, 320–21, 334.

28. GW to Rev. Jacob Van Vleck, June 14, 1797, ibid., 35:466. One of Washington's great-nieces did attend the Moravian school in Bethlehem, Pennsylvania, at this time. According to the school's records, among the new students in 1796 was Eleanor Lee, who was the daughter of Thomas Lee of Park Gate, near Dumfries, Virginia, and step-daughter of George Washington's niece, Mildred Washington Lee, who was the daughter of his brother and sister-in-law, John Augustine and Hannah Bushrod Washington. According to the school, Eleanor had come with a recommendation from President Washington (e-mail communications, October 19 and 20, 2005, between Natalie Bock of the staff at the Sun Inn in Bethlehem, Pennsylvania, and Mary V. Thompson, Research Specialist at Mount Vernon).

29. "Invoice of Sundry's to be Shipd by Robert Cary Esq. & Co.," October 12, 1761; "Invoice of Goods to be Shipd by Robert Cary & Co.," July 20, 1767; GW to Rev. Jonathan Boucher, May 30, 1768; and "Catalogue of Books for Master Custis Referred to on the Otherside, viz.," GW to Capel and Osgood Hanbury, July 25, 1769, *GW Writings*, 2:369–70, 463–64, 486–87, 515–17; "Washington's Household Account Book," July 24, 1794, 30:312; Nelly Custis to Elizabeth Bordley, July 2, 1797, MVLA (typescript).

30. GW to George Steptoe Washington, December 5, 1790, *GW Papers, Presidential Series*, 7:32.

31. GW to George Washington Parke Custis, November 28, 1796, *GW Writings*, 35:294–95.

32. For Washington as a vestryman and as church warden (1763–64, 1766–67, 1774–75) at Pohick, see *Minutes of the Vestry*, 85, 87–88, 90–91, 94–95, 97–101, 103–4, 106–11, 113–15, 117, 122, 124–25, 128, 132–35, 138–39, 142, 149 [159]; *Mount Vernon: An Illustrated Handbook*, 108; and Freeman, *George Washington*, note and illustration between 3:137 and 138. For Washington's resignation as a vestryman from Truro parish, see GW to Daniel McCarty, February 22, 1784, *GW Papers, Confederation Series*, 1:147.

33. Nelson, *A Blessed Company*, 41.

34. For Washington's attendance at vestry meetings, see *GW Diaries*, 2:11, 28, 76, 111, 132, 140, 167; 3:113, 234. For the role of vestrymen in the church in Virginia, see Isaac, *Transformation of Virginia*, 65, 68; Goodwin, *Colonial Church*, 78–79; *Virginia Statutes at Large*, 5:226, 10:198. For the description of the work of churchwardens, see Nelson, *A Blessed Company*, 41–42, 70–79.

35. The fact that Washington had been a burgess for three years before taking on the duties of a vestryman should effectively counter at least one of the arguments of an

earlier writer on this subject, who contended: "That Washington was a vestryman had no special significance religiously. In Virginia, this office was also political. The vestry managed the civil affairs of the parish, among others, the assessment of taxes. Being the largest property holder in the parish, Washington could hardly afford not to be a vestryman, which office he would have to hold before he could become a member of the House of Burgesses. Thomas Jefferson, a pronounced unbeliever, was also a vestryman, and for the same reasons" (Steiner, *Religious Beliefs of Our Presidents*, 18–19). It is true that Thomas Jefferson, who expressed more doubts about Christianity than Washington, was also elected to the vestry of his two parishes, and accepted the office because he "wished to be [a man] of influence" (see Meade, *Old Churches, Ministers, and Families*, 1:191; 2:43n, 49).

36. *Minutes of the Vestry*, 86–139. Several of these meetings lasted multiple days; I have counted each day as a separate meeting.

37. For Washington's activities on the dates when he did not make it to vestry meetings, see *GW Diaries*, 2:44, 199, 323; 3:143, 186, 216, 277, 293.

38. *Minutes of the Vestry*, 86–87, 89, 91–92, 92–93, 94–95, 100–101, 107–8, 111–12, 117–18, 120, 122–23, 126, 130, 137–38.

39. Holmes, *Faiths of the Founding Fathers*, 67–68.

40. Henriques, "A Few Simple Beliefs," 182.

41. Virginia House of Burgesses, *Journals, 1766–1769*, 190, 211, 228. For the renewal in 1772 and 1774, see Virginia House of Burgesses, *Journals, 1770–1772*, 204, and *Journals, 1773–1776*, 102.

42. Virginia House of Burgesses, *Journals, 1770–1772*, 78, 79.

43. Ibid., 204, 209, 210, 241, 292.

44. Virginia House of Burgesses, *Journals, 1773–1776*, 88.

45. Nelson, *A Blessed Company*, 32.

46. "Parish Collection," 1765–68, in Ledger A, MVLA (bound photostat), 224–25. For discussion that it was typical for church wardens, vestrymen, and/or ministers to supply wine for the service of Holy Communion in Virginia Anglican churches at this period, for which they would be reimbursed, see Nelson, *A Blessed Company*, 67.

47. Nelson, *A Blessed Company*, 65.

48. For purchases for Pohick Church, see *GW Diaries*, 3:113n, 234n–35n; and *Minutes of the Vestry*, 134 and 135. Specifically for the purchase of "6 Books of best gold leaf" by Washington, see "Enclosure: Invoice to Robert Cary & Co.," *GW Papers, Colonial Series*, 9:274 and 275n–76n. For more on Sears and his work at Mount Vernon, Gunston Hall, and Mount Airy plantations, as well as Pohick Church, see Dalzell and Dalzell, *George Washington's Mount Vernon*, 103, 104–7, 164–69.

49. Goodwin, *Colonial Church*, 106.

50. Nelson, *A Blessed Company*, 295–99, 301–2.

51. See entries for May 1782 in "Hard Money pd. on Acct. of General Washington"; for February 3, 1783 in "Cash pd. on Acct. of General Washington"; and for November 1783 in "Tobacco pd. on Acct. of Genrl. Washington," Lund Washington Account Book, 1774–86, MVLA (typescript), 110, 117, 118. For the story about Griffith's covert meeting with Washington concerning Lee, see Custis, *Recollections and Private Memoirs*, 289–92.

52. See entries for February 7, 1785, and April 8, 1786, "Cash pd. on Acct. of Genrl. Washington," Lund Washington Account Book, 1774–86, MVLA (typescript), 146, 159; George Washington, November 5, 1787 [*sic*], in GW "Cash Memoranda," March 1788–May 1789, MVLA (bound photostat), 22, [23]. For additional information on David Griffith and his relationship to George Washington, see *GW Papers, Confederation Series*, 1:70n, 284, 286, 499–500; 2:61, 138n; 3:303n, 338; 4:5, 147, 170, 226; 5:50–51, 51n, 76–77, 77n, 156; 6:185, 185n–86n; *GW Papers, Presidential Series*, 1:89–90, 90n; and *GW Diaries*, 4:76, 113, 128, 206, 207, 220, 221, 272, 274, 303, 304; 5:98, 99, 108, 109, 117, 192, 249, 293, 293n, 351.

53. GW, November 20, 1794, in GW "Cash Memoranda," Sept. 1794–Dec. 1799, MVLA, A-55 (bound photostat), 2 [4].

54. GW, January 8, 1798; February 24, 1798; April 24, 1799, in ibid., 11 [51], 17 [57], 46 [88].

55. Wayland, *Washingtons and Their Homes*, 140.

56. Felder, *Fielding Lewis and the Washington Family*, 107–10, 133, 137, 138, 143–44, 157, 240, 240n.

57. Fielding Lewis, Last Will and Testament, October 19, 1781, MVLA, RM-104/PS-2272 (photostat).

58. Griffin, *Catalogue of the Washington Collection*, 234–73; Thomas Birch's Sons, *Catalogue No. 663*, 48.

59. Thomas Birch's Sons, *Catalogue No. 663*, 29.

60. Thompson and Cummins, *This Day in Baptist History*, 77–78, 381–82; Varon, *We Mean to Be Counted*, 23.

61. Meade, *Old Churches, Ministers, and Families*, 2:208n, 236–37. For a wonderful story about the local minister wearing a suit of GW's while spending Christmas with the next generation of Washingtons at Mount Vernon, see page 2:237 of this same source.

62. Ibid., 2:236–37.

63. Jane Charlotte Blackburn Washington to John Augustine Washington III, February 23, 1838, in Lee, "Jane C. Washington, Family, and Nation at Mount Vernon," 35.

64. Jane Charlotte Blackburn Washington, Last Will and Testament, October 3, 1854, MVLA, RM-480/PS-3906 (photostat), 1.

65. See Nelly Custis Lewis to Elizabeth Bordley Gibson, [October 28, 1820] and November 27, 1820, in Lewis, *George Washington's Beautiful Nelly*, 89 and 89n, 94 and 94n. For additional references to Bishop White and Mr. Wilmer in this same source, pages 110, 127, 166, 177, 182, 251, 254.

66. Meade, *Old Churches, Ministers, and Families*, 2:231–32.

4. SUNDAYS

1. Nelson, *A Blessed Company*, 189–93.

2. For Wren's drawing of the plans for Christ Church in Alexandria, see *GW Papers, Colonial Series*, 9:181n.

3. Meade, *Old Churches, Ministers, and Families*, 2:226–27; Netherton and Netherton, *History and Architecture of Pohick Church*, 2–5.

4. Regarding the completion date of the church, see *GW Papers, Colonial Series,* 9:349n.

5. See entry dated December 23, 1773 in Ledger B, MVLA (bound photostat), 98a.

6. For the pews, see *GW Papers, Colonial Series,* 9:463n–64n.

7. GW, "Cash Accounts," August 15, 1774, *GW Papers, Colonial Series,* 10:140, 140n–41n. In an interesting aside, Lund Washington, who was George Washington's cousin and farm manager for many years, paid one pound on July 29, 1782, on behalf of George Washington, "for a stone that was taken from Pohick Church for Dineg Room Hearth" at Mount Vernon (see "Hard Money pd. on Acct. of General Washington," Lund Washington Account Book, 1774–86, MVLA [typescript], 110).

8. See entry dated 1774, in the account with George Mason, in Ledger B, MVLA (bound photostat), 6a.

9. For the story of the construction of Christ Church and Washington's pew there, see *GW Papers, Colonial Series,* 9:181n–83n.

10. The minimum time needed to get to church was determined from several sources. According to an oral communication from Kevin Kelly from the staff at Colonial Williamsburg on July 8, 1999, Richard Nicholls, another staff member at the same institution, estimated that a horse, going at a pretty good pace from 4 a.m. until 8 p.m. could travel about sixty miles in that time (3.75 miles/hour), while a large carriage would make half that distance in the same time (1.88 miles/hour), and a smaller carriage would travel somewhere in between (maybe 45 miles, at 2.8 miles/hour). Using their figures, it would take 2.66 hours to reach Christ Church and 1.87 hours to get to Pohick Church (on horseback), and the journey would have taken 5.33 hours and 3.73 hours, respectively (in a large carriage), or 3.57 hours and 2.5 hours (in a light carriage). Washington once noted in his diary that when traveling by horseback, he typically averaged a rate of 5 miles per hour (see entry for September 12, 1784, in *GW Diaries,* 4:19). At that speed, it would have taken him 2.0 hours to get to Christ Church and 1.4 hours to reach Pohick Church. Of course, when traveling to church with the family, he probably took a carriage, which would suggest that travel times were probably closer to those suggested by the staff at Colonial Williamsburg.

11. GW to Burwell Bassett, August 28, 1762, *GW Papers, Colonial Series,* 7:147. Burwell Bassett of Eltham Plantation, following in the footsteps of his father, was a long-time vestryman at Blissland Parish in New Kent County, Virginia (see Meade, *Old Churches, Ministers, and Families,* 2:496).

12. Jonathan Boucher, excerpt from his published autobiography, in *GW Writings,* 2:486n–87n.

13. Meade, *Old Churches, Ministers, and Families,* 2:247.

14. Bonomi and Eisenstadt, "Church Adherence in the Eighteenth-Century British American Colonies," 254n and 258n–59n; Bond, *Damned Souls in a Tobacco Colony,* 240.

15. Boller, *George Washington & Religion,* 28–31. In the case of foxhunting, it is a bit of a stretch to say that GW often engaged in this practice on Sundays: he may have gone foxhunting on January 24 and February 28 of 1768; on two other occasions (September 17 and 24, 1769), he and his friends hunted the day before and his foxhunt-

ing buddies spent the night, but there is no record of them hunting on the Sunday (see entries for those dates in *GW Diaries*, 2:32, 40, 181, 182).

16. Blassingame, *Slave Testimony*, 248–50.

17. *GW Diaries*, 5:173.

18. Quoted in *GW Papers, Confederation Series*, 5:271n.

19. GW to Bryan Fairfax, January 20, 1799, *GW Papers, Retirement Series*, 3:325, 325n.

20. Lund Washington to GW, August 17, 1767, *GW Papers, Colonial Series*, 8:18.

21. Nelly Custis to Elizabeth Bordley, July 2, 1797, MVLA (typescript).

22. Nelly Custis to Elizabeth Bordley, March 20, 1798, *George Washington's Beautiful Nelly*, 49.

23. For Charles Green's appointment at the suggestion of Augustine Washington and his hiring, see *Minutes of the Vestry*, 13, 18.

24. For a fine overview of this long-forgotten case, see Henriques, "Major Lawrence Washington versus the Reverend Charles Green," 233–64; for the quotes used here, see pages 261 and 262. For letters testifying to the warm and easy relationship between Martha Washington and her pastor's wife, Margaret Green, see Fields, *Worthy Partner*, 131, 135, 137.

25. *Minutes of the Vestry*, 93, 100, 107, 111. For background on Rev. James Scott, see Nelson, *A Blessed Company*, 171–73, 318. For the little that is known about the Reverend John Andrews, see Nelson, *A Blessed Company*, 303, and Meade, *Old Churches, Ministers, and Families*, 2:272–73.

26. See *GW Papers, Colonial Series*, 10:187n. For more on Reverend Dade's background, see Nelson, *A Blessed Company*, 307.

27. Cresswell, October 23, 1774; October 30, 1774; December 4, 1774; January 1, 1775; March 19, 1775, *Journal*, 43, 45, 48, 52, 59.

28. Ibid., 165.

29. Nelson, *A Blessed Company*, 315.

30. For the description of Reverend Massey, see Meade, *Old Churches, Ministers, and Families*, 2:225–26.

31. For ministerial problems at Pohick and Christ Churches, see Moore, *Seaport in Virginia*, 131; Netherton and Netherton, *History and Architecture of Pohick Church*, 5, 10; Powell, *History of Old Alexandria*, 85; *Minutes of the Vestry*, 100, 107, 111.

32. "Alexandria—1795," in Miller, *Pen Portraits of Alexandria*, 39. In this passage, the unnamed "European Emigrant" writes to a friend in London, confiding that he found Alexandria to be "one of the most wicked places I ever beheld in my life." He goes on to give evidence for why he feels this way, including the statement that "Here is one protestant church, where service is performed once a month; one presbyterian, methodist and roman catholic chapel." From the way this is written, I've assumed that Christ Church was the "one protestant church."

33. Meade, *Old Churches, Ministers, and Families*, 1:17.

34. Bond, *Damned Souls*, 240–42. For discussion that Byrd was probably staying away on days when he would not be able to hear a sermon, see Nelson, *A Blessed Company*, 200–201.

35. For absences from church, see *GW Diaries*: sickness in family, March 6, 1768,

January 17, 1790, April 4, 1790, May 9, 1790, September 1, 1799, September 29, 1799; bad
weather, April 6, 1766, December 27, 1789, April 18, 1790; carriage loaned out, January 6,
1760, see also September 16, 1770; traveling, April 20, 1760, see also May 4, 1760, May 18,
1760, October 15, 1763, April 13, 1766, October 23, 1768, and others too numerous to
mention; minister sick, September 27, 1772; broken chariot, April 17, 1774. It should
also be noted that an architectural historian was recently taken to task by a specialist
in church history for criticizing George Washington's habits of church attendance. In
a review of Dell Upton's *Holy Things and Profane,* Joan R. Gundersen noted, "Other
examples of emphasizing the negative include labeling George Washington a 'private
scoffer' for attending church once a month" (188).

36. *GW Diaries,* 2:257n.

37. GW to the secretary of war, April 23, 1799, *GW Writings,* 37:187–88. See also the
statement by Nelly Custis Lewis that her step-grandfather "attended the church in Alexandria, when the weather and roads permitted a ride of ten miles," recorded in Nelly
Custis Lewis to Jared Sparks, February 26, 1833, in Sparks, *Life of Washington,* 521.

38. GW to Jonathan Boucher, May 30, 1768, *GW Writings,* 2:487.

39. GW to Samuel Hanson, August 6, 1788; GW to George Steptoe Washington,
August 6, 1788; Samuel Hanson to GW, August 7, 1788; and George Steptoe Washington
to GW, August 8, 1788, in *GW Papers, Confederation Series,* 6:429, 430, 431–32, 433–34.

40. Chinard, *George Washington as the French Knew Him,* 120–21; and Bishop
William White to the Rev. B. C. C. Parker, December 21, 1832, in Wilson, *Memoir of
Reverend William White,* 193.

41. Decatur, *Private Affairs,* 90, 231–32; GW to The Rector, Church Wardens,
and Vestrymen of the United Episcopal Churches of Christ Church and St. Peter's
(March 2, 1797), *GW Writings,* 35:410–11.

42. GW to George Steptoe Washington, March 23, 1789, *GW Papers, Presidential
Series,* 1:439–40.

43. GW to Tobias Lear, June 26, 1791, *GW Papers, Presidential Series,* 8:300.

44. For the Washington family's standard practice on Sundays, see Custis, *Recollections and Private Memoirs,* 171, 173, 174; Nelly Custis Lewis to Jared Sparks, quoted in
Sparks, *Life of George Washington,* 521.

45. Decatur, *Private Affairs,* 90.

46. The book, which was published in London and Dublin in 1765, was probably
the work of either British poet Charles Churchill or his father. It was purchased by
Washington on November 3, 1772, apparently during a trip to Williamsburg (see Griffin, *A Catalogue of the Washington Collection,* 498, and *GW Papers, Colonial Series,*
7:349n and 9:116).

47. Niemcewicz, *Under Their Vine and Fig Tree,* 99, 104. In addition to his journal,
Niemcewicz also wrote a biography of George Washington, which was published in
Poland in 1803. In the biography, Niemcewicz wrote that, "Every Sunday he [Washing-
ton] goes to church with his family" (see Rusinowa, "Julian Ursyn Niemcewicz's Biography of George Washington," 8). This statement is particularly interesting because,
in the journal, Niemcewicz makes no mention of the family going to church on either

of the Sundays he was with them, nor does George Washington's diary (see entries for June 3 and 10, 1798, in *GW Diaries*, 6:299, 301).

48. For the purchase of Watts's book of psalms and hymns, see GW to Samuel Loudon, December 30, 1782, GW Writings, 25:495. That book, *The Beauties of the late Revd. Dr. Isaac Watts; Containing the Most Striking & Admired Passages in the Works of That Justly Celebrated Divine, Philosopher, Moralist, & Poet: Equally Calculated for the Communication of Polite & Useful Knowledge & the Increase of Wisdom and Happiness. To Which Is Added the Life of the Author,* was published in London in 1782; Martha Washington's original copy survives today (MVLA, W-385).

49. For purchases of religious books during the presidency, see "Washington's Household Account Book," 29:392, 30:159, 168, 169, 327.

50. For the commentary on Psalms, see MVLA, "Report of the Library Committee," *Minutes of the Council,* 51.

51. Jenyns's book bears the signatures of both Martha Washington and her grandson's wife, Mary Lee Fitzhugh Custis (MVLA, W-1201).

52. "Klopstock, Friedrich Gottlieb," *New Encyclopaedia Britannica,* 15th ed., 6:911.

53. For titles dealing with religion in George Washington's library, see Bixby, *Inventory of Mount Vernon,* 16, 17, 19, 22, 23, 24, 25, 26, 27, 36. One of those, bearing George Washington's signature, was published in Boston in 1794 by Shippie Townsend, a member of the Boston Universalist Society, who had produced a catechism for Universalist children in 1787. Interestingly, the Townsend book in Washington's library was given the decidedly evangelical title *Gospel News, Divided into Eleven Sections. Peace and Joy: Being a Brief Attempt to Consider the Evidences of the Truth of the Gospel, in Which We Have the Witness of Peace with God, through Jesus Christ . . . ,* (MVLA, ML-28-W). Information on Shippie Townsend's membership in the Universalist Society was found in item number bMS 407/1(3), at http://www.harvard.edu/library/bms/bms00407.html. Information about Townsend's catechism for Universalist children was at http://onlineskm.edu/univ/education/robertson_early_univ_edu.html (both accessed June 2, 2004).

54. For an indication that many of the earlier pamphlets and sermons may have been bound together during George Washington's presidency, see GW to Howell Lewis, August 4, 1793, *GW Writings,* 33:42n. Washington also shared sermons with his wife (see GW to Tobias Lear, March 28, 1791, in *GW Papers, Presidential Series,* 8:22).

55. In looking, for example, at the collecting habits of President James Monroe, one historian has written: "James and Elizabeth Monroe did own a substantial collection of art that included religious subjects. . . . But the inclusion of religious art was typical in a collection of that time and says little about religious belief. Monroe's selection of art parallels that of Jefferson and of other Virginia and English contemporaries. A typical Protestant gentleman's home might have paintings of religious subjects by continental Roman Catholic artists, mixed with landscapes, old masters, contemporary art, engravings and prints, and classical sculpture. In addition, the evidence indicates that Elizabeth Kortright Monroe, who was especially interested in art and architecture, was instrumental in the collecting" (see Holmes, *Faiths of the Founding Fathers,* 104).

56. GW, Circular to the States, June 8, 1783, *GW Writings,* 26:485.

57. "An Inventory &c. of Articles at Mount Vernon," in Prussing, *The Estate of George Washington,* 410. For more on the artwork collected by George Washington for the mansion, see Reeves, "The Prints," 502–11.

58. Ayres, "The Virgin Mary's Homecoming," 22–25.

59. Curl, *Art and Architecture of Freemasonry,* 25, 44, 113–14, 244; Hamilton, *Material Culture of the American Freemasons,* 167, 203.

60. "An Inventory &c. of Articles at Mount Vernon," in Prussing, *The Estate of George Washington,* 414. A duplicate of the original engraving now hangs in the Yellow Bedroom (MVLA, M-93/K).

61. "An Inventory &c. of Articles at Mount Vernon," in Prussing, *The Estate of George Washington,* 412; Reeves, "The Prints," 503; "Alfred," in *New Encyclopaedia Britannica,* 15th ed., 1:259–60. For the engraving *Alfred the Great Dividing His Loaf With the Pilgrim,* see MVLA, M-93/CC. For the legend of Alfred and the Pilgrim, see http://www.orthodoxengland.btinternet.co.uk/athlifea.htm, and http://www.somerset .gov.uk/museums/alfred/legends.htm; and Erffa and Staley, *Paintings of Benjamin West,* 187–88.

62. "An Inventory &c. of Articles at Mount Vernon," in Prussing, *The Estate of George Washington,* 412; Reeves, "The Prints," 503. For specific information on the engraving currently hanging in the mansion, which is a duplicate of the original, see MVLA, M-93/N. For background on the print itself, see Fowble, *Two Centuries of Prints in America,* 202–3.

63. Lillback, *Proclaim Liberty,* 16–24.

64. GW to the Society of Quakers, (October 1789), *GW Papers, Presidential Series,* 4:266.

65. GW, Farewell Address, September 19, 1796, *GW Writings,* 35:231.

66. For more on the quilt, see MVLA, W-365 (an illustration of the quilt can be found in Allen, *First Flowerings,* 29). For discussion that the scene in the engraving was symbolic of brotherly love and that dealers were selling the fabric in Philadelphia in the late 1780s, see Montgomery, *Printed Textiles,* 279 and 285. Apparently, the first of the treaty negotiations between William Penn and the Indians was held under a large tree. Also in the Mount Vernon collections is a nineteenth-century box, lined with wood, which is said to be from that tree (see MVLA, W-660).

67. "An Inventory &c. of Articles at Mount Vernon," in Prussing, *The Estate of George Washington,* 416; for the original print, see MVLA, W-2621.

68. Goethe, *Sufferings of Young Werther,* 79–85.

69. For identification of the Countess of Huntingdon, see *GW Papers, Confederation Series,* 2:199–200. For additional information about the countess, see "Making History: The Countess of Huntingdon's Connexion," at http://www.bbc.co.uk/ education/beyond/factsheets/makhist/makhist7-prog5d.shtml; "Selina Hastings: Countess of Huntingdon, Patroness of Revival," at http://www.historyswomen.com/ selina.html; Cook, "Selina: Countess of Huntingdon," at http://www.evangelical-times .org/articles/oct01/oct01all.htm; "Selina Shirley Huntingdon: Countess of Huntingdon, 1707–1791," at http://www.cyberhymnal.org/bio/h/u/huntingdon-c.htm; and Osborn

Music MS.525, Acc. 71.8.64, in "Yale University, Beinecke Rare Book and Manuscript Library, The James Marshall and Marie-Louise Osborn Collection, Osborn Music Manuscripts," at http://webtext.library .yale.edu/beinflat/osborn.MUSIC.HTM. Information about the hymn writers was taken from http://www.cyberhymnal.org/index .htm (accessed June 8, 2004).

70. Mason, *Poems of Phyllis Wheatley,* 7–8, 44, 56–57, 78n, 132–35, 150n, 184–85, 184n–86n, 193–95, 193n–94n, 196n.

71. For a detailed treatment of the countess's life, as well as the source for the George III quote, see Cook, *Selina, Countess of Huntingdon,* 299.

72. For an outline of the countess's plan, see *Papers of GW, Confederation Series,* 2:199–200. For the quotes, see the Countess of Huntingdon to GW (March 1784), in *GW Papers, Confederation Series,* 2:206. For discussion that the countess and George Washington may have been related, see GW to Bryan Fairfax, January 20, 1799, in *GW Papers, Retirement Series,* 3:325 and 325n, and Cook, *Selina, Countess of Huntingdon,* 3.

73. The information that the portrait was a gift from the countess comes from a list of original Washington objects that were sold to the Smithsonian Institution in 1878 by descendants of Martha Washington's youngest granddaughter, Nelly Custis Lewis (see "The Washington Relics [Lewis Collection]," at http://www.150.si.edu/siarch/guide/washing.htm). The engraving is still part of the Political History Collection at the National Museum of American History, Smithsonian Institution, Washington, D.C. The quote from Bowyer is found in Smith, *Selina Hastings, the Countess of Huntingdon,* 53.

74. GW to Robert Bowyer, January 8, 1792, in *GW Papers, Presidential Series,* 9:395. Within just a few years, Washington's friend the Reverend Bryan Fairfax would become friends with the countess's successor, Lady Anne Agnes Erskine (see Bryan Fairfax to GW, August 21, 1798; GW to Bryan Fairfax, January 20, 1799; and Bryan Fairfax to GW, April 28, 1799, *GW Papers, Retirement Series,* 2:551, 3:325, 4:32, 33n.).

75. Baker, *Washington After the Revolution,* 232n; Decatur, Private Affairs, 221–22.

76. Oliver, "A Fine Kettle of Fish," 19, 20–21.

77. For the Washingtons' behavior during church services, see Nelly Custis Lewis to Jared Sparks, February 26, 1833, in Sparks, *Life of George Washington,* 521.

78. Bishop William White to the Rev. B. C. C. Parker, November 28, 1832, in Wilson, *Memoir of the Reverend William White,* 189.

79. M'Guire, *Religious Opinions and Character of Washington,* 154–55. The only time Washington is known to have attended Christ Church in the summer of 1799 was on Sunday, June 2, as he was heading home from the Federal City to Mount Vernon; the story in M'Guire's book is corroborated by Washington's diary account of the day (see *GW Diaries,* 6:350). Reverend M'Guire's commentary on this story is particularly intriguing in light of Washington's previously mentioned statements about how the distance of Mount Vernon from church and the presence of guests often prevented him from getting to church. It is also a good example of how overstatement by well-meaning proponents of Washington as a Christian have not only muddied the waters but have cast doubt on the very points they hoped to make.

80. Steiner, *Religious Beliefs of Our Presidents,* 22. Steiner then continued: "If he did not kneel in church, who will believe that he did so on the ground, covered with snow,

with his hat off, when the thermometer was probably below zero?" This remark was a reference to the praying-in-the-snow stories, popular in the nineteenth century, which portrayed Washington as a pietist (ibid.).

81. Holmes, *The Faiths of the Founding Fathers*, 62.

5. CONFIRMATION AND COMMUNION

1. Nelson, *A Blessed Company*, 194–95.

2. For religious practice in Virginia at this period, see Isaac, *Transformation of Virginia*, 120; Bonomi and Eisenstadt, "Church Adherence in the Eighteenth-Century British American Colonies," 260–61.

3. Nelson, *A Blessed Company*, 196.

4. Ibid., 196–99. So common was it for people to have scruples against taking communion, that one of the prayer books (catalogue number M-1804) in the Mount Vernon collections, which was published in Edinburgh in 1701, contains a chapter entitled "A Companion to the Altar: Shewing the Nature and Necessity of a Sacramental Preparation, in Order to Our Worthy Receiving the Holy Communion; Wherein Those Fears and Scruples about Eating and Drinking Unworthily, and of Incurring Our Own Damnation Thereby, Are Proved Groundless and Unwarrantable. Unto Which Are Added Prayers and Meditations, Preparative to a Sacramental Preparation, according to What the Church of England Requires from Her Communicants."

5. Ibid., 218–20.

6. Holmes, *Faiths of the Founding Fathers*, 62, 94, 104, 112–15, 136, 138, 140. For more on the confirmation of Mrs. Madison, see Meade, *Old Churches, Ministers, and Families*, 2:91–92.

7. For the connection of Bishop James Madison to the future president of the same name, see Holmes, *Faiths of the Founding Fathers*, 104. For Bishop Madison's actions as bishop of Virginia, see Meade, *Old Churches, Ministers, and Families*, 1:17–18, 22, 30, 37, 95; 2:70, 91–92, 257, 267–68, 272, 274, 322, 346, 422, 496.

8. For the assertion that Washington took communion before the Revolution but changed his practice later, see Nelly Custis Lewis to Elizabeth Bordley Gibson, December 1, 1826, MVLA (typescript), and Nelly Custis Lewis to Jared Sparks, February 26, 1833, in Sparks, *Life of George Washington*, 522.

9. David L. Holmes, who is the Walter G. Mason Professor of Religious Studies at the College of William and Mary, is one of the rare modern scholars who accepts Nelly Custis Lewis's statements about her grandparents' religious practices as valid. In one passage, he notes, "Because the sacrament would have represented a curiosity to a young adult, no substantial reason exists to doubt the story [that Washington took communion before the Revolution]." A little later in the same essay, he writes, "Far more persuasive is the account of Nelly Custis that she and Washington always left church at the end of the Desk and Pulpit service on Communion Sundays and then sent the carriage back from Mount Vernon to pick up Martha, who had remained" (Holmes, *Faiths of the Founding Fathers*, 62 and 63).

10. Col. Hugh Mercer to Bishop William White, August 13, 1835, and Bishop William White to Col. Hugh Mercer, August 15, 1835, in Wilson, *Memoir of the Life of the Right Reverend William White*, 196–97.

11. Ashbel Green to Bernard Whitman, March 8, 1834, in MVLA, *Annual Report 1956*, 41–42. In addition to this wartime incident, apparently the widow of Alexander Hamilton told her great-grandson that she witnessed Washington taking communion during the church service following his first inauguration in New York. This story has problems of credibility: first, knowing how infrequently communion was part of Anglican/Episcopal services in the eighteenth century, it seems strange that this rite would have taken place at a more official service, when nonmembers of the congregation were present. Second, Mrs. Hamilton is said to have related this incident to her great-grandson at a family reunion in May of 1854, when she was alleged to be ninety-seven years old and he was only seven. While elderly people tend to retain long-term memories better than short-term ones, and the inauguration would surely have been an important and impressive event in her life, there were still sixty-five years between the event and the relation of the tale to Mrs. Hamilton's great-grandchild. One also has to wonder about how clearly a seven-year-old would remember a specific conversation. Third, the story was not made public until the 1920s, seventy years after the initial telling of the story. Even though two other individuals also are said to have heard Mrs. Hamilton make similar statements, there are too many problems with the sources to give the story serious credence. A number of these issues would pertain to another story in the Hamilton family, told by Mrs. Hamilton to the same great-grandson at the same family reunion, that while she was at Valley Forge with her father during the Revolution, she heard "George Washington praying fervently for all to be well for the soldiers." I would like to thank Dr. Peter A. Lillback of the Providence Forum for bringing this Hamilton family lore to my attention (Peter A. Lillback, "Mrs. Alexander Hamilton, Witness That Washington Was a Communicant of the Church," undated memo enclosed with a letter to the author dated June 2, 2005). When a later member of the Washington family, Jane Charlotte Blackburn Washington (Mrs. John Augustine Washington II), indicated in 1838 that she had doubts "as to the certainty of the General's having been a Communicant in the Church while residing in the City of New York after the Revolution," an elderly gentleman from that city wrote to put her mind at ease. His recollections are quite interesting, and perhaps more credible than the Hamilton oral history for several reasons: the writer/witness was speaking of something he himself had witnessed, more than once; he was well into adulthood (in his late thirties or early forties) at the time of the incidents he described; and he put these stories into writing during his own lifetime (see Maj. William Popham to Jane Charlotte Blackburn Washington, March 14, 1838, in Popham, *The Churchman*, 796–97, MVLA [typescript]). The Popham correspondence was also published in Meade, *Old Churches, Ministers, and Families*, 2:490–91, along with the reminiscences of Gen. Robert Porterfield, who also claimed to have seen Washington "on his knees to receive the Sacrament of the Lord's Supper in —— Church, in Philadelphia" (see Gen. S. H. Lewis to the Rev. Mr. Dana, December 14, 1855, in Meade, *Old Churches, Ministers, and Fami-*

lies, 2:491–92). There was also an oral tradition passed down in the family of the Rev. Lee Massey, who had been at Pohick Church, that Washington had been a communicant (see Meade, *Old Churches, Ministers, and Families,* 2:254).

12. Boller, *George Washington & Religion,* 33–34.

13. For the biographer's interpretation about this change in practice, see Sparks, *Life of George Washington,* 523. Another notable American who was contemporary with Washington and also did not take communion, despite the fact that he was a professing Christian and was active in the church, was John Marshall, the fourth chief justice of the U.S. Supreme Court (see Baker, *John Marshall,* 751–52). Abstaining from communion when one was not in the proper state of mind would have been in keeping with traditional Christian theology and practice as propounded by the apostle Paul (see 1st Corinthians 11:27–29).

14. Meade, *Old Churches, Ministers, and Families,* 2:495.

15. Gaustad, *Faith of Our Fathers,* 17–18. Not surprisingly, examples of similar beliefs about episcopacy, monarchy, and democracy can be found in British documents from this period as well (see Serle, *American Journal,* 93, 115–16).

16. GW to Daniel McCarty, February 22, 1784, *GW Writings,* 27:341–42.

17. For information on Seabury and the state of the Anglican/Episcopal Church during and after the Revolution, see Bryden, *Virginia's Mother Church,* 117–18, 212–16, 223; Goodwin, *Colonial Church in Virginia,* 102–22, 127–35; Clarence H. Vance, "Seabury, Samuel," *DAB,* 16:529; Manross, *History of the American Episcopal Church,* 121, 174–75, 178, 179, 192–209, 214; and Thompson, *United States Army Chaplaincy,* 82–83, 204.

18. Emphasis in the original (see *GW Diaries,* 4:203–4).

19. Thompson, *United States Army Chaplaincy,* 245–67.

20. Undated marginal note by Charles Cecil Wall, long-time director at Mount Vernon, in the MVLA copy of Meade, *Old Churches, Ministers, and Families,* 2:255.

21. For more on Washington's change of heart about slavery, see Flexner, "George Washington and Slavery," in *George Washington: Anguish and Farewell,* 112–25; Flexner, "Washington and Slavery," 5–10; Twohig, "That Species of Property," 114–38; and Thompson, "The Only Unavoidable Subject of Regret," 6–8.

22. Jack D. Warren Jr., former assistant editor of the *Papers of George Washington* at the University of Virginia, 1993–98, and author of *The Presidency of George Washington* (Mount Vernon, VA: Mount Vernon Ladies' Association, 2000), conversation with the author and Michael Quinn, Mount Vernon, Virginia, July 20, 1999.

23. Clarence H. Vance, "Letters of a Westchester Farmer," in Seabury, *Letters of a Westchester Farmer,* 3. For examples of how similar beliefs—and outright persecution—were used to enforce both British rule and Anglican supremacy over dissenters for several hundred years within Britain and its burgeoning empire, see Thompson and Cummins, *This Day in Baptist History,* 28–29, 33–34, 136–37, 255–56, 359–60, 414–15, 470–71, 497–98; Rusten and Rusten, *One Year Book of Christian History,* 52–53, 96–97, 130–31, 160, 244–45, 260–1, 264–65, 408–9, 620–21; and Webb, *Born Fighting,* 85, 92, 97–98, 110, 142.

24. Thompson, *United States Army Chaplaincy,* 245–67.

25. Thompson and Cummins, *This Day in Baptist History,* 49, 184–85, 521.

26. Thompson, *United States Army Chaplaincy,* 182, 255.

27. GW, October 2, 1785, *GW Diaries,* 4:200, 200n, and 201. David Jones was not the only former chaplain to visit the Washingtons at Mount Vernon. Abraham Baldwin, a Congregationalist who had been chaplain to the Second Connecticut Regiment during the Revolution, stopped by Mount Vernon on December 13, 1785, but, according to his host, "would not stay [to] dinner" (*GW Diaries,* 4:249, 249n–50n; see also Thompson, *United States Army Chaplaincy,* 205, 246.)

28. Thompson, *United States Army Chaplaincy,* 195–96. For the information about Caldwell managing spies, see the Marquis de Lafayette to Elias Boudinot, July 15, [1778], in Lafayette, *Lafayette in the Age of the American Revolution,* 2:107–8.

29. Thacher, *Military Journal of the American Revolution,* 198–99.

30. Thompson, *United States Army Chaplaincy,* 196; GW to Elias Boudinot, December 14, 1782, and GW to the president of Congress, January 8, 1783, *GW Writings,* 25:427 and 26:17.

31. Still another factor in Washington's change in practice regarding communion might be his role during the war itself. My father, Chaplain (Col.) Parker Campbell Thompson (U.S. Army, retired), served as a chaplain in the United States Army for thirty-two years, including service with combat units in both the Korean and Vietnam Wars. In a conversation in the summer of 2001, Chaplain Thompson noted that it had been his experience that officers in positions of authority, with responsibility for sending hundreds of young men into actions that might cause their deaths, often have trouble later continuing to practice their religious beliefs, because they feel like they have blood on their hands and are unworthy.

32. Frank Grizzard to Richard Holway, September 12, 2005 (e-mail communication forwarded to me by the recipient, September 13, 2005).

33. GW to James Madison, March 2, 1788, *GW Writings,* 29:431.

34. GW to Lund Washington, August 15, 1778, ibid., 12:327.

35. Marquis de Lafayette to GW, February 5, 1783, ibid., 26:300n.

36. GW to the Marquis de Lafayette, April 5, 1783, ibid., 26:300.

37. William Gordon to GW, August 30, 1784, *GW Papers, Confederation Series,* 2:64.

38. The Marquis de Lafayette to GW, February 6, 1786, ibid., 3:121, 544.

39. GW to the Marquis de Lafayette, May 10, 1786, ibid., 4:43.

40. GW to Arthur Young, December 12, 1793; GW to Tobias Lear, September 11, 1797; and GW to Richard Parkinson, November 28, 1797, *GW Writings,* 33:174–83, 36:31 and 80.

41. Robert Pleasants to GW, December 11, 1785, *GW Papers, Confederation Series,* 3:449–51, 451n.

42. GW to Robert Morris, April 12, 1786, *GW Writings,* 28:408.

43. GW to the Marquis de Lafayette, May 10, 1786, *GW Papers, Confederation Series,* 4:43–44.

44. GW to John Francis Mercer, September 9, 1786, *GW Writings,* 29:5.

45. Kolchin, *American Slavery,* 76–79; Robinson, *Slavery in the Structure of American Politics,* 23–24, 29–30, 35, 55n.

46. For discussion of how Washington's concern with preserving the new country may have overridden his objections to the continuation of slavery, see Hirschfeld, *George Washington and Slavery,* 233; Wiencek, *An Imperfect God,* 268–70.

47. *Virginia Statutes at Large,* 6:112, and 11:39–40; Finkelman, "Thomas Jefferson and Antislavery," 217; and Finkelman, "Jefferson and Slavery," 186–88.

48. *Last Will and Testament of George Washington,* 2.

49. John C. Fitzpatrick, "The Will of Martha Washington of Mount Vernon," in ibid., 62.

50. Ibid., 2–4. For Virginia laws dealing with the estate issues and manumission requirements faced by the Washingtons, see *Virginia Statutes at Large,* 5:445, 446, 464; 11:39–40; 12:145, 146, 150.

51. Comment by GW, recorded by his former secretary, David Humphries, in Zagarri, *David Humphreys' "Life of General Washington,"* 78.

<h3 style="text-align:center">6. PRAYER</h3>

1. Weems, *Life of Washington,* ix–xiii, xvii–xviii, 181–82.

2. Thorburn, "Letter from Grant Thorburn," 179. For an earlier publication of a similar story, see M'Guire, *Religious Opinions and Character of Washington,* 159. For another similar story, see Custis, *Recollections and Private Memoirs,* 275n.

3. For the prayers themselves, their appearance in the 1891 auction, and the debate about their authenticity as it stood in the early twentieth century, see Burk, *Washington's Prayers,* and Steiner, *Religious Beliefs of Our Presidents,* 20–21. Information on the latest scholarly opinion about the prayers comes from a conversation I had with Dorothy Twohig, retired senior editor of the Papers of George Washington project at the University of Virginia, at the Virginia Historical Society in Richmond, Virginia, in the fall of 1999; and from Grizzard, *Ways of Providence,* 51–52.

4. Sullivan, *Familiar Letters,* 74; also quoted in Custis, *Recollections and Private Memoirs,* 493n.

5. For more on Porterfield's military career, see GW, general orders, January 8, 1779, and GW to John Marshall, June 6, 1799, in *GW Writings,* 13:485 and 485n, 37:228 and 228n. For Porterfield's recollections of this incident, see Gen. S. H. Lewis to the Rev. Mr. Dana, December 14, 1855, in Meade, *Old Churches, Ministers, and Families,* 2:491–92.

6. Chinard, *George Washington as the French Knew Him,* 119.

7. "Enclosure: Invoice to Robert Cary & Co.," July 18, 1771, in *GW Papers, Colonial Series,* 8:509, for Washington's order. See also page 563 of the same volume for the invoice, dated December 3, 1771, of what was actually sent by the London bookseller Francis Newbery.

8. GW, general order, September 13, 1777, *GW Writings,* 9:211.

9. Nelly Custis Lewis to Jared Sparks, February 26, 1833, quoted in Sparks, *Life of George Washington,* 521–22. In discussing the last two sentences of Nelly's statement about Washington and prayer, Nicholas F. Gier, professor of religion, Continental philosophy, and Eastern philosophy at the University of Idaho and senior fellow at the

Martin Institute for Peace Studies and Conflict Resolution, offered the following opinion about her reliability on this issue: "Sparks' editing and commentary are considered inaccurate, unreliable, and even fraudulent by professional historians today. Sparks was definitely building a pious monument and not writing objective history. This comment by Washington's daughter [*sic*] runs so much against the utmost piety that Sparks attempts to instill in Washington that I believe its credibility is thereby strengthened" (see Gier, "Religious Liberalism and the Founding Fathers," 24n39).

10. M'Guire, *Religious Opinions and Character of Washington*, 160–61.

11. Sparks, *Life of George Washington*, 522–23; Sparks, *Writings of George Washington*, 12:407. Backing up the evidence in Sparks's published work is a letter dated February 25, 1828, in which the author tells Lewis, "I was particularly gratified with your account of Gen. Washington's devotional habits, and shall introduce it into some part of his works" (MVLA, RM-862/MS-5319 [photostat]). For Sparks's dates and more on his life, see Samuel Eliot Morison, "Sparks, Jared," *DAB*, 17:430–34.

12. Rusinowa, "Julian Ursyn Niemcewicz's Biography of George Washington," 8. A second visitor's statements on Washington and prayer, unfortunately, have to be taken with more caution. The Reverend Jedidiah Morse, a Congregationalist who has been called the "Father of American Geography," came to Mount Vernon on Monday, November 27, 1786, with a friend and stayed to dinner. Three years later, in his *American Geography or a View of the Present Situation of the United States of America,* he published a description of Washington's life at Mount Vernon. Ten years later, in the eulogy he wrote for Washington, Morse described Washington's daily schedule, stating: "In his allotments for the revolving hours, religion was not forgotten. Feeling, what he so often publicly acknowledged, his entire dependence on God, he daily, at stated seasons, retired to his closet, to worship at his footstool, and to ask his divine blessing. He was remarkable for his strict observation of the Sabbath, and exemplary in his attendance on public worship." It is hard to believe, given Washington's famous reticence, how Morse might have gleaned this information in the course of a very brief visit; one suspects that his statements were primarily based on Washington's reputation. For Morse's visit to Mount Vernon, see *GW Diaries,* 5:72, 72n. For Morse's publications about Mount Vernon and Washington, including the quote, see Baker, *Character Portraits of Washington*, 30–34, 34n, 76–78, 78n–79n.

13. For the first description of Patsy Custis's death, see Sparks, *Life of George Washington,* 522. For the second description of the same event, see Eliza Parke Custis [Law], "Self-Portrait: Eliza Custis, 1808," 92.

14. From *The Book of Common Prayer, and Administration of the Sacraments, and Other Rites and Ceremonies of the Church, according to the Use of the Church of England; Together with the Psalter or Psalms of David, Pointed as They Are to Be Sung or Said in Churches.* The pages are not numbered, but this prayer is taken from a section entitled "The Order for the Visitation of the Sick."

15. Ibid.

16. "Washington's Runaway Slave, and How Portsmouth Freed Her," *Frank W. Miller's Portsmouth, New Hampshire, Weekly,* June 2, 1877.

17. For Martha Washington's daily routine, see Berard, "Arlington and Mount Vernon 1856," 162; Thane, *Mount Vernon Family,* 74. For the surviving prayer book, see

MVLA, W-409. For Mrs. Washington's daily religious practice and the purchase of a Bible and religious pamphlets for her, see Decatur, *Private Affairs,* 50 and 313. For the purchase of prayer books for various members of the family, see MW to Fanny Bassett Washington, July 1789, in Fields, *Worthy Partner,* 217.

18. GW, January 18, 1798, in GW "Cash Memoranda," Sept. 1794–Dec. 1799, 13 [53], MVLA (bound photostat).

19. Fithian, *Journal & Letters,* 42. Fithian was a Presbyterian who would later serve as chaplain to Colonel Newcomb's Battalion of the New Jersey Militia, and died during the Revolution (see Thompson, *United States Army Chaplaincy,* 252).

20. Staples, "A Day at Mount Vernon," 8–11, MVLA, "Early Descriptions Notebook" (photostat).

21. Journal of John Latta, July 3, 1799, MVLA, "Early Descriptions Notebook" (photostat); for the information that Latta had been a Presbyterian chaplain during the war, see Thompson, *The United States Army Chaplaincy,* 256; and Green, *The Life of Ashbel Green,* 267.

22. Chinard, *George Washington as the French Knew Him,* 66.

23. Baker, *Washington after the Revolution,* 138.

24. John Parke Custis to MW, July 5, 1773, in Fields, *Worthy Partner,* 152–53.

25. William Gordon to GW, February 16, 1789, *GW Papers, Presidential Series,* 1:314–15, 316n.

26. Thomas Birch's Sons, *Catalogue No. 663,* 29.

27. Perry, *Mrs. Robert E. Lee,* 10, 71–80, 91, 96, 104–6.

28. Journal of Elizabeth Foote Washington, November 1779 to December 1796, MVLA, RM-573/PS-4259 (photostat and typescript), 28–29.

29. Meade, *Old Churches, Ministers, and Families,* 2:196.

30. Perry, *Mrs. Robert E. Lee,* 37–39, 41–43, 47.

31. Lossing, *Hours with the Living Men and Women of the Revolution,* 173 and 174.

32. For examples of the Custis's grandchildren teaching the slaves on Sundays, see Lee, *Growing Up in the 1850s,* 9, 40, 64–65. For services by seminary students, see Berard, "Arlington and Mount Vernon, 1856," 161, 161n.

7. EVIDENCE OF BELIEF

1. See, for example, Henriques, *He Died as He Lived,* 24; and Boller, *George Washington and Religion,* 68–76.

2. GW, speech to the Delaware chiefs, May 12, 1779, *GW Writings,* 15:55–56.

3. GW, Circular to the States, June 8, 1783, ibid., 26:496. Historian Peter Henriques argues that the phrase "Divine Author of our blessed Religion" may well refer to Jesus but could be a reference to Jehovah (see Henriques, "A Few Simple Beliefs," 175). This argument makes no sense in light of the words that both precede and follow the phrase in Washington's original statement; the idea that the United States cannot hope to be a happy nation unless its citizens humbly imitate the example of charity, humility, and pacific temper of mind shown to them by the Divine Author of Christianity can refer only to Jesus, because God gave no such example.

4. Freeman, *George Washington,* 5:493.

5. Boller, *George Washington and Religion,* 59–64.

6. John C. Fitzpatrick, "Introductory Note," in *GW Writings,* 1:xliii–xliv. For examples of others who have looked at this question, see Philander D. Chase, Preface to *GW Papers, Revolutionary War Series,* 1:xvii–xviii; Holmes, *Faiths of the Founding Fathers,* 65; Kahler, "Gentlemen of the Family," 76–79.

7. Dr. James Craik to GW, November 25, 1757, *GW Papers, Colonial Series,* 5:64–65.

8. Dr. James Craik to GW, January 6, 1778, *GW Papers, Revolutionary War Series,* 13:161.

9. Frances Bassett Washington to GW, November 22, 1793, MVLA, A-301 (typescript).

10. George Washington Parke Custis to GW, June 8, [1797], *GW Papers, Retirement Series,* 1:175, 176.

11. Hannah Bushrod Washington to GW, October 15, 1797, ibid., 1:410.

12. Elizabeth Foote Washington, Journal, MVLA (typescript), 1–2.

13. Ibid., 33. For discussion that Elizabeth was holding morning and evening prayers, "never failing if it was possible to get two or three together," see page 18 of the journal typescript.

14. Ibid., 6–7, 9–10, 17–21, 28–29, 38.

15. Ibid., 25.

16. Ibid., 34.

17. Ibid., 26–27, 36.

18. McGroarty, "Elizabeth Washington of Hayfield," 157, 162–63.

19. Eliza Parke Custis [Law] to E[dmund] L[aw] Rogers, January 22, 1831, MVLA (photostat and typescript).

20. Washington, "Jane Charlotte Blackburn Washington to Major William Popham, May 24, 1839," 798.

21. Lewis, *Pursuit of Happiness,* 41–43, 45–46.

22. Ibid., 51.

23. Lee, *Growing Up in the 1850s,* 79, 95.

24. GW to Robert Stewart, [April 27, 1763], *GW Papers, Colonial Series,* 7:206. In this same vein, historian Frank Grizzard, an associate editor at the Papers of George Washington project at the University of Virginia at the time, commented, in a discussion about George Washington's religious beliefs, that he thought Washington, himself, would have taken issue with anyone who said he wasn't Christian (statement made on November 7, 1998, at a symposium entitled "George Washington: Mourning and Memory," held at Mount Vernon, November 6 and 7, 1998).

25. John Parke Custis to MW, July 5, 1773, in Fields, *Worthy Partner,* 153.

26. GW to John Christian Ehler, December 23, 1793, *GW Writings,* 33:215.

27. GW to Maj. Gen. Israel Putnam, October 19, 1777, ibid., 9:400–401.

28. GW, general orders, May 2, 1778, ibid., 11:342–43.

29. Jones, *George Washington,* 27.

30. "Providence," *OED,* 8:1522.

31. Godbeer, *Devil's Dominion,* 11, 27, 56, 77, 127.

32. Bond, *Spreading the Gospel,* 496n, 500, 505. For another example of Stith's use

of the term "Providence," or "Divine Providence," this time in a sermon from 1753, see ibid., 512.

33. Novak, *On Two Wings,* 136.

34. Ibid., 15, 16.

35. Thompson, *United States Army Chaplaincy,* 290.

36. The Rev. Uzal Ogden to George Washington, September 20, 1785, *GW Papers, Confederation Series,* 3:269.

37. The Rev. William Gordon to GW, February 16, 1786, ibid., 3:559.

38. MW to Mercy Otis Warren, March 7, 1778, in Fields, *Worthy Partner,* 177.

39. Neill, *The Fairfaxes of England and America,* 179.

40. Frances Bassett Washington to GW, March 5, 1793, *GW Papers, Presidential Series,* 12:269–70.

41. Ibid., March 28, 1793, 12:388.

42. Fanny Bassett Washington to MW, [Summer 1794], in Fields, *Worthy Partner,* 271.

43. GW to John Augustine Washington, July 18, 1755, *GW Writings,* 1:152.

44. GW to Joseph Reed, January 4, 1776, ibid., 4:211–12.

45. GW to the Rev. William Gordon, March 9, 1781, ibid., 332.

46. GW to the Hebrew Congregations of Philadelphia, New York, Charleston, and Richmond, (December 1790), ibid., 31:185–86.

47. Nathanael Greene to the Rev. John Murray, after September 1, 1778, in Greene, *Papers,* 2:506.

48. For Langdon's military service, see Thompson, *United States Army Chaplaincy,* 41, 44, 113–14, 217–18.

49. Samuel Langdon to GW, July 8, 1789, *GW Papers, Presidential Series,* 3:149–51, 151n.

50. GW to Samuel Langdon, September 28, 1789, ibid., 4:104.

51. Bryan Fairfax to GW, February 17, 1793; GW to Bryan Fairfax, March 6, 1793; and Bryan Fairfax to GW, March 19, 1793, ibid., 12:157, 271, 346.

52. GW to David Humphreys, March 23, 1793, *GW Writings,* 32:398.

53. MW to the Marquis de Lafayette, October 31, 1800, transcribed by Dale Limbert and George Lupone, http://web.ulib.csuohio.edu/Lafayette/documents/doc4.shtml (accessed April 18, 2005).

54. William Augustine Washington to GW, March 23, 1798, *GW Papers, Retirement Series,* 2:151.

55. Flexner, *George Washington,* 3:212. This story, which seems to have first come down in a biography of Dr. Bard, is also given in Custis, *Recollections and Private Memoirs,* 398n. For additional references to Dr. Bard's care of Washington during this illness, see Decatur, *Private Affairs,* 27–28, 68.

56. Zagarri, *David Humphreys' "Life of General Washington,"* 57. Humphreys would later remind Martha Washington of this incident in his condolence letter to her following George Washington's death (see David Humphreys to MW, July 5, 1800, in Fields, *Worthy Partner,* 389).

57. George Washington to Pierre Charles L'Enfant, April 28, 1788, *GW Writings,* 29:481.

58. See, for example, the opening words of the Lord's Prayer (Matthew 6:9; Luke 11:2), the parable of the prodigal son (Luke 15:11–32), and Jesus's words after being

nailed to the cross (Luke 23:34, 46). Other examples are too numerous to list but can be found easily using a good concordance.

59. GW, general orders, August 3, 1776, *GW Writings*, 5:367. See also Thompson, *United States Army Chaplaincy*, 56, 110. For other examples in which Washington either denounced the practice of swearing or had soldiers punished for cursing, see *GW Writings*, 1:179, 382, 392, 396; 3:309, 410; 5:32; 8:152–53; 13:118–19; 16:13.

60. GW, Farewell Address, September 19, 1796, *GW Writings*, 35:231.

61. GW to Burwell Bassett, April 20,(1773), *GW Papers, Colonial Series*, 9:219.

62. Remarks by George Grieve, the eighteenth-century translator of Chastellux, *Travels in North America*, 1:298–99.

63. GW to Jonathan Trumbull, December 4, 1788, *GW Writings*, 30:149.

64. GW to the attorney general, August 26, 1792, ibid., 32:136. For an example of the same words, "the allwise disposer of events," in place of "God" in a sermon by an Anglican chaplain in the French and Indian War, see Thompson, *United States Army Chaplaincy*, 271. For an example of Martha Washington using the same terminology, see MW to Fanny Basset Washington, February 20, 1793, in Fields, *Worthy Partner*, 243.

65. MW to Fanny Bassett Washington, September 29, 1794, in Fields, *Worthy Partner*, 276.

66. Hannah Bushrod Washington to GW, October 15, [17]97, *GW Papers, Retirement Series*, 1:410.

67. GW to Lund Washington, December 17, 1778, *GW Writings*, 13:408.

68. GW to Maj. Gen. Robert Howe, August 17, 1779, ibid., 16:119.

69. GW to Edmund Randolph, January 8, 1788, ibid., 29:357.

70. GW to Burwell Bassett, June 20, 1773, ibid., 3:138.

71. Letters of GW to Fanny Bassett Washington, February 24, 1793, and Tobias Lear, March 30, 1796, ibid., 32:354 and 35:6; also quoted in McCallister, "Reason and Resignation," 28.

72. Henriques, "The Final Struggle between George Washington and the Grim King," 95.

73. Burgess Ball to GW, August 25, 1789, *GW Papers, Presidential Series*, 3:536.

74. GW to Betty Washington Lewis, September 13, 1789, *GW Writings*, 30:399; also quoted in Flexner, *George Washington and the New Nation (1783–1793)*, 227.

75. See *GW Diaries*, 4:26.

76. GW to Thomas Smith, December 7, 1785, *GW Papers, Confederation Series*, 3:438–39.

77. GW to Benjamin Harrison, March 21, 1781, *GW Writings*, 21:341–42.

78. GW to Mary Ball Washington, February 15, 1787, ibid., 29:159–60.

79. GW to Gov. Robert Dinwiddie of Virginia, May 29, 1754, ibid., 1:59–60.

80. GW to Henry Knox, January 10, 1788, ibid., 29:378. Thomas Jefferson, in an effort to comfort his daughter after his death, left her a poem he had written in which he appears to express a belief in an afterlife, including a possible reunion with loved ones (see Randolph, *Domestic Life of Thomas Jefferson*, 429).

81. Caleb Gibbs to GW, October 24, 1785, *GW Papers, Confederation Series*, 3:316.

82. MW to Burwell Bassett, December 22, 1777, in Fields, *Worthy Partner*, 175–76.

83. John Parke Custis to MW, July 5, [1773], ibid., 152–53.

84. Nelly Custis Lewis to Jared Sparks, February 26, 1833, in Sparks, *Life of George Washington,* 522.

85. MW to Jonathan Trumbull, January 15, 1800, in Fields, *Worthy Partner,* 339.

86. Meadows, "A Mourning Tribute," 20–25, 43.

87. Eliza Parke Custis [Law] to E[dmund] L[aw] Rogers, January 22, 1831, MVLA (photostat and typescript).

88. Zagarri, *David Humphreys' "Life of General Washington,"* 78.

89. Eliza Parke Custis [Law] to E[dmund] L[aw] Rogers, January 22, 1831, MVLA (photostat and typescript).

8. OUTWARD ACTIONS

1. GW to Lund Washington, November 26, 1775, *GW Writings,* 4:115

2. Ibid.; Lund Washington to GW, January 1776, quoted in Mount Vernon Ladies' Association, *Mount Vernon: A Handbook,* 95, 113.

3. MW to Mr. Devenport, November 5, 1775, in Fields, *Worthy Partner,* 163.

4. Nelly Custis Lewis to Elizabeth Bordley Gibson, April 29, 1823, in Lewis, *George Washington's Beautiful Nelly,* 134. Although much of what Parson Mason Locke Weems has written about the Washingtons is suspect, his statements on the subject of Martha Washington's beneficence fit well with the remarks of Lund Washington and Nelly Custis Lewis (see Weems, *Life of Washington,* 54).

5. GW to the Reverend William White, December 31, 1793, *GW Writings,* 33:220–21. The fact that Washington wanted to provide his charitable gifts anonymously would have been in keeping with principles propounded in the New Testament (see, for example, Matthew 6:2–4).

6. GW to Bushrod Washington, January 15, 1783, *GW Writings,* 26:40.

7. Two relatively rare exceptions to this rule are found in Washington's cash memoranda. In the first, dated April 29, 1760, Washington recorded giving £1.1.3 "at the Charity Sermon." Two months later, he gave £12 "for the Sufferers at Boston by Fire," a disaster in which over four hundred homes and businesses were lost (see GW, "Cash Accounts," [April 1760 and June 1760], *GW Papers, Colonial Series,* 6:406, 430).

8. Decatur, *Private Affairs,* 48–49, 54, 55, 64, 87, 88, 113, 115, 179, 182, 193, 196, 202, 203, 208, 214, 228, 233, 254, 257, 265, 292, 312, 313, 321, 322, 323. Also, entries for July 23, 1793; August 14, 1793; December 27, 1793; January 21, 1794; May 8, 1794; May 23, 1794; January 26, 1795; October 22 and 23, 1795; December 20 and 21, 1796; and January 7, 1797, in "Washington's Household Account Book," 30:35, 40, 55, 162, 179, 181, 463; 31:64, 331, 334.

9. See cash account entry dated January 5, 1799, Mount Vernon Farm Ledger, 1797–1798, MVLA (bound photostat), 194.

10. Decatur, *Private Affairs,* 38, 90, 91, 112, 201, 231–32, 254, 310; entries for July 18, 1793, January 28, 1794, and December 30, 1796, in "Washington's Household Account Book," 30:33, 163; 31:332.

11. Reverend Charles Green, Fairfax County List of Titheables for 1749, MVLA, PS-789c/R-203 (photostat).

12. GW to the Marquis de Lafayette, August 15, 1787, *GW Writings*, 29:259.

13. GW to Sir Edward Newenham, October 20, 1792, ibid., 32:190.

14. Decatur, *Private Affairs*, 232.

15. McCullough, *John Adams*, 84.

16. Samuel Hanson to GW, January 12, 1786, *GW Papers, Confederation Series*, 3:504, 503n–4n.

17. [Wharton], *Poetical Epistle*, 23–24.

18. Ibid.

19. *GW Diaries*, 3:162; 6:351, 351n. For Carroll's desire to bring Christianity to the Indians, see GW to John Carroll, April 10, 1792, *GW Writings*, 32:19–20.

20. For Washington's attendance at non-Anglican churches, see entries for September 25, 1774; October 9, 1774; May 27, 1787; October 18, 1789; July 3, 1791; and October 4, 1794, in *GW Diaries*, 3:280, 285; 5:163, 466; 6:168, 182; and Freeman, *George Washington*, 4:77n.

21. *GW Diaries*, 3:285.

22. For Adams's devoutness, see McCullough, *John Adams*, 84, 650, and Adams, Sunday, [October 9], 1774, *Diary and Autobiography*, 2:149 and 150.

23. John Adams to Abigail Adams, October 9, 1774, *Adams Family Correspondence*, 1:166–67, 167n; McCullough, *John Adams*, 84.

24. Francis A. Christie, "Murray, John," *DAB*, 13:360.

25. Skemp, *Judith Sargent Murray*, 21; Francis A. Christie, "Murray, John," *DAB*, 13:362.

26. Col. James M. Varnum to the Rev. John Murray, May 24, 1775, in Greene, *Papers*, 1:81.

27. For Reverend Murray's acceptance of the chaplaincy, see Nathanael Greene to Col. James M. Varnum, June 2, 1775, in ibid., 1:83. For the incident that had so upset people, see ibid., 1:81n.

28. Nathanael Greene to Catharine Greene, September 10, 1775, ibid., 1:116; *GW Papers, Revolutionary War Series*, 2:1n–2n.

29. For the quote from Greene, see Nathaniel Greene to [Samuel Ward Jr.], October 9, 1772, in Greene, *Papers*, 1:49, 50n.

30. GW, general orders, September 17, 1775, *GW Papers, Revolutionary War Series*, 2:1, 1n–2n.

31. Nathanael Greene to whom it may concern, May 27, 1777, in Greene, *Papers*, 2:96 and 96n. Opposition to Murray continued after he left the army. One of the complaining chaplains, John Cleaveland, a Congregationalist from Ipswich, Massachusetts, even published a pamphlet in May of 1776 against Murray, which he entitled "An Attempt to Nip in the Bud the Unscriptural Doctrine of Universal Salvation" (see Francis A. Christie, "Murray, John," *DAB*, 13:362; Thompson, *United States Army Chaplaincy*, 116–17, 249). Army surgeon James Thacher made a point of hearing Murray preach in September of 1779, and left an interesting description of his experience and people's

reaction to the minister (see Thacher, *Military Journal of the American Revolution,* 178–79).

32. Milton Ellis, "Murray, Judith Sargent Stevens," *DAB,* 13:364–65.

33. Judith Sargent Murray to her parents, August 14, 1790, in Murray, *From Goucester to Philadelphia,* 10, 244–59. Information about Judith Sargent Murray's work on the Universalist catechism was taken from the Web site of The Judith Sargent Murray Society, http://hurdsmith.com/judith/publications.htm (accessed June 9, 2004). See also Skemp, *Judith Sargent Murray,* 28–29, 129–32.

34. Judith Sargent Murray to GW, March 29, 1798, and GW to Judith Sargent Murray, June 4, 1798, *GW Papers, Retirement Series,* 2:162, 162n–64n. For a more readily available edition of the two essays "Necessity of Religion, Especially in Adversity" and "Spirit Independent of Matter," see Murray, *Selected Writings,* 69–77, 78–84.

35. *GW Diaries,* 4:145, 145n–46n; Stukenbroeker, *A Watermelon for God,* 4–6, 39. For more on General Roberdeau, see *GW Diaries,* 3:287, 287n; *GW Papers, Confederation Series,* 1:152n–53n; James H. Peeling, "Roberdeau, Daniel," *DAB,* 15:646–47; Stukenbroeker, *A Watermelon for God,* 90–93.

36. Coke, *Extracts of the Journals,* 45. For Asbury's description of the meeting at Mount Vernon, see Asbury, *Journal and Letters,* 1:489, 489n. Many thanks to my friend Sheridan Harvey, the women's studies specialist at the Library of Congress, for copying the entries from Coke's and Asbury's diaries and forwarding them on to me. The Methodist petition was read in the Virginia legislature on November 8, 1785, and rejected by that body two days later (see *GW Papers, Confederation Series,* 3:357n.).

37. Francis Asbury to GW, April 24, 1786, *GW Papers, Confederation Series,* 4:27, 27n.

38. Griffin, *Catalogue of the Washington Collection,* 50, 221.

39. Clark, *Joseph Priestley,* 11–15, 45–56, 63–65, 73, 214–15.

40. For Priestley's following among these prominent Americans, see Clark, *Joseph Priestley,* 32, 128–29, 140–44, 188, 220–21, 223–24, 229–33. For more on Samuel Vaughan himself and on the gift of the pamphlets, see *GW Papers, Confederation Series,* 1:46n; and GW to Samuel Vaughan, August 25, 1791, *GW Papers, Presidential Series,* 8:454–55, 455n–56n. For Vaughan's relationship with Priestley, see Clark, *Joseph Priestley,* 179. In addition to the reading materials, Vaughan gave Washington a lovely marble mantel, a set of Worcester vases, and a painted battle scene, all of which can be seen today at Mount Vernon.

41. Griffin, *Catalogue of the Washington Collection,* 169, 169n.

42. Clark, *Joseph Priestley,* 219.

43. GW to Joseph Priestley, April 14, 1796, *GW Writings,* 35:21–22.

44. GW to Tobias Lear, March 10, 1797, *GW Papers, Retirement Series,* 1:27, 28n.

45. George Washington Parke Custis to GW, July 14, 1797, ibid., 1:249–50.

46. Griffin, *Catalogue of the Washington Collection,* 170.

47. GW to the bishops of the Methodist Episcopal Church, May 29, 1789, *GW Papers, Presidential Series,* 2:412.

48. GW to Tench Tilghman, March 24, 1784, *GW Writings,* 27:367.

49. *GW Diaries,* 2:100, 195n, 197n, 201n, 202n.

50. Hirschfeld, *George Washington and the Jews,* 122–23.

51. Receipt from Solomon Levy to Martha Washington, June 17, 1790, MVLA (photostat). Information on Solomon and Hayman Levy was found in an e-mail communication from Gretchen Goodell to the Collections Department, May 31, 2006, MVLA. For more on Shearith Israel, see Hirschfeld, *George Washington and the Jews,* 13–14, 60, 62–63, 71, 134–35, 136, 140, 144, 147.

52. GW, May 1, 1766, Ledger A, MVLA (bound photostat), 216; George Washington, *GW Papers, Colonial Series,* 7:440n; entry dated August 12, 1793, "Washington's Household Account Book," 30:40.

53. Agreement with Burgis Mitchell, May 1, 1762, *GW Papers, Colonial Series,* 7:132; George Washington to the Overseers at Mount Vernon, July 14, 1793, *GW Writings,* 33:12.

54. For a much fuller treatment of the religious beliefs and practices of the slaves at Mount Vernon, see Thompson, "They Appear to Live Comfortable Together," 99–100; Thompson, "Religious Practice in the Slave Quarters of Mount Vernon," 10–14; and Thompson, "And Procure for Themselves a Few Amenities," 187–90.

55. MW to Fanny Bassett Washington, April 6, 1795, in Fields, *Worthy Partner,* 284. It should be noted in this case that Eliza was then nineteen years old and considered old enough to decide not to go to church each week, unlike the case, mentioned earlier, in which Washington's nephew, then only thirteen years old, was punished for not attending church.

56. Decatur, *Private Affairs,* 41, 125, 185, 189, 252, 254, 255.

57. See entries dated May 10, 1793; July 23, 1793; July 14, 1794; and November 24, 1796, in "Washington's Household Account Book," 29:397, 30:35, 311, and 31:327. For similar contributions by Benjamin Franklin and Thomas Jefferson, see Holmes, *Faiths of the Founding Fathers,* 56, 84.

9. CHURCH AND STATE

1. Many thanks to my colleague Scott Casper, of the History Department at the University of Nevada at Reno, for his help in clarifying the themes in this chapter.

2. GW to Edward Newenham, October 20, 1792, *GW Papers, Presidential Series,* 11:246.

3. GW to the Hebrew congregations of Philadelphia, New York, Charleston, and Richmond, December 1790, *GW Writings,* 31:185.

4. GW, Farewell Address, September 9, 1796, ibid., 35:229–30.

5. For a study of the development of what one author has called America's "public religion," which Washington was instrumental in forming, see Meacham, *American Gospel.*

6. GW, June 2, 1754, in *GW Diaries,* 1:199. It is not known exactly what Washington meant by "Prayers," but the most likely possibility is that the Anglican service was read, as it would have been in any Virginia church on the Sundays when the pastor was absent and not able to officiate.

7. William Fairfax to GW, October 7, 1754, *GW Papers, Colonial Series,* 1:177–78. This rather enthusiastic statement by William Fairfax of Belvoir Plantation is interesting because historians have recently credited the Belvoir Fairfaxes with introduc-

ing GW to the ancient philosophy of Stoicism, a "simple, practical, reasonable, and humanitarian" belief system, which "embraced the classical virtues and reinforced the Deist beliefs current in the eighteenth century," and which supposedly drew the young Washington away from his Christian upbringing (Henriques, *He Died as He Lived*, 11–12; also Grizzard, *George Washington*, 269 [for quotes]).

8. Adam Stephen to GW, July 25, 1756, *GW Papers, Colonial Series*, 3:295; for biographical information on Stephen, see ibid., 1:80n.

9. GW to Robert Dinwiddie, September 23, 1756, *GW Writings*, 1:470.

10. GW to Gov. Robert Dinwiddie, September 28, 1756, ibid., 1:498.

11. For example, the Anglican Church was named the state church in Maryland in 1691, in New York in 1692, in South Carolina in either 1704 or 1706 (depending on the source), in North Carolina in 1732, and in Georgia in 1758. In addition, Congregationalism was the state church in Massachusetts, New Hampshire, and Connecticut, while four of the British colonies (Rhode Island, New Jersey, Delaware, and Pennsylvania) had no state church (see Lillback, *Proclaim Liberty*, 14; Thompson and Cummins, *This Day in Baptist History*, 14–15).

12. Boucher, *Reminiscences of an American Loyalist*, 113.

13. Ibid., 118–24, 141.

14. Thacher, *Military Journal of the American Revolution*, 18–19.

15. Cresswell, *Journal*, 189.

16. Serle, *American Journal*, 131.

17. For the debate in Congress on having the opening prayer, as well as remarks on Reverend Duché's performance, see John Adams, September 7, 1774, in Adams, *Diary and Autobiography*, 2:126; and Continental Congress, *Journals*, 1:26, 26n, 27, 27n. For the minister's early career and letter to Washington, see *GW Papers, Revolutionary War Series*, 1:247n.

18. Jacob Duché to GW, August 5, 1775, *GW Papers, Revolutionary War Series*, 1:246–47.

19. Thacher, *Military Journal of the American Revolution*, 120 and 121.

20. See *GW Papers, Revolutionary War Series*, 1:247n; Thacher, *Military Journal of the American Revolution*, 120.

21. GW to Francis Hopkinson, November 21, 1777, *GW Papers, Revolutionary War Series*, 12:341.

22. Ibid. According to an Englishman serving in America at the time, "Washington is said to have been much offended at his Letter to himself. 'Tis a Performance, wch does but little Honor either to the Head or the Heart of its Author" (see Serle, *American Journal*, 269).

23. GW to the Reverend Jacob Duché, August 10, 1783, *GW Writings*, 27:91–92.

24. *GW Papers, Revolutionary War Series*, 1:247n.

25. Freeman, *George Washington*, 3:351–52. For an example of Washington encouraging ministers to exhort their flocks to do their political duty, see GW to Townshend Dade Jr., November 19, 1774, in *GW Papers, Revolutionary War Series*, 10:187, 187n.

26. See entry for June 1, 1774, in *GW Diaries*, 3:254, 254n–55n. Interestingly, although Reverend Price was opposed to Britain's actions toward the colonies, his belief that he

"could not violate his ordination vows to George III as head of the Anglican Church" led to his service as a British chaplain during the American Revolution. For Price's career, see Thompson, *United States Army Chaplaincy*, 204; and Nelson, *A Blessed Company*, 317.

27. Freeman, *George Washington*, 3:357–58.

28. GW to Col. Benedict Arnold, September 14, 1775, *GW Writings*, 3:492.

29. GW, general orders, November 5, 1775, ibid., 4:65.

30. Baker, *Character Portraits of Washington*, 12.

31. Continental Congress, *Journals*, 2:112, 121, 220.

32. Thompson, *United States Army Chaplaincy*, 106, 245–67.

33. GW, general orders, July 4, 1775, *GW Writings*, 3:309. See also Thompson, *United States Army Chaplaincy*, 57, 107–10.

34. Thacher, *Military Journal of the American Revolution*, 206; Thompson, *United States Army Chaplaincy*, 247.

35. GW to the Reverend John Rodgers, June 11, 1783, *GW Writings*, 27:1, 1n. Several years after their correspondence on the subject of Bibles for the troops, in 1788, Rodgers would come to Mount Vernon for dinner (see entry for March 21, 1788, in *GW Diaries*, 5:288, 288n.).

36. Adams, *Diary and Autobiography*, 3:353, 371; McCullough, *John Adams*, 113–14.

37. Thacher, *Military Journal of the American Revolution*, 30.

38. GW, general orders, November 18, 1775, *GW Writings*, 4:98. For other days of thanksgiving, see GW, general orders, November 30, 1777 and December 17, 1777; GW to Maj. Gen. John Sullivan, December 20, 1778; GW, general orders, December 22, 1778 and November 27, 1779; GW to Thomas McKean, November 15, 1781, ibid., 10:123 and 168; 13:441 and 450; 17:189–90; 23:342–43.

39. GW, general orders, March 6, 1776, ibid., 4:369. For other fast days, see GW, general orders, July 16, 1775; May 15, 1776; and May 16, 1776; February 4, 1777 and February 5, 1777; April 12, 1778; April 12, 1779; May 5, 1779; April 6, 1780; April 27, 1781; April 22, 1782, and GW to the President of Congress, April 2, 1779, and March 23, 1780, ibid., 3:341–42; 5:43, 50; 6:354n; 7:98, 102; 11:252; 14:328, 369, 504; 18:146, 225; 22:2; 24:151. The contrast in language between Washington's orders for days of prayer and fasting and those of Confederate general Robert E. Lee, a nineteenth-century member of his extended family, are striking (see Rusten and Rusten, *One Year Book of Christian History*, 468). Additional information about this incident, including the date of Lee's order, can be found in Hayward, "Prayers before Battle," 32–40.

40. Thacher, *Military Journal of the American Revolution*, 126.

41. GW, after orders, May 5, 1778, and an excerpt from the *Military Journal of George Ewing*, both in *GW Writings*, 11:354–56, 356n–57n. For the text of the sermon given by one of the chaplains on that occasion, see "Sermon delivered at Valley Forge on May 6, 1778, to members of the 1st and 2nd Virginia Brigade, in celebration of France's entry into the War," in Thompson, *United States Army Chaplaincy*, 289–91.

42. Thacher, *Military Journal of the American Revolution*, 126–27.

43. Thompson, *United States Army Chaplaincy*, 254.

44. Thacher, *Military Journal of the American Revolution*, 126–27.

45. Muhlenberg, May 7, 1778, *Notebook*, 195. Reverend Muhlenberg was the father of

three prominent men in the life of the new United States, all of whom were also pastors (see George Harvey Genzmer, "Muhlenberg, Frederick Augustus Conrad," "Muhlenberg, Gotthilf Henry Ernst," "Muhlenberg, Henry Melchior," and "Muhlenberg, John Peter Gabriel," *DAB,* 13:307–9, 310–13).

46. See George Harvey Genzmer, "Muhlenberg, John Peter Gabriel," *DAB,* 13:312.

47. For a description of the service and other events of the day, see *GW Papers, Revolutionary War Series,* 3:558n–59n.

48. Thacher, *Military Journal of the American Revolution,* 42–43.

49. GW, speech to the Delaware chiefs, May 12, 1779, *GW Writings,* 15:55.

50. GW, general orders, April 18, 1783, ibid., 26:335–36.

51. GW, Circular to the States, June 8, 1783, ibid., 26:496.

52. Muhlenberg, July 28, 1783, *Notebook,* 228–29.

53. "Nantes, Edict of," *New Encyclopaedia Britannica,* 15th ed., 8:504.

54. The Marquis de Lafayette to GW, May 11, 1785, *GW Papers, Confederation Series,* 2:550.

55. GW to the Marquis de Lafayette, September 1, 1785, ibid., 3:215–16.

56. The Marquis de Lafayette to GW, October 26, 1786, ibid., 4:312.

57. GW to the Marquis de Lafayette, February 4, 1788, ibid., 6:86.

58. Jonathan Boucher to GW, May 25, 1784, ibid., 1:405–7, 407n.

59. Richard Henry Lee, as quoted in Nelson, *A Blessed Company,* 297.

60. GW to George Mason, October 3, 1785, *GW Writings,* 28:285, 285n

61. *Papers of James Madison,* 8:295–304.

62. Countess of Huntingdon to GW, (March 1784), *GW Papers, Confederation Series,* 2:206–7.

63. GW to the Countess of Huntingdon, February 27, 1785, ibid., 2:392.

64. GW to Richard Henry Lee, February 8, 1785, ibid., 2:330–33.

65. GW to the Countess of Huntingdon, June 30, 1785, ibid., 3:93, 93n.

66. *World Almanac and Book of Facts, 1995,* 459.

67. Hirschfeld, *George Washington and the Jews,* 13, 134.

68. For the licensing of dissenting ministers and congregations, see Bond, *Spreading the Gospel,* 33–36. For Gershom Mendes Seixas, see Hirschfeld, *George Washington and the Jews,* 134–35.

69. For the address, as well as background on Moses Seixas, see Moses Seixas to GW, August 17, 1790, *GW Papers, Presidential Series,* 6:286n; and Hirschfeld, *George Washington and the Jews,* 30–31. Seixas was also one of the signers of an address to Washington from his Masonic Lodge (see GW to the Masons of King David's Lodge, Newport, Rhode Island, [August 18, 1790]; and the Masons of King David's Lodge to GW, August 17, 1790, ibid., 6:287, 287n–88n).

70. GW to the Hebrew Congregation in Newport, Rhode Island [August 18, 1790], ibid., 6:284–85. For the suggestion that Thomas Jefferson, David Humphreys, or even Tobias Lear might have written the draft of Washington's response, see Hirschfeld, *George Washington and the Jews,* 31–33, and *GW Papers, Presidential Series,* 6:285n.

71. Hirschfeld, *George Washington and the Jews,* 31–33; *GW Papers, Presidential Series,* 6:285n.

72. The General Assembly of the Presbyterian Church to GW [May 1789], *GW Papers, Presidential Series,* 2:421n–22n.

73. GW to the General Assembly of the Presbyterian Church, [May 1789], ibid., 2:420–21.

74. Ibid.

75. The Presbytery of the Eastward, October 28, 1789, ibid., 4:275n.

76. Ibid.

77. GW to the Presbyterian ministers of Massachusetts and New Hampshire, [November 2, 1789], ibid., 4:274.

78. GW to the members of the New Jerusalem Church of Baltimore, [January 27, 1793], ibid., 12:52–53. For the earlier letter of the church to Washington, see the members of the New Jerusalem Church of Baltimore, [January 22, 1793], ibid., 12:40–41 and 41n.

79. Thompson and Cummins, *This Day in Baptist History,* 5–6, 16–18, 19, 25, 30–31, 47–48, 50–51, 79–80, 103, 123, 153–54, 155, 167–68, 183–84, 198–99, 215–16, 227, 230–31, 233–34, 241, 245, 274, 290, 319–20, 331–32, 335–36, 337; and Bond, *Spreading the Gospel,* 33–34, 36.

80. Thompson and Cummins, *This Day in Baptist History,* 15, 25–26, 31, 32–33, 48, 66, 178, 191, 233, 242–43, 290, 242–43, 396–98, 460, 514. See also Novak, *On Two Wings,* 52–61.

81. Thompson and Cummins, *This Day in Baptist History,* 32–33.

82. Ibid., 242.

83. Address of the General Committee representing the United Baptist Churches in Virginia, assembled in the City of Richmond, May 8–10, 1789, *GW Papers, Presidential Series,* 2:425.

84. GW to the United Baptist Churches in Virginia, May 10, 1789, *GW Writings,* 30:321n.

85. According to one scholar of religious history in America, the Quakers were "Plain in appearance" and believed "in an Inner Light that was the presence of Christ within each person, asserting the fundamental equality of all men and women, and opposing not only trained clergy and formal worship but also military service and the swearing of oaths" (Holmes, *Faiths of the Founding Fathers,* 4–5).

86. GW to the Society of Quakers, [October 1789], *GW Papers, Presidential Series,* 4:266.

87. Ibid.

88. The Roman Catholics of America to GW, March 15, 1790, *GW Papers, Presidential Series,* 5:300n–301n.

89. Ibid., 5:299–300.

90. "Ten Original Amendments: The Bill of Rights," *World Almanac and Book of Facts, 1995,* 460.

91. Text of the treaty and information about its passage is available through the Avalon Project at Yale Law School, http://www.yale.edu/lawweb/avalon/diplomacy/barbary/bar1796t.htm.

92. For discussion that Barlow is probably responsible for this clause, as well as questions about it not being in the Arabic version of the treaty, see Gier, "Religious

Liberalism and the Founding Fathers," 11, 22–23. For Barlow's life and career, see GW to the secretary of war, September 13, 1782; GW to Mrs. John Penn, September 18, 1787; GW to the Comte de Rochambeau, May 28, 1788; GW to the Marquis de la Luzerne, May 28, 1788; GW to Richard Henderson, June 19, 1788; GW, "List of Government Officers," [March 1795], all in *GW Writings*, 25:154 and 154n; 29:276, 503–4, 521; 34:168; Thompson, *United States Army Chaplaincy*, 205, 216, 217, 246; and Theodore A. Zunder and Stanley Thomas Williams, "Barlow, Joel," *DAB*, 1:609–13. For Barlow's later fall from grace in the eyes of both George Washington and John Adams, which led Adams to compare Barlow to Thomas Paine, see GW to the president of the United States, February 1, 1799 and March 3, 1799, *GW Writings*, 37:119–20, 120n, 143–44.

93. GW to the secretary of state, August 1, 1796, *GW Writings*, 35:161–62.

94. GW to the president of the United States, March 3, 1799, ibid., 37:143.

95. GW to James Madison, [August 1789], ibid., 30:394.

96. *GW Papers, Presidential Series*, 4:129n–30n.

97. GW, circular to the governors of the states, October 3, 1789, *GW Papers, Presidential Series*, 4:129, 130n, 131–32, 132n; GW, "Thanksgiving Proclamation," October 3, 1789, *GW Writings*, 30:427–28. For Washington's donation to the poor in connection with the day of prayer and thanksgiving, see Tobias Lear to the Reverend John Rodgers, November 28, 1789, in *GW Papers, Presidential Series*, 4:130n.

98. For more on the 1795 day of thanksgiving and prayer, see *GW Writings*, 34:76n. Bishop White's thanksgiving sermon was published in March of 1795 (see Baker, *Washington after the Revolution*, 297, 297n; Carroll and Ashworth, *George Washington*, 235, 235n.).

99. GW to the Society of United Brethren for Propagating the Gospel among the Heathen, July 10, 1789, *GW Writings*, 30:355n.

100. GW to the United States Senate and House of Representatives, October 25, 1791, *GW Papers, Presidential Series*, 9:111–12.

101. GW to Rev. John Carroll, April 10, 1792, *GW Writings*, 32:19–20. For Carroll's letter to the president, see John Carroll to GW, March 20, 1792, *GW Papers, Presidential Series*, 10:135–36.

10. CONCLUSIONS

1. Lear, *Letters and Recollections*, 129–36.

2. Ibid., 130.

3. F[rances] P[arke] Butler, born Lewis, undated affidavit concerning a miniature portrait of Martha Washington painted by Robert Field in 1801, MVLA, in the Washingtoniana Unowned file of the Moorehead Collection (photostat). While Parke, as she was known in the family, was certainly too young to have recalled Washington's visit herself, the visit to her sickroom by her beloved grandfather on the night before his death must have been a favorite memory of Nelly Custis Lewis, who undoubtedly shared the story many times with her eldest daughter.

4. See, for example, Henriques, *He Died as He Lived*, 44–45.

5. Custis, *Recollections and Private Memoirs,* 510.

6. Henriques, *He Died as He Lived,* 11–12; also, Grizzard, *George Washington,* 269.

7. For the Stoic work, see Griffin, *Catalogue of the Washington Collection,* 179.

8. Gay, *Deism,* 19.

9. Neill, *Fairfaxes of England and America,* 63, 65, 67, 70.

10. *Minutes of the Vestry,* 71, 73, 76.

11. Ibid., 76, 86–87, 91, 94–100, 104, 107, 109, 110, 114, 115, 117, 121, 122, 124, 125, 128, 129. For the register of Pohick Church, showing both George Washington's and George William Fairfax's signatures as vestrymen, see Klapthor and Morrison, *Figure upon the Stage,* 164.

12. *Minutes of the Vestry,* 105, 133.

13. Samuel Athawes to GW, July 20, 1787, *GW Papers, Confederation Series,* 5:264.

14. John Carlyle to his brother, December 3, 1747, in Munson, *Colo. John Carlyle, Gent.,* 11.

15. Sarah Fairfax Carlyle to GW, June 17, 1754, *GW Papers, Colonial Series,* 1:145.

16. Neill, *Fairfaxes of England and America,* 175–82.

17. Bryan Fairfax to GW, May 15, 1798, and GW to Rufus King, May 15, 1798, *GW Papers, Retirement Series,* 2:268, 269.

18. See Bryan Fairfax to GW, August 21[–23], 1798, and April 28, 1799, *GW Papers, Retirement Series,* 2:550, 551; 4:32, 33n. For more on Lady Anne Agnes Erskine, see Cook, *Selina, Countess of Huntingdon,* 235, 239, 258, 356–57, 366–67, 409–10, 416–19, 423, and 438–39.

19. Neill, *Fairfaxes of England and America,* 175–82.

20. Wilson, *Memoir of the Life of the Right Reverend William White,* 265.

21. Ibid., 266–67.

22. Ibid., 264–65.

23. Eliza Willing Powel to MW, December 24, 1799, in Fields, *Worthy Partner,* 325.

24. Catherine Livingston Garretson to MW, February 27, 1800, ibid., 357–58.

25. MW to Catherine Livingston Garretson, March 15, 1800, drafted by Tobias Lear, ibid., 364.

26. Lear, *Letters and Recollections,* 135.

27. Cornelia Lee to Mrs. Eliza Lee, March 14, 1802, MVLA, "Early Descriptions Notebook" (typescript).

28. Cope, *Philadelphia Merchant,* 111–12, 113.

29. Thomas Law to John Law, May 23, 1802, in [McCallister], "This Melancholy Scene," 15.

30. Custis, *Recollections and Private Memoirs,* 513.

31. *Last Will and Testament of George Washington,* 1, 2–5, 9–10, 56, 60. In a manner similar to George and Martha Washington, GW's brother, John Augustine Washington, and his wife, Hannah Bushrod Washington, both began their wills with the words "In the Name of God Amen." The only other statement about their religious faith was a clause in John Augustine's will, to the effect that he was undertaking the writing of that document, "considering the uncertainty of life" (see John Augustine Washington,

Last Will and Testament, June 22, 1784, MVLA, RM-502/MS-4086 [manuscript and typescript]; see also Hannah Bushrod Washington, Last Will and Testament, April 26, 1801, MVLA, RM-251/TYP-2748/a-g (retro) [photostat and typescript]).

32. For a biographical sketch of Elisha Cullen Dick, as well as his dates, see McGroarty, *Washington,* 240. For the December 16 article, see Kahler, "Washington in Glory, America in Tears," 1:40–41; and McGroarty, *Washington,* 6. The article published after the funeral is quoted in McGroarty's work on pages 5, 7–11.

33. Kahler, "Washington in Glory, America in Tears," 1:56, 58, 59.

34. Ibid., 1:8; 2:345–46.

35. Madison, *A Nation Mourns,* 15–18, 33.

36. Quoted in Kahler, "Washington in Glory, America in Tears," 2:338–39.

37. Quoted in ibid., 2:340–41. For Dwight's background, see Harris Elwood Starr, "Dwight, Timothy," and Francis A. Christie, "Edwards, Jonathan," both in *DAB,* 5:573–77, 6:30–37. Dwight's point was echoed by early Washington biographer Jared Sparks, who wrote: "I must end, as I began, by saying that I conceive any attempt at argument in so plain a case would be misapplied. If a man, who spoke, wrote, and acted as a Christian through a long life, who gave numerous proofs of his believing himself to be such, and who was never known to say, write, or do a thing contrary to his professions, if such a man is not to be ranked among the believers of Christianity, it would be impossible to establish the point by any train of reasoning" (Sparks, *Life of George Washington,* 525).

38. Wilson, *Memoir of the Life of the Right Reverend William White,* 351.

39. The quote is taken from the section entitled "The Order for the Burial of the DEAD," in *The Book of Common Prayer, and Administration of the Sacraments, and Other Rites and Ceremonies of the Church, according to the Use of the Church of England; Together with the Psalter or Psalms of David, Pointed as They Are to Be Sung or Said in Churches;* the pages in this volume are unnumbered.

40. Newport, [Rhode Island], June 5, 1802, MVLA, Martha Washington/Personal Items Notebook, R-333 (clipping and typescript).

41. *Augusta [Georgia] Herald,* June 9, 1802, MVLA, RM-35/News-204/a/b (photostat). The primary difference between the two articles is that the earlier one began with the words "DIED—At Mount Vernon, on Saturday evening last . . ." (MVLA, Martha Washington/Personal Items Notebook [photostat]). For a similar article, which appeared in the *Port Folio* on June 5, 1802, see Custis, *Recollections and Private Memoirs,* 513n–14n.

42. *The New England Palladium,* [May 22, 1802, date incorrect], MVLA, PS-179 (photograph). *The Alexandria, [Virginia] Advertiser and Commercial Intelligencer,* Tuesday, May 25, 1802, MVLA, Martha Washington/Personal Items Notebook (typescript).

43. Boller, *George Washington and Religion,* 89–90. One of my favorite summations of George Washington's religious beliefs was made by Mount Vernon's longtime director, Charles Cecil Wall: "Most students who have approached the question objectively have concluded that George Washington was a true Christian who attached no great significance to form and ritual. His broad tolerance toward all who shared his own

belief in a Supreme Being and his feeling of unity with them is eloquently expressed in his own writings. The discerning reader would discover in this mature and benevolent attitude the outstanding characteristic of George Washington's religion" (Charles C. Wall to Maj. Louis Osborne, August 5, 1954, MVLA [copy]).

44. See Romans 5:1 and Galatians 2:16.

45. See, for example, Luke 13:6–9; John 15:1–2.

46. GW to James Anderson, December 21, 1797, *GW Writings*, 36:113.

47. For examples from the Old Testament, see 1 Samuel 16:7 and Second Chronicles 6:29–30. For a New Testament example, see Matthew 7:1 and 2. Also applicable are the parable of the Pharisee and the publican (Luke 18:9–14) and the story of the dying thief (Luke 23:39–43).

48. See Matthew 6:1–7, 16–18; Mark 12:38–44; Luke 20:46–47; John 23:1–33.

49. 1st Corinthians 13:1–3.

50. For teachings on this subject, see Matthew 22:15–22, Mark 12:14–17, and Romans 23:1–7. For reformed Protestant theology on the subject of submission to earthly rulers, see John Calvin's *On God and Political Duty*.

51. Quoted in Kahler, "Washington in Glory, America in Tears," 2:340–41.

BIBLIOGRAPHY

Adams, Abigail. *New Letters of Abigail Adams, 1788–1801.* Edited by Stewart Mitchell. Boston: Houghton Mifflin, 1947.

Adams Family. *Adams Family Correspondence.* Edited by L. H. Butterfield. 2 vols. Cambridge, MA: Belknap Press of Harvard University Press, 1963.

Adams, John. *Diary and Autobiography of John Adams.* Edited by L. H. Butterfield. 4 vols. Cambridge, MA: Belknap Press of Harvard University Press, 1961.

Allen, Gloria Seaman. *First Flowerings: Early Virginia Quilts.* Washington, DC: DAR Museum, 1987.

"The Apostles' Creed." http://www.creeds.net/ancient/apostles.htm (accessed August 23, 2004).

Asbury, Francis. *The Journal and Letters of Francis Asbury.* Edited by Elmer T. Clark, J. Manning Potts, and Jacob S. Payton. 3 vols. Nashville, TN: Abingdon Press, 1958.

Ayres, Linda. "The Virgin Mary's Homecoming: Generous Descendant Contributes Period Pastel." In *The Annual Report of the Mount Vernon Ladies' Association of the Union, 2003,* 22–25. Mount Vernon, VA: Mount Vernon Ladies' Association of the Union, 2004.

Baker, John. *John Marshall: A Life in Law.* New York: Macmillan, 1974.

Baker, William Spohn. *Character Portraits of Washington, as Delineated by Historians, Orators, and Divines, Selected and Arranged in Chronological Order with Biographical Notes and References.* Philadelphia: Robert M. Lindsay, 1887.

———. *Washington after the Revolution, 1784–1799.* Philadelphia: J. B. Lippincott, 1898.

Bassett, A. L. "Reminiscences of Washington: From Unpublished Family Records." *Scribner's Monthly* (May 1887): 77–78.

Berard, Augusta Blanche. "Arlington and Mount Vernon 1856 as Described in a Letter of Augusta Blanche Berard." Edited by Clayton Torrence. *Virginia Magazine of History and Biography* 57, no. 2 (April 1949): 140–75.

Bixby, W. K. *Inventory of the Contents of Mount Vernon, 1810.* With a prefatory note by Worthington Chauncey Ford. Cambridge, U.S.A.: University Press, 1909.

Blassingame, John W., ed. *Slave Testimony: Two Centuries of Letters, Speeches, Interviews, and Autobiographies.* Baton Rouge: Louisiana State University Press, 1977.

Bogard, Ben M. *President Washington a Baptist: An Example for American Youth.* Texarkana, AR: Baptist Sunday School Committee, n.d.

Boller, Paul F., Jr. *George Washington & Religion*. Dallas, TX: Southern Methodist University Press, 1963.

Bond, Edward L. "Anglican Theology and Devotion in James Blair's Virginia, 1685–1743: Private Piety in the Public Church." *Virginia Magazine of History and Biography* 104, no. 3 (Summer 1996): 313–40.

———. *Damned Souls in a Tobacco Colony: Religion in Seventeenth-Century Virginia.* Macon, GA: Mercer University Press, 2000.

———. *Spreading the Gospel in Colonial Virginia: Sermons and Devotional Writings.* Lanham, MD: Lexington Books, in association with the Colonial Williamsburg Foundation, 2004.

Bonomi, Patricia U., and Peter R. Eisenstadt. "Church Adherence in the Eighteenth-Century British American Colonies." *William and Mary Quarterly,* 3rd ser., 39, no. 2 (April 1982): 245–86.

The Book of Common Prayer. N.p.: Protestant Episcopal Church in America, ca. 1790.

The Book of Common Prayer, and Administration of the Sacraments, and Other Rites and Ceremonies of the Church, According to the Use of the Church of England; together with the Psalter or Psalms of David, Pointed as They Are to be Sung or Said in Churches. Edinburgh, UK: Printed by Alexander Kincaid, 1701.

Boucher, Jonathan. *Reminiscences of an American Loyalist, 1738–1789: Being the Autobiography of The Revd. Jonathan Boucher, Rector of Annapolis in Maryland and afterwards Vicar of Epsom, Surrey, England.* Edited by Jonathan Bouchier. Boston: Houghton Mifflin, 1925.

Bowen, Clarence Winthrop, ed. *The History of the Centennial Celebration of the Inauguration of George Washington as First President of the United States.* New York: D. Appleton and Company, 1892.

Briggs, Martha. "To Be Alone with God." *William and Mary Quarterly,* 3rd Ser., 12, no. 3 (July 1955): 476–78.

Brookhiser, Richard. *Founding Father: Rediscovering George Washington.* New York: Free Press, 1996.

Brooks, Joshua. "A Dinner at Mount Vernon: From the Unpublished Journal of Joshua Brookes (1773–1859)." Edited by R. W. G. Vail. *New-York Historical Society Quarterly* 31, no. 2 (April 1947): 72–85.

Brydon, G. MacLaren. "The Clergy of the Established Church in Virginia and the Revolution." *Virginia Magazine of History and Biography* 41, nos. 1–4 (1933): 11–23, 123–43, 231–43, 297–309.

———. *Virginia's Mother Church and the Political Conditions under Which It Grew.* Richmond: Virginia Historical Society, 1947.

Burk, W. Herbert. *Washington's Prayers.* Norristown, PA: Published for the benefit of the Washington Memorial Chapel, 1907.

Calvin, John. *On God and Political Duty.* Indianapolis, IN: Bobbs-Merrill Educational Publishing, 1956.

Carroll, John Alexander, and Mary Wells Ashworth. *George Washington: First in Peace, Completing the Biography of Douglas Southall Freeman.* New York: Charles Scribner's Sons, 1957.

Bibliography

Cary, Wilson Miles. "Descendants of Rev. Rowland Jones, First Rector of Bruton Parish, Va." *William and Mary College Quarterly Historical Magazine,* 1st ser., 5, no. 3 (January 1897): 192–97.

Chamberlayne, C. G., ed. *The Vestry Book and Register of St. Peter's Parish, New Kent and James City Counties, Virginia, 1706–1786.* 1937. Reprint, Richmond: Virginia State Library and Archives, 1989.

Chastellux, Marquis de. *Travels in North America in the Years 1780, 1781 and 1782.* Translated by Howard C. Rice Jr. 2 vols. Chapel Hill: Published for the Institute of Early American History and Culture by the University of North Carolina Press, 1963.

Chinard, Gilbert, ed. and trans. *George Washington as the French Knew Him: A Collection of Texts.* Princeton, NJ: Princeton University Press, 1940.

Clark, John Ruskin. *Joseph Priestley: A Comet in the System.* Northumberland, PA: Friends of Joseph Priestley House, 1994.

Coke, Thomas. *Extracts of the Journals of the Rev. Dr. Coke's Five Visits to America.* London: Printed by G. Paramore, 1793.

Connell, Janice T. *Faith of Our Founding Father: The Spiritual Journey of George Washington.* New York: Hatherleigh Press, 2004.

Continental Congress. *Journals of the Continental Congress, 1774–1789.* Edited by Worthington C. Ford et al. 34 vols. Washington, DC: Government Printing Office, 1904–37.

Cook, Faith. *Selina, Countess of Huntingdon: Her Pivotal Role in the 18th Century Evangelical Awakening.* Carlisle, PA: Banner of Truth Trust, 2001.

Cook, Jane Hampton. *The Faith of America's First Ladies.* Chattanooga, TN: Living Ink Books, 2006.

Cope, Thomas P. *Philadelphia Merchant: The Diary of Thomas P. Cope, 1800–1851.* Edited by Eliza Cope Harrison. South Bend, IN: Gateway Editions, 1978.

Coulling, Mary P. *The Lee Girls.* Winston-Salem, NC: John F. Blair, 1987.

Cresswell, Nicholas. *The Journal of Nicholas Cresswell, 1774–1777.* New York: Dial Press, 1924.

Cromartie, Alan. *Sir Matthew Hale, 1609–1676: Law, Religion, and Natural Philosophy.* Cambridge: Cambridge University Press, 1995.

Curl, James Stevens. *The Art and Architecture of Freemasonry: An Introductory Study.* Woodstock, NY: Overlook Press, 1993.

Cushing, Stanley Ellis. *The George Washington Library Collection.* Boston: Boston Athenaeum, 1997.

Custis, George Washington Parke. *Recollections and Private Memoirs of Washington, by His Adopted Son, George Washington Parke Custis, with a Memoir of the Author, by His Daughter; and Illustrative and Explanatory Notes, by Benson J. Lossing.* 1860. Reprint, Bridgewater, VA: American Foundation Publications, 1999.

Cutler, William Parker, and Julia Perkins Cutler. *Life Journals and Correspondence of Rev. Manasseh Cutler, LL.D. By His Grandchildren.* Vol. 2. Cincinnati: Robert Clarke & Company, 1888.

Dalzell, Robert F. Jr., and Lee Baldwin Dalzell. *George Washington's Mount Vernon: At Home in Revolutionary America.* New York: Oxford University Press, 1998.

Decatur, Stephen, Jr. *Private Affairs of George Washington: From the Records and Ac-counts of Tobias Lear, Esquire, his Secretary.* Boston: Houghton Mifflin, 1933.

Dictionary of American Biography. 20 vols. New York: Charles Scribner's Sons, 1928–36.

Dreisbach, Daniel L., Mark D. Hall, and Jeffry H. Morrison, eds. *The Founders on God and Government.* Lanham, MD: Rowman & Littlefield, 2004.

Erffa, Helmut von, and Allen Staley. *The Paintings of Benjamin West.* New Haven, CT: Yale University Press, 1986.

Felder, Paula S. *Fielding Lewis and The Washington Family: A Chronicle of 18th Century Fredericksburg.* Fredericksburg, VA: American History Company, 1998.

Fields, Joseph E., comp. *"Worthy Partner": The Papers of Martha Washington.* With an introduction by Ellen McCallister Clark. Westport, CT: Greenwood Press, 1994.

Finkelman, Paul. "Jefferson and Slavery: Treason against the Hopes of the World." In *Jeffersonian Legacies,* edited by Peter S. Onuf, 181–221. Charlottesville: University Press of Virginia, 1993.

———. "Thomas Jefferson and Antislavery: The Myth Goes On." *Virginia Magazine of History and Biography* 102, no. 2 (April 1994): 193–228.

First Federal Congress. *Documentary History of the First Federal Congress, 1789–1791.* Edited by Charlene Bangs Bickford, Kenneth R. Bowling, Helen E. Veit, and William Charles DiGiacomantonio. Vol. 15, *Correspondence, First Session: March–May 1789.* Baltimore: Johns Hopkins University Press, 2004.

Fithian, Philip Vickers. *Journal & Letters of Philip Vickers Fithian, 1773–1774: A Plantation Tutor of the Old Dominion.* Edited by Hunter Dickinson Farish. Williamsburg, VA: Colonial Williamsburg, 1957.

Flexner, James Thomas. *George Washington and the New Nation (1783–1793).* Boston: Little, Brown and Company, 1970.

———. *George Washington: Anguish and Farewell (1793–1799).* Boston: Little, Brown and Company, 1972.

———. "Washington and Slavery." *Constitution* 3, no. 2 (Spring–Summer 1991): 5–10.

Fowble, E. McSherry. *Two Centuries of Prints in America, 1680–1880: A Selective Catalogue of the Winterthur Museum Collection.* Charlottesville: Published for the Henry Francis du Pont Winterthur Museum by the University Press of Virginia, 1987.

Freeman, Douglas Southall. *George Washington: A Biography.* 6 vols. New York: Charles Scribner's Sons, 1948–54.

Gaustad, Edwin S. *Faith of Our Fathers: Religion and the New Nation.* San Francisco, CA: Harper & Row, 1987.

———. *Sworn on the Altar of God: A Religious Biography of Thomas Jefferson.* Grand Rapids, MI: William B. Eerdmans Publishing, 1996.

Gay, Peter. *Deism: An Anthology.* Princeton, NJ: D. Van Nostrand Company, 1968.

"George Washington's Chaplain." *Pentecostal Evangel,* February 2, 1970.

Gibbs, Dr. David C., Jr., with Jerry Newcombe. *One Nation under God: Ten Things Every Christian Should Know about the Founding of America.* 2nd ed. Seminole, FL: Christian Law Association, 2005.

Gier, Nicholas F. "Religious Liberalism and the Founding Fathers." In *Two Centuries of Philosophy in America,* edited by Peter Caws, 22–45. Oxford, UK: Basil Blackwell Publishers, 1980. Additional material on John Adams (added August 2003) and George Washington (added March and June 6/2005), available at http://users .adelphia.net/~nickgier/foundfathers.htm (accessed July 7, 2006).

Godbeer, Richard. *The Devil's Dominion: Magic and Religion in Early New England.* Cambridge: Cambridge University Press, 1992, 1994.

Goethe, Johann Wolfgang von. *The Sufferings of Young Werther, Die Leiden des Jungen Werther: A Bantam Dual-Language Book.* Edited and translated by Harry Steinhauer. New York: Bantam Books, 1962.

Goodwin, Edward Lewis. *The Colonial Church in Virginia, with Biographical Sketches of the First Six Bishops of the Diocese of Virginia and Other Historical Papers, together with Brief Biographical Sketches of the Colonial Clergy of Virginia.* Milwaukee, WI: Morehouse Publishing, 1927.

Green, Ashbel. *The Life of Ashbel Green, V.D.M.* Edited by Joseph H. Jones. New York: Robert Carter and Brothers, 1949.

Greene, Nathanael. *The Papers of General Nathanael Greene.* Edited by Richard K. Showman and Dennis M. Conrad. 9 vols. Chapel Hill: Published for the Rhode Island Historical Society by the University of North Carolina Press, 1976–97.

Griffin, Appleton P. C. *A Catalogue of the Washington Collection in the Boston Athenaeum . . . in Four Parts . . . with an Appendix . . . by William Coolidge Lane.* Cambridge, MA: Boston Athenaeum, 1897.

Griffin, Martin I. J. *American Catholic Historical Researches* 17 (1900): 126–29.

Griswold, Rufus Wilmot. *The Republican Court, or American Society in the Days of Washington.* New York: D. Appleton and Company, 1856.

Grizzard, Frank E. Jr. *George Washington: A Biographical Companion.* Santa Barbara, CA: ABC-CLIO, 2002.

———. *The Ways of Providence: Religion and George Washington.* Buena Vista and Charlottesville, VA: Mariner Publishing, 2005.

Gundersen, Joan R. "Review of *Holy Things and Profane: Anglican Parish Churches in Colonial Virginia,* by Dell Upton." *William and Mary Quarterly,* 3rd ser., 46, no. 2 (April 1989): 379–82.

Hadfield, Joseph. *An Englishman in America, 1785, Being the Diary of Joseph Hadfield.* Edited by Douglas S. Robertson. Toronto, Canada: Hunter-Rose Company, 1933.

Haller, William. *The Rise of Puritanism; or, The Way to the New Jerusalem as Set Forth in Pulpit and Press from Thomas Cartwright to John Lilburne and John Milton, 1570–1643.* 1938. Reprint, Philadelphia: University of Pennsylvania Press, 1972.

Hamilton, John D. *Material Culture of the American Freemasons.* Lexington, MA: Museum of Our National Heritage, 1994.

Hayward, Joel. "Prayers before Battle: The Spiritual Utterances of Three Great Commanders." *The [U.S.] Army Chaplaincy* (Winter–Spring 2002): 32–40. Available at http://www.joelhayward.org/prayersbeforebattle.htm (accessed August 22, 2006).

Henriques, Peter R. "A Few Simple Beliefs: George Washington and Religion." Chap. 9 in *Realistic Visionary: A Portrait of George Washington,* 166–85. Charlottesville: University of Virginia Press, 2006.

———. "The Final Struggle between George Washington and the Grim King: Washington's Attitude toward Death and an Afterlife." *Virginia Magazine of History and Biography* 107, no. 1 (Winter 1999): 73–97.

———. *He Died as He Lived: The Death of George Washington.* Mount Vernon, VA: Mount Vernon Ladies' Association, 2000.

———. "Major Lawrence Washington versus the Reverend Charles Green: A Case Study of the Squire and the Parson." *Virginia Magazine of History and Biography* 100, no. 2 (April 1992): 233–64.

Hirschfeld, Fritz. *George Washington and the Jews.* Newark: University of Delaware Press, 2005.

———. *George Washington and Slavery: A Documentary Portrayal.* Columbia: University of Missouri Press, 1997.

Holmes, David L. *The Faiths of the Founding Fathers.* New York: Oxford University Press, 2006.

———. *The Religion of the Founding Fathers.* Charlottesville, VA: Ash Lawn-Highland, the Home of James Monroe, and the Clements Library of the University of Michigan, 2003.

Honeywell, Roy J. *Chaplains of the United States Army.* Washington, DC: Office of the Chief of Chaplains, 1958.

Hoppin, Charles Arthur. *The Washington Ancestry and Records of The McClain, Johnson, and Forty Other Colonial American Families.* 3 vols. Greenfield, OH: Privately printed, 1932.

Hutson, James H. *The Founders on Religion: A Book of Quotations.* Princeton, NJ: Princeton University Press, 2005.

———. *Religion and the Founding of the American Republic.* Washington, DC: Library of Congress, 1998.

Isaac, Rhys. *The Transformation of Virginia, 1740–1790.* Chapel Hill: Published for the Institute of Early American History and Culture by the University of North Carolina Press, 1982.

Jefferson, Thomas. *The Papers of Thomas Jefferson.* Edited by Julian Boyd and Mina R. Bryan. Vol. 13. Princeton, NJ: Princeton University Press, 1956.

———. *The Writings of Thomas Jefferson.* Edited by Andrew A. Lipscomb and Albert Ellery Bergh. Vol. 1. Washington, DC: Thomas Jefferson Memorial Association of the United States, 1903.

"The John Gano Sword." *SAR Magazine* (Summer 1999): 12–13.

Johnson, William J. *George Washington: The Christian.* Arlington Heights, IL: Christian Liberty Press, n.d.

Jones, Robert F. *George Washington: Ordinary Man, Extraordinary Leader.* New York: Fordham University Press, 2002.

Kahler, Gerald Edward. "Gentlemen of the Family: General George Washington's Aides-de-Camp and Military Secretaries." Master's thesis, University of Richmond, May 1997.

———. "Washington in Glory, America in Tears: The Nation Mourns the Death of George Washington, 1799–1800." 2 vols. Ph.D. diss., College of William and Mary, 2003.

Kennedy, Dr. James D. *The Faith of Washington.* Fort Lauderdale, FL: Coral Ridge Ministries, n.d.

Klapthor, Margaret Brown, and Howard Alexander Morrison. *G. Washington: A Figure upon the Stage.* Washington, DC: Smithsonian Institution Press, 1982.

Kolchin, Peter. *American Slavery, 1619–1877.* New York: Hill and Wang, 1993.

Lafayette, Marquis de. *Lafayette in the Age of the American Revolution: Selected Letters and Papers.* Edited by Stanley J. Idzerda and Robert Rhodes Crout. 5 vols. Ithaca, NY: Cornell University Press, 1977–83.

[Law], Eliza Parke Custis. "Self-Portrait: Eliza Custis, 1808." Edited by William D. Hoyt Jr. *Virginia Magazine of History and Biography* 53, no. 2 (April 1945): 89–100.

Lear, Tobias. *Letters and Recollections of George Washington.* New York: Doubleday, Page & Company, 1906.

Lee, Agnes. *Growing Up in the 1850s: The Journal of Agnes Lee.* Edited by Mary Custis Lee DeButts. Chapel Hill: Published for the Robert E. Lee Memorial Association by the University of North Carolina Press, 1984.

Lee, Jean B. "Jane C. Washington, Family, and Nation at Mount Vernon, 1838–1855." In *Women Shaping the South: Creating and Confronting Change,* edited by Angela Boswell and Judith N. McArthur, 30–49. Columbia: University of Missouri Press, 2006.

Lewis, Eleanor Parke. *George Washington's Beautiful Nelly: The Letters of Eleanor Parke Custis Lewis to Elizabeth Bordley Gibson, 1794–1851.* Edited by Patricia Brady. Columbia: University of South Carolina Press, 1991.

Lewis, Jan. *The Pursuit of Happiness: Family and Values in Jefferson's Virginia.* Cambridge: Cambridge University Press, 1983.

Library of Dr. S. Weir Mitchell, Author of Hugh Wynne, Books, Autographs, Prints, and Historical Relics, to be Sold at Unrestricted Public Sale on Monday, May 19th, 1941 at 2:15 and 8:15 P.M. Philadelphia: Wm. D. Morley, Inc., Auctioneers-Appraisers, 1941.

Lillback, Peter A. *Proclaim Liberty: A Broken Bell Rings Freedom to the World.* Bryn Mawr, PA: Providence Forum, 2001.

Lillback, Peter A., with Jerry Newcombe. *George Washington's Sacred Fire.* Bryn Mawr, PA: Providence Forum Press, 2006.

Lossing, Benson J. *Hours with the Living Men and Women of the Revolution: A Pilgrimage.* New York: Funk & Wagnalls, 1889.

———. *Mount Vernon and Its Associations, Historical, Biographical, and Pictorial.* New York: W. A. Townsend & Company, 1859.

Madison, James. *A Nation Mourns: Bishop James Madison's Memorial Eulogy on the Death of George Washington.* Edited by David Holmes. Mount Vernon, VA: Mount Vernon Ladies' Association, 1999.

Madison, James. *The Papers of James Madison.* Vol. 8. Edited by Robert A. Rutland, William M. E. Rachal, Barbara D. Ripel, and Fredericka J. Teute. Chicago: University of Chicago Press, 1973.

Manross, William Wilson. *A History of the American Episcopal Church.* New York: Morehouse Publishing Company, 1935.

Mapp, Alf J., Jr. *The Faiths of Our Fathers: What America's Founders Really Believed.* Lanham, MD: Rowman & Littlefield, 2003.

Marshall, Dorothy. *Eighteenth Century England.* London: Longman Group, 1962.

Marshall, John. *The Life of George Washington, Commander in Chief of the American Forces, during the War Which Established the Independence of His Country, and First President of the United States. Compiled under the Inspection of the Honourable Bushrod Washington, from Original Papers Bequeathed to Him by His Deceased Relative, and Now in Possession of the Author. To Which Is Prefixed, an Introduction, Containing a Compendious View of the Colonies Planted by the English on the Continent of North America, from Their Settlement to the Commencement of That War Which Terminated in Their Independence.* 5 vols. New York: William H. Wise & Company, 1925.

————. *The Papers of John Marshall.* Vol. 7. Edited by Charles F. Hobson. Chapel Hill: University of North Carolina Press, in association with the Institute of Early American History and Culture, 1993.

Mason, Julian D., Jr. *The Poems of Phyllis Wheatley.* Revised and enlarged edition. Chapel Hill: University of North Carolina Press, 1989.

Massey, Don W., and Sue Massey. *Colonial Churches of Virginia.* Charlottesville, VA: Howell Press, 2003.

[McCallister, Ellen Land]. "Reason and Resignation." In *Annual Report 1980,* 27–31. Mount Vernon, VA: Mount Vernon Ladies' Association, 1981.

————. "This Melancholy Scene." In *Annual Report 1981,* 13–15. Mount Vernon, VA: Mount Vernon Ladies' Association of the Union, 1982.

McCullough, David. *John Adams.* New York: Simon & Schuster, 2001.

McGroarty, William Buckner. "Elizabeth Washington of Hayfield." *Virginia Magazine of History and Biography* 33, no. 2 (April 1925): 154–65.

————, ed. *Washington, First in the Hearts of His Countrymen: The Orations by Men Who Had Known Washington in Person and Who Thus Could Speak with Authority.* Richmond, VA: Garrett & Massie, 1932.

Meacham, Jon. *American Gospel: God, the Founding Fathers, and the Making of a Nation.* New York: Random House, 2006.

Meade, Bishop [William]. *Old Churches, Ministers, and Families of Virginia.* 2 vols. Philadelphia: J. B. Lippincott Company, 1857.

Meadows, Christine. "The Furniture." *Antiques* 135, no. 2 (February 1989): 480–89.

————. "A Mourning Tribute." In *Annual Report 1991,* 20–25. Mount Vernon, VA: Mount Vernon Ladies' Association, 1992.

M'Guire, E[dward] C[harles]. *The Religious Opinions and Character of Washington.* New York: Harper & Brothers, 1836.

Miller, T. Michael, comp. *Artisans and Merchants of Alexandria, Virginia, 1780–1820.* 2 vols. Bowie, MD: Heritage Books, 1991.

————, ed. *Pen Portraits of Alexandria, Virginia, 1739–1900.* Bowie, MD: Heritage Books, 1987.

Minutes of the Vestry: Truro Parish Virginia, 1732–1785. Lorton, VA: Pohick Church, 1974.

Montgomery, Florence M. *Printed Textiles: English and American Cottons and Linens,*

1700–1850. New York: Published for The Henry Francis du Pont Winterthur Museum by Viking Press, 1970.

Moore, Gay Montague. *Seaport in Virginia: George Washington's Alexandria*. Richmond, VA: Garret and Massie, Inc., 1949.

Mount Vernon Ladies' Association. *Annual Report 1956*. Mount Vernon, VA: Mount Vernon Ladies' Association of the Union, 1957.

———. *Minutes of the Council of the Mount Vernon Ladies' Association of the Union, Held at Mount Vernon, Virginia, May Eighth to Sixteenth, Nineteen Forty-One*. Mount Vernon, VA: Mount Vernon Ladies' Association of the Union, 1941.

———. *Mount Vernon: A Handbook*. Mount Vernon, VA: Mount Vernon Ladies' Association, 1985.

———. *Mount Vernon: An Illustrated Handbook*. Mount Vernon, VA: Mount Vernon Ladies' Association of the Union, 1974.

Muhlenberg, Henry Melchior. *The Notebook of a Colonial Clergyman: Condensed from the Journals of Henry Melchior Muhlenberg*. Translated and edited by Theodore G. Tappert and John W. Doberstein. Eugene, OR: Wipf & Stock Publishers, 1987.

Munson, James D. *Colo. John Carlyle, Gent.: A True and Just Account of the Man and His House, 1720–1780*. [Alexandria, VA?]: Northern Virginia Regional Park Authority, 1986.

Murray, Judith Sargent. *From Gloucester to Philadelphia in 1790: Observations, Anecdotes, and Thoughts from the 18th-century Letters of Judith Sargent Murray, with a Biographical Introduction*. Edited by Bonnie Hurd Smith. Cambridge, MS: Judith Sargent Murray Society and Curious Traveller Press, 1998.

———. *Selected Writings of Judith Sargent Murray*. Edited by Sharon M. Harris. New York: Oxford University Press, 1995.

Neill, Edward D. *The Fairfaxes of England and America in the Seventeenth and Eighteenth Centuries, including Letters from and to Hon. William Fairfax, President of Council of Virginia, and His Sons Col. George William Fairfax and Rev. Bryan, Eighth Lord Fairfax, the Neighbors and Friends of George Washington*. Albany, NY: Joel Munsell, 1868.

Nelson, John K. *A Blessed Company: Parishes, Parsons, and Parishioners in Anglican Virginia, 1690–1776*. Chapel Hill: University of North Carolina Press, 2001.

Netherton, Nan, and Ross Netherton, comps. *Notes on the History and Architecture of Pohick Church, Truro Parish, Fairfax County, Virginia*. Fairfax County, VA: Fairfax Historical Landmarks Preservation Commission, 1968.

Niemcewicz, Julian Ursyn. *Under Their Vine and Fig Tree: Travels through America in 1797–1799, 1805, with Some Further Account of Life in New Jersey*. Edited and translated by Metchie J. E. Budka. Elizabeth, NJ: Grassman Publishing Company, 1965.

Novak, Michael. *On Two Wings: Humble Faith and Common Sense at the American Founding*. San Francisco: Encounter Books, 2002.

Novak, Michael, and Jana Novak. *Washington's God: Religion, Liberty, and the Father of Our Country*. New York: Basic Books, 2006.

Oliver, Sandra. "A Fine Kettle of Fish." *Cultural Resource Management: What's for Lunch? Food in American Life* 24, no. 4 (2001): 18–22.

Bibliography

Perry, John. *Mrs. Robert E. Lee: The Lady of Arlington.* Sisters, OR: Multnomah Publishers, 2001.

Popham, William. "Major William Popham to Jane Charlotte Blackburn Washington, March 14, 1838." *The Churchman: An Illustrated Weekly News-Magazine* 79, no. 22 (June 3, 1899): 796–97.

Powell, Mary G. *The History of Old Alexandria, Virginia, from July 13, 1749 to May 24, 1861.* Richmond, VA: William Byrd Press, 1928.

Prussing, Eugene E. *The Estate of George Washington, Deceased.* Boston: Little, Brown, and Company, 1927.

Pyle, Andrew. "The Boyle Lectures (1692–1732)." Paper prepared for the University of Bristol, 2000. http://www.thoemmes.com/theology/boylelec_intro.htm.

Quitt, Martin H. "The English Cleric and the Virginia Adventurer: The Washingtons, Father and Son." *Virginia Magazine of History and Biography* 97, no. 2 (April 1989): 163–84.

Randolph, Sarah N. *The Domestic Life of Thomas Jefferson.* Charlottesville: University Press of Virginia, 1978.

Reeves, Wendy Wick. "The Prints." *Antiques* 135, no. 2 (February 1989): 502–11.

Remsburg, John E. "George Washington." Chap. 3 in *Six Historic Americans.* 1906. http://www.infidels.org/library/historical/john_remsburg/six_historic_americans/chapter_3.html (accessed June 11, 1999).

Ribblett, David L. *Nelly Custis: Child of Mount Vernon.* Mount Vernon, VA: Mount Vernon Ladies' Association, 1993.

Robinson, Donald L. *Slavery in the Structure of American Politics, 1765–1820.* New York: Harcourt Brace Jovanovich, 1971.

Rusinowa, Izabella. "Julian Ursyn Niemcewicz's Biography of George Washington." *American Studies* 17 (1999): 5–14.

Rusten, E. Michael, and Sharon Rusten. *The One Year Book of Christian History.* Carol Stream, IL: Tyndale House Publishers, 2003.

Sanford, Charles B. *The Religious Life of Thomas Jefferson.* Charlottesville: University Press of Virginia, 1984.

Sayen, William Guthrie. "George Washington's 'Unmannerly' Behavior: The Clash between Civility and Honor." *Virginia Magazine of History and Biography* 107, no. 1 (Winter 1999): 5–36.

Schwarz, Philip J., ed. *Slavery at the Home of George Washington.* Mount Vernon, VA: Mount Vernon Ladies' Association, 2001.

Seabury, Samuel. *Letters of a Westchester Farmer (1774–1775) by the Reverend Samuel Seabury (1729–1796).* Edited by Clarence H. Vance. White Plains, NY: Westchester Historical Society, 1930.

Serle, Ambrose. *The American Journal of Ambrose Serle, Secretary to Lord Howe, 1776–1778.* Edited by Edward H. Tatum. San Marino, CA: Huntington Library, 1940.

Sheridan, Eugene R. *Jefferson and Religion.* Charlottesville, VA: Thomas Jefferson Memorial Foundation, 1998.

Skemp, Sheila L. *Judith Sargent Murray: A Brief Biography with Documents.* Boston, MA: Bedford Books/St. Martin's, 1998.

Smith, Wanda Willard. *Selina Hastings the Countess of Huntingdon* [exhibition catalogue]. Dallas: Bridwell Library, Perkins School of Theology, Southern Methodist University, 1997.

Sorley, Merrow Egerton, ed. *Lewis of Warner Hall: The History of a Family*. 1935. Reprint, Baltimore: Genealogical Publishing Company, 1979.

Sparks, Jared. *The Life of George Washington*. Boston: Published by Ferdinand Andrews, 1839.

Spellman, W. M. *The Latitudinarians and the Church of England, 1660–1700*. Athens: University of Georgia Press, 1993.

Steiner, Franklin. *The Religious Beliefs of Our Presidents: From Washington to F.D.R.* [1936?]. Reprint, Amherst, NY: Prometheus Books, 1995.

Stokes, I. N. Phelps. *The Iconography of Manhattan Island*. Vol. 5. New York: Robert H. Dodd, 1926.

Stukenboeker, Fern C. *A Watermelon for God: A History of Trinity Methodist Church, Alexandria, Virginia, 1774–1974*. Alexandria, VA: Fern C. Stukenboeker, 1974.

Sullivan, William. *Familiar Letters on Public Characters, and Public Events, from the Peace of 1783, to the Peace of 1815*. Boston: Russell, Odiorne, and Metcalf, 1834.

Thacher, James. *Military Journal of the American Revolution, from the Commencement to the Disbanding of the American Army; Comprising a Detailed Account of the Principal Events and Battles of the Revolution, with Their Exact Dates, and a Biographical Sketch of the Most Prominent Generals*. Hartford, CT: Hurlbut, Williams & Company, American Subscription Publishing House, 1862.

Thane, Elswyth. *Mount Vernon Family*. New York: Crowell-Collier Press, 1968.

Thomas Birch's Sons, Auctioneers. *Catalogue No. 663, The Final Sale of the Relics of General Washington Owned by Lawrence Washington, Esq., Bushrod C. Washington, Esqr., Thos. B. Washington, Esq., and J.R.C. Lewis, Esq., Embracing the Most Important Collection Ever Brought Together, of Letters, Deeds, Leases, Legal Documents, Receipts, Bills, Account Books, and Memoranda, Belonging to and Written by General Washington . . . to Be Sold in Our Book Salesroom . . . April 21st, 22d, 23d, 1891. . . .* Philadelphia: Catalogue Compiled and Sale Conducted by Stan V. Henkels, 1891.

Thompson, E. Wayne, and David L. Cummins. *This Day in Baptist History: 366 Daily Devotions Drawn from the Baptist Heritage*. Greenville, SC: Bob Jones University Press, 1993.

Thompson, Mary V. "'And Procure for Themselves a Few Amenities': The Private Life of George Washington's Slaves." *Virginia Cavalcade* 48, no. 4 (Autumn 1999): 178–90.

———. "'The Only Unavoidable Subject of Regret': George Washington and Slavery." Lecture presented at a symposium entitled "George Washington and Alexandria, Virginia: Ties That Bind," Alexandria, VA, February 20, 1999. http://www.mountvernon.org/learn/collections/index.cfm/pid/242/cfid/132224/cftoken/70263683.

———. "Religious Practice in the Slave Quarters at Mount Vernon." *Colonial Williamsburg Interpreter* 21, no. 1 (Spring 2000): 10–14.

———. "'They Appear to Live Comfortable Together': Private Lives of the Mount Vernon Slaves." In *Slavery at the Home of George Washington*, edited by Philip J. Schwartz, 78–109. Mount Vernon, VA: Mount Vernon Ladies' Association, 2001.

Bibliography

Thompson, Parker C. *The United States Army Chaplaincy: From Its European Anteced-ents to 1791*. Washington, DC: Office of the Chief of Chaplains, Department of the Army, 1978.

Thorburn, Grant. "Letter from Grant Thorburn—Anecdote of Gen. Washington." *Mount Vernon Record* 2, no. 9 (March 1860): 179.

Thornton, Edward. "A Young Englishman Reports on the New Nation: Edward Thorn-ton to James Bland Burges, 1791–1793." Edited by S. W. Jackman. *William and Mary Quarterly*, 3rd ser., 18, no. 1 (January 1961): 85–121.

Toner, Joseph M., ed. *Wills of the American Ancestors of General George Washington in the Line of the Original Owner and the Inheritors of Mount Vernon: From Original Documents and Probate Records*. Boston: New-England Historic Genealogical Society, 1891.

Twohig, Dorothy. "That Species of Property: Washington's Role in the Controversy over Slavery." In *George Washington Reconsidered*, edited by Don Higginbotham, 114–38. Charlottesville: University Press of Virginia, 2001.

Tyler, Lyon G. "Bruton Church." *William and Mary College Quarterly Historical Maga-zine* 3, no. 3 (January 1895): 169–80.

Varon, Elizabeth R. *We Mean to Be Counted: White Women and Politics in Antebellum Virginia*. Chapel Hill: University of North Carolina Press, 1998.

Virginia. *The Statutes at Large: Being a Collection of All the Laws of Virginia, from the First Session of the Legislature, in the Year 1619*. 13 vols. Edited by William Waller Hening. Richmond: Printed by and for Samuel Pleasants, Junior, Printer to the Commonwealth, 1809–23.

Virginia. General Assembly. House of Burgesses. *Journals of the House of Burgesses of Virginia, 1766–1769*. Edited by John Pendleton Kennedy. Richmond: [The Colonial Press, E. Waddey Co.], 1906.

———. *Journals of the House of Burgesses of Virginia, 1770–1772*. Edited by John Pend-leton Kennedy. Richmond: [Colonial Press, E. Waddey Co.], 1906.

———. *Journals of the House of Burgesses of Virginia, 1773–1776: Including the records of the Committee of Correspondence*. Edited by John Pendleton Kennedy. Rich-mond: [E. Waddey Co.], 1905.

Wall, Charles C. "Letter to the Editor." *William and Mary Quarterly*, 3rd ser., 12, no. 4 (October 1955): 678–79.

Waring, E. Graham, ed. *Deism and Natural Religion: A Source Book*. New York: Freder-ick Unger Publishing, 1967.

Warren, Jack D., Jr. "The Childhood of George Washington." *Northern Neck of Virginia Historical Magazine* 49, no. 1 (December 1999): 5785–5809.

Washington, George. *The Diaries of George Washington*. Edited by Donald Jackson and Dorothy Twohig. 6 vols. Charlottesville: University Press of Virginia, 1976–79.

———. *The Last Will and Testament of George Washington and Schedule of His Property, to which Is Appended the Last Will and Testament of Martha Washington*. 4th ed. Edited by John C. Fitzpatrick. Mount Vernon, VA: Mount Vernon Ladies' Association of the Union, 1972.

———. *Maxims of George Washington: Political, Military, Social, Moral, and Religious*.

Rev. ed. Edited by John Frederick Schroeder. Mount Vernon, VA: Mount Vernon Ladies' Association, 1989.

————. *The Papers of George Washington, Colonial Series*. Edited by W. W. Abbot and Dorothy Twohig. 10 vols. Charlottesville: University Press of Virginia, 1983–95.

————. *The Papers of George Washington, Confederation Series*. Edited by W. W. Abbot and Dorothy Twohig. 6 vols. Charlottesville: University Press of Virginia, 1992–97.

————. *The Papers of George Washington, Presidential Series*. Edited by W. W. Abbot, Dorothy Twohig, and Philander D. Chase. 12 vols. to date. Charlottesville: University Press of Virginia, 1987–.

————. *The Papers of George Washington, Revolutionary War Series*. Edited by W. W. Abbot, Dorothy Twohig, Philander D. Chase, and Theodore J. Crackel. 16 vols. to date. Charlottesville: University of Virginia Press, 1985–.

————. *The Papers of George Washington, Retirement Series*. Edited by W. W. Abbot and Dorothy Twohig. 4 vols. Charlottesville: University Press of Virginia, 1998–99.

————. *Rules of Civility & Decent Behaviour in Company and Conversation*. Mount Vernon, VA: Mount Vernon Ladies' Association, 1989.

————. *The Writings of George Washington: Being His Correspondence, Addresses, Messages, and Other Papers, Official and Private, Selected and Published from the Original Manuscripts, with a Life of the Author, Notes, and Illustrations*, by Jared Sparks. 12 vols. Boston: American Stationers' Co., 1834–37.

————. *The Writings of George Washington from the Original Manuscript Sources, 1745–1799*. Edited by John C. Fitzpatrick. 39 vols. Washington, DC: United States Government Printing Office, 1931–44.

Washington, Jane Charlotte Blackburn. "Jane Charlotte Blackburn Washington to Major William Popham, May 24, 1839." *The Churchman: An Illustrated Weekly News-Magazine* 79, no. 22 (June 3, 1899): 798.

"Washington's Household Account Book, 1793–1797." Published in 8 pts. *Pennsylvania Magazine of History and Biography* 29, no. 4 (1906): 385–406; 30 (1906), no. 1: 30–56, no. 2: 159–86, no. 3: 309–31, no. 4: 459–78; 31 (1907), no. 1: 53–82, no. 2: 176–94, no. 3: 320–50.

"Washington's Runaway Slave, and How Portsmouth Freed Her." *Frank W. Miller's Portsmouth, New Hampshire, Weekly*, June 2, 1877.

Wayland, John W. *The Washingtons and Their Homes*. Staunton, VA: Press of McClure Printing Company, 1944.

Webb, James. *Born Fighting: How the Scots-Irish Shaped America*. New York: Broadway Books, 2004.

Weems, Mason L. *The Life of Washington*. Edited by Marcus Cunliffe. Cambridge, MA: Belknap Press of Harvard University Press, 1962.

West, John G., Jr. "George Washington and the Religious Impulse." In *Patriot Sage: George Washington and the American Political Tradition*, edited by Gary L. Gregg II and Matthew Spalding, 267–86. Wilmington, DE: ISI Books, 1999.

[Wharton, Charles Henry]. *A Poetical Epistle to His Excellency George Washington, Esq. Commander in Chief of the Armies of the United States of America, from an Inhabitant of the State of Maryland. To Which Is Annexed a Short Sketch of General*

Washington's Life and Character. Annapolis, MD, 1779. Reprinted for C. Dilly and others in London, 1780.

White, John. *The First Century of Scandalous, Malignant Priests, Made and Admitted into Benefices by the Prelates, in Whose Hands the Ordination of Ministers and Government of the Church Hath Been. Or, a Narration of the Causes for Which the Parliament Hath Ordered the Sequestration of the Benefices of Severall Ministers Complained of before Them, for Vitiousness of Life, Errors in Doctrine, Contrary to the Articles of Our Religion, and for Practicing and Pressing Superstitious Innovations against Law, and for Malignancy against the Parliament*. London: Printed by George Miller, 1643.

Wiencek, Henry. *An Imperfect God: George Washington, His Slaves, and the Creation of America*. New York: Farrar, Straus and Giroux, 2003.

Wilson, Bird. *Memoir of the Life of the Right Reverend William White, D.D., Bishop of the Protestant Episcopal Church in the State of Pennsylvania*. Philadelphia: James Kay, Jun. & Brother; Pittsburgh: C. H. Kay & Co., 1839.

Zabriskie, Alexander Clinton. "The Rise and Main Characteristics of the Anglican Evangelical Movement in England and America." 1943. http://www.episcopalian.org/gambeirevangelicals/Background/AnglicanEvangelicalismB1.htm.

Zagarri, Rosemarie, ed. *David Humphreys' "Life of General Washington," with George Washington's "Remarks."* Athens: University of Georgia Press, 1991.

INDEX

Index